# Past Life Regression and Conversations with the Higher Self

Chelsey Perry CCH

# Dedicated to:

To my amazing family. My husband and children. They have helped and supported me through every step of my journey. This book was possible because of you.

To my friends who have walked this journey with me.

And to my clients who have allowed me to grow into the person I am today. Thank you for trusting me with your journey. I am forever grateful.

# Table of Contents

# Introduction

I want to preface this book by saying, I know it can be difficult for some to believe in past lives or if it is even real. Some are just opening the door to the possibility. Some believe and some do not. There is a wide range of where you, the reader, might be on that scale.

My only request is for you to keep an open mind. This book is created from sessions that have covered nine years at the time of publishing. I have grown; from someone who only wondered about past lives as a possibility, to exploring other worlds and civilizations. I can preface this by saying, buckle up! This book will stretch your mind to new possibilities and potentials. Each one of these sessions changed me in ways I cannot explain. I hope that sharing with you a window into this world that I now live in, you might expand, even if only a little, your belief that we are not alone in the world, and the things we experience are only the smallest tip of the iceberg. There is so much more we have yet to discover about being human and about our souls.

We are so much more than our physical body. These clients have given me the opportunity to share with you a window into another world, another existence. These people have come in sometimes not even believing if they have lived a past life or believed it might be real, only to find that door they opened showed them how vast their soul really is. I cannot begin to convey to you how powerful a journey it has been for me to be allowed this opportunity to tag along with each and every person. It has truly been my own awakening as well.

Each one of these sessions holds a piece of my own heart. I have wept in sorrow, cried tears of joy, felt the deep wells of anger, and I've been overwhelmed at all of the things I've experienced alongside people over the years through this journey. From death by stoning, to suicide, to simple, peaceful lives, and other planets and civilizations. This book shows the raw, unfiltered human lives we experience and the vast journeys of our souls to get to where we are right now. The Great Awakening.

We are all in this together; each and every one of us. I see now how we each came here to make a difference. Not a single person is unimportant. A ripple effect in the cosmos. I am so lucky to watch people bloom from the confines in which they have placed themselves. Waking up to their true purposes and why they really came here.

This book is full of experiences. Some may not be easily understood but they are seen from unique points of view. If only for a moment while you read these pages, put your beliefs aside and you may find that a glimmer of change begins to start within you. Breaking out of the boxes we so quickly put ourselves in for security that ultimately stifles us; we can find comfort in the unknown, just beyond the fear, and open to the unique and endless world we really live in. Our souls are waiting for us to open the door and look, just once, and see what's beyond. If you picked up this book, it's not by accident. It's calling you and you heard the call. In the whispers, in the nudges. The more you look, the more you will realize it is calling us to more. We can still be human and awaken to the vast universe beckoning just beyond us. It is not ever to be feared, but to be explored. And you may find that you will become more of who you truly are and are meant to be.

Stepping into your power is a choice, but it is not a journey easily walked. It asks much of you. Peeling back each layer of self and peering into the vast depths of our own souls. Healing the deepest, darkest corners that have been long neglected and forgotten or buried. For in the darkness, there is a light. Brighter and stronger than anything else. We are led in light down the path of greatness, heeding the call of our soul, to who we are, and what we are meant to be. When you answer the call, your own soul will lead the way, hand in hand, every step of the way. You will find that there are many others walking the same path to discovery and freedom of self. I pose the question to you; what would you find, if only you opened that door and peered inside?

---

My name is Chelsey Perry, and I am a Clinical Hypnotherapist. I work within many different areas of hypnosis, but I specialize in Past Life Regression Hypnosis, and I am also a Quantum Healing Hypnosis Technique (QHHT) level two practitioner. QHHT is a method of Past Life Regression that includes conversations with the Higher Self. I will explain that in greater detail later.

I began my journey into hypnosis by training for the Clinical Hypnotherapist title at Southwest Institute of Healing Arts in 2015. I had no prior experience in hypnosis, nor had I ever been hypnotized. I was, however, fascinated with past life experiences. I was not able to find someone near me at the time to experience one myself, so I signed up for school and knew that I was going to get my answers one way or another. I wanted to know more about the other side. Do we live more than once? Do we die and never come back? How many lives can we have IF we actually do reincarnate? I grew up in the western world and my entire exposure to everything in my younger years came from the church.

The problem was, I asked too many questions. (I still do today, which is why I believe I am so well suited for this line of work.) You see, I used to see and experience things of the supernatural growing up as a child, and no one knew how to answer my questions about it. What was it? Are ghosts real? No, well… why can I see them? I never got clarity or answers to the things I experienced and knew as truth for myself, as a kid. So, I kept asking questions to anyone who might know the answer. No one had those answers.

The churches I went to as a child, none of them could give me what felt like truth. (It was the normal thing to do, going to church, so I went with friends or anyone who asked me.)

Anytime I'd ask people at the church to explain some of my experiences, the answers were varied but went something like this: "It was the devil." (I wish I was exaggerating.) "It's not real." "It's your mental state." "You need to talk to a therapist." "It's trauma." "You need to repent." "Demons are trying to steal your soul." Other responses too, but you get the point. It felt defeating. I knew deep inside there was more to life and I really, REALLY wanted someone to have answers to something about this world beyond us. However, in a small town in Alabama, I couldn't find those kinds of answers. There was no internet access or other people who seemed to be like me, not at the time anyhow. I am in no way vilifying the church. Everything has its own place and fills a need. I only share with you my experience, so you understand how this journey unfolded.

At the time, our area was not diverse in beliefs, or people and I spent most of my years locking away my abilities and experiences to live a normal life. Deep down though, I knew I wasn't normal in the general sense, and I knew I couldn't exist like that forever. There was a part of my being withering away from being hidden and neglected. I didn't know that at the time, but looking back, I can see how much I hurt myself by denying myself. I wanted, like everyone else in this world, to fit in. I tried my best to live life normally and it worked, for a while, on the surface.

Funny thing about being human though, when we try to deny ourselves, our true self, it WILL find a way out. It knocks on that door within our mind. It gets louder and louder until you can't ignore it anymore. Everyone is different in how long they can deny themselves. Mine was noticeably short.

Everyone I'd talked to didn't believe in ghosts, past lives, or any life beyond this one. I was "weird" for bringing odd topics up or trying to find someone to talk to about it. My closest friends just accepted me with my quirks and looked past them, thankfully. Looking back, I appreciate them so very much for tolerating my brand of different. To fit into general society, I stayed quiet about my experiences and went on about life as usual.

I lived that "normal" life. I graduated high school, went to college, found my soul mate, got married, and became pregnant. I was twenty-five with my first child and was going through school to become a hypnotherapist, soaking up ANY information about past life regression I possibly could.

The problem for me was, in the entire curriculum, there was only one past life class in the course. It just wasn't something widely requested, or used, even for hypnotherapists. I understood why, but it didn't make learning about this subject any easier. I absorbed every word and book that I had access to for my classes and quickly began practicing on classmates to see what came of it. Mostly, we discovered normal living scenarios, day-to-day living things. Deep down, I knew there was more to be discovered though. I wanted to learn more about what happens beyond human life and why.

I was still limited in many ways. When I ran into something I didn't understand, or had never heard of, most of the time the teachers or classmates hadn't either. I was again at a stalemate. I was doing hypnosis sessions and getting fascinating information but there was a lot I didn't understand. I only had access to the books that had already been written about on the topic of past lives (of which there weren't many), and the thoughts or possibilities supplied by the people around me.

I made the most of it at the time and opened my hypnotherapy business a little over a year later. I spent countless hours devouring anything and everything about the topic. I was still a general hypnotherapist, but I wanted to focus on past life regression. I knew I needed to offer general hypnosis to be able to keep my business open as not many in my area were seeking information on past lives, so that's what I did. I thrived on the days I was able to do past life sessions and somehow, the universe delivered. I began noticing the synchronicities and seeing the odd ways new clients began finding me. This was really where I began to see the magic of the unseen playing a role in my life.

I was able to explore the most amazing lifetimes with clients, cried with them, got angry when lives seen were unfair, felt sorrow when life was cut short and celebrated when the "why's of life" were discovered. I truly began to live lives, within my own life, and with the new people I was meeting. I began to grow in ways I didn't know were even possible.

I LOVED what I did, but there was a point in these explorations I felt something was missing. I got answers to a lot of things clients wanted to know by exploring in many different ways, however I felt there was still a stone left unturned. Somewhere, it felt like there was a missing puzzle piece and missing it didn't keep the motivation fire lit to continue hypnotherapy. Eventually, as life would have it, I shut my business down and decided to stop doing hypnotherapy for good. I'd discovered a lot of answers to the questions I had, I'd met a lot of amazing people, and my life had changed drastically. At the time, I just felt it was necessary to close this chapter and move on. I knew I would always be pulled to the unknown and unseen aspects of life, but it was still just "too weird" for me to continue. I wasn't comfortable with the nonconformist part of this life just yet.

Fast forward - a few years later, with a few major medical problems I'd been going through, and my second child having been born. I had repressed and almost felt embarrassed about that phase of my life where I had accepted who I was and how I'd tried to shine. The people we were surrounded by liked *normal* people. It's funny how society is really good at beating people into submission with the promise of a *normal* life. So again, I'd closed that door on myself and lived life as a *normal* stay at home mom, with a thriving *normal* life. Except this time, that door wasn't going to stay closed for as long. I tried though; I really did.

A friend that had been in my life since my teenage years, contacted me and said, "Here, you should read this book, it sounds just like what you do." She sent me the title of one of the most inspirational books for me at the time, book one of Conversations with Nostradamus. Books are the best way to get me to pay attention to a message. Initially I didn't think much of it, but eventually I pulled up the book and began reading it. I felt like a lightbulb lit up and alarm bells started ringing in my head!

THIS, THIS was the missing piece! I just KNEW it. Just getting a few pages into the book, I knew the universe was delivering to me something I'd been seeking. I bought her books as fast as I could find them and devoured them in what felt like just days. I felt like a piece of my soul had ignited and sparked a flame that was burning so hot, I was going to go up in flames with it. It felt that extreme; like those moments where your entire life converges to one moment in time. I felt like a piece of my soul had finally "clicked" into place.

I ordered one book after another, digesting every ounce of information I could get from her books, and I was at another crossroads in my life. I was fine living a *normal* and easy life. (I was lying to myself.) I had friends, family, an extended family, and a *normal* existence. That's all you're supposed to ask out of life, right? That's the dream. The best life you can ask for.

But I was drowning.

I was living a life of untruth. Untruth to my true self, my true nature. That tug within my soul calling me, beckoning me to listen, was getting louder and louder. Like many people, I was in denial of who I was because if I showed the true me, I might be unlovable. I might be too much, too weird, too "crazy" to handle. I might lose everyone and everything I knew. I was at war with myself. Sometimes there is nothing worse than our own minds and the lies we tell ourselves. The excuses are always very viable and convincing, but they aren't serving us.

So, I put feelers out. I had been contacted since I closed my business because people still wanted to experience past life regression sessions. I wondered, if I opened it again, would it be worth it? Would I be able to live as my true self and be unafraid, be proud of who I was? I really didn't know.

I began by offering sessions to those who were interested just to see if these sessions were worth doing. I began with a friend. She was always up for the new and unusual. She had become my friend over the years. She started as a client so I knew I could trust her and whatever came through would help me know whether this was my path.

I put her under hypnosis and the box that I had put myself in once again shattered. I began with no idea what I was going to find but I knew I was forever changed after we finished. We both spent the next few days trying to digest the information we'd received and how to put it into place within the context of what we knew. You see, when you receive a broader perspective from the soul, the mind has to catch up. Changing the belief system is always challenging and we were definitely challenged to incorporate the information!

I had strongly and stubbornly held onto my own belief systems and my own soul, through these sessions, was forcing me to grow and expand. It physically felt like it hurt because I was at war with myself and didn't know how to put things into perspective.

I began doing more sessions with others to see if the information was able to be replicated. To my own surprise, it was. I am, however, a person that likes proof as I am a healthy skeptic. In the sessions you'll read here, take note of the replication through different people who are complete strangers to one another. I will not try to convince you, the reader, of the proof I've discovered, but I will share the follow-ups to some of these individuals' sessions. The discoveries that were made for these clients shocked even them with some of the answers and their personal changes after the session. Some clients had radiographs (x-rays) to verify changes, and some went on to prove to themselves in other ways that what they received was real. Each person finds their own path to believing or knowing. Spirit is always with us, orchestrating the bigger picture. We are all so loved and guided.

These sessions have all been done through the course of eight years. Some are very basic because I was only just learning and beginning. Some are in depth and incredibly detailed. I am sharing the entirety of my journey. It's time for humans to be raw, to be unfiltered, and be who they are meant to be. I cannot say that without showing the raw and messy that was my beginning to the growth of where I am today.

It's built into us to judge, to flock to those who are like us, to point out flaws. I am here in my light, my vulnerability, my truth. I hope you feel that same openness within these pages and with these clients who have so kindly let me share their experiences and their growth. There is an energy within these pages which is conveyed as you read the transcripts. The energy of growth, of power, of Spirit, who guides us, whatever you may believe in or call it. The Higher Self works in mysterious ways and that is shared here beyond the words that are written. You can feel them. I hope you enjoy this journey with me and the people within these pages. This is only the beginning of a very long, very exciting journey.

## What is Past Life Regression?

All of this talk of past life regression hypnosis, but what is it really?

Hypnosis itself is an amazing form of working with the subconscious mind or the unconscious mind. There are many names for it and there are many aspects to our own mind, and each part is particularly important in the role it plays.

The conscious mind is our day-to-day mind. The part of which we are most aware. Where all our thoughts seem to be sitting as they flow throughout our day.

The unconscious mind or subconscious mind is the part that is always working in the background 24/7. It never stops processing. We are rarely ever aware that it is there. This part of our mind is what we work with in hypnosis. We are calming the conscious mind to begin working with the unconscious, where all of our programs are stored. You see, if you have a major life event happen to you, the unconscious is what takes that event and programs it into the mind. It can create a fear loop, a habit, or a trauma response. It is essentially 'protecting" you in the only ways it's been taught to.

During hypnosis, we work with where that program has been stored to either remove it or alter it in a way that allows you to live again without that extreme fear or response that hinders you.

Psychology has come a long way in understanding how our mind works. Hypnosis is a straightforward way to make changes in a much faster manner. It has a high success rate for working with many things when it comes to the mind. We are, after all, what we believe and think. Our world around us is shaped by our very thoughts and feelings. One person will experience the same thing as another and have quite a different response. One person's experience may be considered positive while the other person would consider the very same thing negative. Two perspectives from the same event. Our subconscious and its patterns of interpretation play a significant role in how we process those events. Through hypnosis, we work with the subconscious to create change which positively reprocesses trauma.

Our souls are vast, ancient, and incredibly wise. There is no time beyond our physical-ness and every experience we have had before (or after) this one human experience we are living now, is contained right there within us. So, why can't we access them? How do some people just KNOW there is life beyond this one, while others are certain this is the only one?

Well, that's complicated. This free-will planet we live on is part of that reason. We knew coming to this life that we were going to forget EVERYTHING. And I mean everything, except just this life; normally. You, by now, have likely heard stories of children remembering past lives or unexplainable things which they could not know that occurred before they were born. How is that possible? Stories of others near-death experiences where they came back forever changed because of the information they have "remembered" they didn't know beforehand.

On the other hand, there are some who claim to remember everything before they came here. All of their Souls' collective memories. There have been enough of those claims that do point towards proof that there is more than we understand. As we begin to discover other civilizations out there, other "beings," other planets that might hold life, of course we begin to question. Is there more beyond us? In this life, and others?

There is a point before we come here physically, our Soul looks at what we want for ourselves while we are in a body here. It chooses what lessons we want to learn, how we want to go about that, and who we want to experience those things with, both the blessings and the challenges. Some choose to come here with their memories intact because it serves their soul's purpose. Not very many though.

One of the many reasons we come here is to learn to reconnect to the larger part of ourselves while remaining physically focused. We've all had that feeling that something bigger is out there and there is a reason we feel "pulled" to something beyond us. My clients and I have seen it in lifetimes from "caveman" to present. There is always a pull to something, anything beyond us. Why do we experience that emptiness or need to reach for something bigger within us, or just beyond us? Well, that's the communication from our souls going "over here, over here, just look beyond." We knew we wanted to grow and experience that feeling of searching, and then finding, that bigger connection within us. Many spend a lifetime searching for that connection to "God" or Self. That bigger, more complete, inner Self.

That connection to something deeper is and always has been, right there within us. That connection to Source is here, right inside if one only dares to look. We ARE of Source and once we find that power, that connection and peace, we begin to explore more in depth and realize that there are many things we have come to believe as a people or culture that might not be exactly what they have seemed to be.

How do we prove something we cannot see? This is where past life regression helps. Though it's not the only way to explore beyond our human senses, it is a tried-and-true method yielding consistent results. The information that comes through can sometimes be verified and other times it cannot. Many regressionists have completed case studies over a lifetime of regressions, piecing together a bigger map of the universe. This is what I have dedicated my life to as well; exploring the depths of the soul beyond just what we experience here physically. It is a world we are only just beginning to truly explore. We have explored Earth and its many depths, but what about the soul and beyond?

Past Life Regression (PLR) hypnosis takes people into those deeper states where they can open that door to the broader part of their soul. The part that has always been there with us, lying dormant and waiting for when we only dare to turn the key and open the door. It's a personal choice that must be made by each person. Free will to begin to look beyond the veil if one chooses. It's no small feat, no matter where you are on your journey of discovery in your life. Past Life Regression has been around for quite some time and even then, as time has gone on, more layers to regressions have been discovered.

PLR allows us to begin opening that door to peek beyond this life and see what might come from it. What life we may see, many times, is a surprise from what we expected. I tell all of the people I regress; you will see what is most important to you at the time you are doing it and what will help the most with where you are in life right in this moment. That is the reason for this; a catalyst to propel you forward in life in the direction you are meant to go. Help to heal those inner parts of self from cycles that may go beyond just this current life. Clearing or understanding unexplainable patterns or blocks that are put in place for reasons you are ready to discover. A depth you wouldn't explore without those placeholders in the way for that very reason. Waking you up to the vastness of your soul and learning there is more to you and who you truly are.

If you've ever asked yourself, "is there more to this life and beyond it?", then you may be ready to see for yourself. That is what the calling of the soul looks like after all. A hint, a nudge, a question only you can begin to answer. If you have felt the pull, or have heard the whisper, then you know that your Soul is ready to open the door. Ready to begin a new journey of deeper self-discovery.

There is so much that goes into coming to Earth that we are not aware of at first, or sometimes at all, but there is a rhyme and a reason to all of this madness. All of these lessons and experiences we must go through; what if you planned it all? Maybe not down to the detail, no because we can never do that. It's too intricate, but what about maybe a blueprint? What if you could look at that blueprint and begin seeing the patterns and lessons? Accept them and move beyond the maze you have found yourself in? It's all for a reason and it's not hard once you begin to see it come together.

Now there is a difference between some of these sessions you will get to explore. I want to show you the depth of which I am speaking. Everyone is in a different place of exploration, so these depths are different for everyone. Some only want to just know there is something more. Some have a million and one questions about that or something more. I'll raise my own hand here. I never stop with the questions, I ask and then ask some more, even when I don't always like the answer.

Past life regression can encompass many things within a single session. There is exploring any life beyond this one, life after death or life as another civilization all together. Sometimes that also includes other dimensions, life planning, and experiencing real time visitations from past loved ones or guides who have a message to pass on to help in the current life.

Then there is something we call the Higher Self. This is the new depth that has recently been discovered over the last forty or fifty years. That may seem like a long time, but it really isn't in the big scheme of things. PLR goes back a long way in use for tapping into deeper levels of the self.

The Higher Self IS the bigger part of us. It's our soul that has the broader view and can answer questions beyond our general knowledge. This connection that is created during a session is powerful in a quite unique way, deeper than just exploring. Exploring itself is powerful and is not to be discounted however, the Higher Self, when accessed via hypnosis, allows communication with your own larger self. There is no go-between, and no way for the information that you are ready for, to be altered in any fashion. It comes straight from within you. That is what our souls want for us ultimately, for us to lean on our own truth. Our own internal connection.

---

## The "Higher Self" Explained.

The Higher Self is what is considered to be the larger part of our soul. The part of us that is beyond the physical body that can see the entire picture. Some people call it the subconscious, some call it the Higher Self and others have other varying names. For the purposes of this book and my training, I shall refer to this part of our souls as the Higher Self.

It has been consistent across the board; each person has their own Higher Self. Here's an example of how this is experienced: Say you're in a valley with a small and narrow point of view (the physical human) and your Higher Self is the bird in the sky that can see everything you cannot. We each have a vast and powerful soul, and a small part of that essence comes into the physical body. We are always connected to the larger part of our Soul i.e., the Higher Self, our entire life. There are varying degrees of connection for each person and each person chooses how much they want to connect with that larger part of themselves. Many feel that connection to something bigger that is beyond their physicality, but do not know how to put it into words or what to call it.

This is the connection we will explore here. There is much more out there; including guides, angels, deceased loved ones, God/Source, etc. but I won't go into that. For the purpose of this book, I will only cover the Higher Self connection.

The Higher Self is always guiding us but has to do so in a manner that is non-invasive. This means that it cannot look as if what we feel or get comes from an outside source. We are on a free will planet and because of that, it is our choice while we are here, whether or not we connect willingly to anything beyond us on a conscious or unconscious level. So, when we get those intuitive feelings or a lightbulb moment that is normally the Higher Self filtering down to us those "energy" messages that get translated in a manner our human minds can interpret. For most of us, we just think it is our own mind coming up with the ideas or thoughts.

Have you noticed that those moments tend to come when we are tuned out and not paying much attention, or maybe doing something else entirely? You see, when we are most receptive and connected is when the conscious mind is busy somewhere else. It's when we are in a light hypnotic state, day-to-day. You could be doing chores, driving, daydreaming, watching TV, doing a hobby, or walking in nature. Those are the moments we tend to get random ideas or ah-ha moments.

These are the moments that are easiest for our Higher Self to filter in hints and ideas. We are most receptive and open when in this state. It may seem as if our mind is the one getting it out of nowhere, but really, it's an orchestration between the bigger parts of our Self that is guiding us and helping us. We just don't realize it's not just the mind doing it and that it's meant to look like this. It's by design.

We have agreed that being human means we forget everything before this so there can be no interference in how we live our lives. This ensures free will, even if life turns out not to be what we had hoped or planned. Those little nudges that come as whispers, those are the course corrections we tend to get from

Spirit or Source. A nudge here, a nudge there. A random book or paper being handed to us that make us stop and realize something big. A song that stops you in your tracks. It's the little things that keep us on our path. Constant course corrections that create a seamless existence within our world.

Now sometimes, there are big course corrections. The Higher Self almost always explains these and why they have to happen in some form or another. If we are not listening to our internal nudges and guidance, there is a need to get our attention in a bigger way. I cannot count the ways the Higher Self has used the physical body or things around us to get our attention. Many times, it is a physical issue that directly relates to the problem a person is not facing, manifesting as maybe a major wreck, injury, illness, death, or such.

So many times, they have explained that in order to wake ourselves up, drastic measures have had to be taken. Our own Souls are trying to find the best way to get us to listen. After all, we are the ones that planned what we wanted from the beginning. We knew coming in there would be difficulties because we forget. So, we have to figure out the best ways to get our own selves to listen. Those are some of the ways that are most effective. I know you have noticed that the biggest changes you have seen in people tend to come after major life events. These events cause us to have major breakdowns and stop us where we are. Only then do humans tend to change. We are creatures of habit, and we are on a planet of growth and change.

We are here to learn and grow, but we do not have to make it so difficult on ourselves. We are our own worst critics, however we can change that and become our own biggest advocates. Our soul team is on our side and cheering us on. Helping us in any way they can, but they cannot live it for us. We are the ones that must do the dirty work. Earth is the hardest school, and we are the graduating class.

As we grow, Spirit grows. As we learn, they learn. It does not matter what name you give to the world beyond us. Names are not important but the feeling inside our hearts are. We can begin to find this deeper connection within the self by allowing ourselves to look inside, to look within. Once you face the inner darkness, they say, you will find the beauty of the rainbow at the end of the storm. It's worth the journey and it's worth wading through the mud. Everyone experiences life's journey in their own unique ways.

Some of these sessions will have conversations with the Higher Self-included. Each Higher Self has its own personality and feelings about a topic. Though most of the time the info may vary slightly, I have found that the core information is always the same. So, while the information or advice may seem odd or unusual, you have to remember its being filtered through the person that needs to hear it in a certain way to understand it. Some are quirky, some are drill sergeants, and some are soft and easy to talk to. But always, it's an extension of the person to whom they are connected. I have found that the Higher Self knows the person better than they know themselves, and they always want what's best for the person they are so lovingly connected to.

So, sit back and enjoy the variety that is life and a peek into the world beyond.

---

## Why share these sessions?

I know I have been asked, what's the point in sharing these? Why write a book about it? I had to sit back and really think about WHY I have wanted to share these for so long. I have known since the first year that I began this journey, that I wanted to put them in this format to share. But what will it do for those who read it? Well, I think there are many bits and pieces of these stories that resonate for people. However, when it truly comes down to the why…

It's the missing piece. There are so many searching and looking for this missing piece that they can't seem to find. It feels elusive, like something you forgot, and you can't quite place your finger on it. And that missing piece for everyone is different.

This can be explained in so many ways, but we come here and we forget. We forget why we chose this and we forget what we wanted to learn and grow from. We forget what lessons we planned for ourselves. Our hopes and desires. And we feel a pull to something that feels just outside of our reach. That fork in the road we can't quite figure out. Or that connection to someone that we know is more than what it seems on the surface. That draw to things that seem unexplainable, and cannot explain to others but we FEEL it. A pain within the body that no one can figure out. A unique feature that tells a story. And we just know there is a reason why. Everyone has felt that inkling of something more beyond what they are experiencing. And for each person, that pull is different. But it's what pushes us forward through times of discomfort and pulls us out of our complacency when we stall.

For these people, they chose this path of exploration to find out why. If you felt called to this book, you may find your soul is asking you to answer that call too. It may not be through this method of exploration, but the soul calls us. It asks us to find a way to discover more about who we are and why we are here. It's time to awaken to who we are outside of the day-to-day world we focus upon. We can live a life of purpose on Earth in a physical way, that is part of why we are here. But we can also grow from the inside out. Dive into the depths of our soul and understand more of why we are here and what we meant to do. It changes how we interact with the world around us, making us better humans, and better companions and friends. Overall I find it makes life a lot easier to understand, and all you have to do is open the door and look inside.

# CHAPTER 1
## "Margie"

I am beginning this book with a session that really shows what a past life regression is all about. I am given a small window into someone's life, and they put their full trust in me while we are together. This process is a door we open to the soul, and this is a beautiful example of that experience.

I usually take clients to a beautiful place before we dive further into a past life and really begin exploring. This allows us to begin to open the door. It allows the client to dip their toes in and fully relax. Then we are able to make a smooth transition into a past life from there. Normally I would not include that opening, but in this session, I noticed it was different than normal, so I included it here. And I was right, it was important, and the reason why is revealed in the conversation with the Higher Self.

This session includes life after death and what we might encounter as well as the life planning before we come back. This client has had an EXTREMELY hard and painful life. She has only ever experienced pain and heartache. She has still somehow prevailed in life and found a way to move forward. She is truly a beautiful soul inside and out.

*Also note, the grammar in these session transcripts is different than how sentence structure normally looks. This is because I am typing up word for word how these sessions transpired. So, if you are an English major or grammar aficionado, please set that hat aside for this book because there are some hard transitions and many, many errors in sentence structure. In the transcripts, I will use the first letter of my name to denote my speech and the first letter of the client's name to denote responses. *

*Session begins

C: Can you find a place like that? (Yes) Tell me about it.

M: It's a beach. It's quiet. Except for the ocean sounds. There are no people around. The palm trees are so green. Healthy. The breeze is warm. It smells so good. Feels like where I belong.

C: Tell me more. What else are you noticing around you?

M: I'm noticing the soft sand under my feet. There's some mountains? Out on the horizon. It's almost like a cove. Hmm. It feels so safe. It feels so, just, the energy is calm. Serene. The water is blue, it's beautiful. The sky is blue. Deep blue. Sparse clouds in the sky. It's almost, it is a safe haven. It's a very, it's the closest place on earth that you can be to God.

C: And when you look behind you, what do you notice?

M: There's a grove of trees. But there is a little cabin. There is a porch. And it's breezy. It's a cute little cabin.

C: Are there any sounds around you?

M: It's the ocean. Ocean and, *Laughs* there's a wind chime on the porch of the cabin and it's pretty big. *Smiling* It has a deep tone to it. And as it blows in the wind it's such a deep tone, I can feel it. I can feel it in my chest, I can feel it in my body. When it sounds...

C: What does it feel like when you feel that vibration? (I knew something was different here.)

M: It feels like it's healing. It's a good feeling frequency. Feels like it's clearing things out.

C: What else do you notice around you as you're experiencing this?

M: Comfort. Like it's all comfortable. Temperature is perfect. And everything is just beautiful. I am happy.

C: Are the wind chimes still chiming?

M: Yes.

C: What else are you noticing as you feel that?

M: That I can breathe better. I can relax. It's taking away all my worries. It's taking away all the fears. And just puts me in a good frame of mind. It just makes me feel as I imagine I'm supposed to feel all the time. I could just stay here forever.

C: It's a lovely feeling that peace. *Suggestions to drift off into a past life as we begin deepening the session. I knew they were up to something with that wind chime. I knew they would shed light on it when it was time but for now, it was time to deep dive into those lives and see what we could find.

C: What is the first thing that you notice?

M: A man. Standing. Tall. Can't see his face.

C: And as it comes into focus, tell me more about what you're noticing?

M: I can't see his face because it's me.

C: That's ok, when you look down at your feet, what do you notice?

M: They are big feet. * Laughs. * They have blue jeans and boots.

C: And what do the shoes look like?

M: They are like, um, work boots.

C: And what else do you notice?

M: Um, moving in and out of the body. It's like I'm inside it and outside it too.

C: That's perfect, as you look at your arms, what do you notice?

M: Notice there is a long sleeve shirt on. He is a very tall, big man. But seems a little older. Maybe 40, late 40s. He is got a watch on.

C: What does the watch look like?

M: Silver.

C: And as you look down at the hands, do they look worn?

M: Yeah. They look older than the rest of him.

C: Are you carrying anything with you?

24

M: I didn't see anything at first. But it looks like a backpack. Like an older, tattered backpack. More of a sling type backpack.

C: And as you look around you, what do you notice?

M: It's kind of blank. I don't really see anything around us. It's like we are just in a cloud. On the ground. It's foggy all around us.

C: As your exploring, the next breath you take, it will clear as it comes into focus. Do you hear any sounds around you?

M: I hear kids playing. They are being loud. But they are having fun.

C: And are there any smells?

M: Wood. I see a wooden fence.

C: Tell me about it.

M: It's a roughhewn fence. It's handmade.

C: What else are you noticing as you look around you?

M: Pastures. Green pastures. It's like the grass is thick but I feel like where the kids are playing in the background there is no grass. But I don't see the kids though. I can just hear them.

C: And as that's coming into focus, what are you doing?

M: Just standing still. I'm looking back at the man, it's almost like I'm merged with him but I'm not. I'm just standing still.

C: As you're standing there, you can press play on the scene and just watch what is going on, what do you notice?

M: He is nervous. But he is afraid and nervous, but excited at the same time. He is coming home.

C: Tell me more.

M: He is coming home for the first time in a long time. I don't know where he has been. But he, he is kind of stuck looking at the fence. He wants to keep moving but he is afraid.

C: What is he afraid of?

M: He is afraid that, he is afraid that they won't want him anymore. He is afraid he won't recognize people.

C: Do you get the feeling he has been gone a very long time?

M: Yes.

C: Just explain to me as he makes his decision what does he do?

M: He just takes a deep breath and gathers courage. And he is walking on the road now.

C: What does the road look like?

M: It's a dirt road.

C: What happens next?

M: He is walking to where the kids are playing. He sees the kids but doesn't recognize them.

C: What else do you notice?

M: There is a house in the distance. It's a big white house. With columns.

C: Does he recognize the house?

M: Yes. It looks more worn than the last time he saw it. Makes him sad.

C: What else is happening?

M: He is walking towards the house. Kind of slowed down a little. Notice the fruit trees. There are fruit trees there that used to be so small.

C: Is he taking that in?

M: Yes. He is confused about the kids. Where did the kids come from? Whose kids are they?

C: Is he worried?

M: Not really worried, he is surprised. Confused.

C: As he gets closer, what is going on?

M: They think, they think I'm dead.

C: Why would they think that?

M: They think I'm dead because I've been gone so long. They might not want me here anymore. (Sad) But this is my home.

* Suggestions for no discomfort as she is preparing to walk into this house. I have no idea what to expect and she is already incredibly sad and confused. I was preparing her for anything. As any person would expect, we all have ideas of what might be waiting, and as always, that's how you know it isn't made up, because it's never as we might first assume. *

C: What do you notice now?

M: He is moving on, but he is very reluctant to go up the steps. He is wondering should he knock on the door. *Laughs* He has never knocked on the door in his life.

C: What does he decide?

M: He stops to start. He stops in front of the door, and he is about to knock but then changes his mind. He opens the screen door. It's loud. He smells… smells the house. It smells like it always did. Familiar smell. Makes him think of his grandmother. She was always so kind.

C: Whis his grandmother's house too?

M: Yes.

C: And who is in the house now?

M: He is not sure. He is thinking he might should have sent word ahead that he was coming.

C: How would he do that?

M: He would have written a letter. Or send someone. There is no phone.

C: What does he find when he goes in the house?

M: There is no one in there. There is no one in there. But things look, look like they did before. Little worn. More worn than it was but still the same furniture.

C: Does it feel good to be home?

M: It does. But it's scary. He doesn't know what he is going to find. He is wondering where his mother is. *Laughs. * He sees his grandmother.

C: He sees her?

M: He sees his grandmother. *Laughs* She sees him. She is confused about him standing there. But he realizes that it's not his grandmother, it's his mother.

C: Wow.

M: She has gotten old.

C: What happens next?

M: She is crying.

C: How does she feel?

M: *Laughs* She feels, she feels happy.

C: What does he do?

M: He drops his backpack. He hugs her. He is sad that she has gotten old without him being a part of it. But he is so glad to see her.

C: Tell me more.

M: They are both crying. She is pulling him in the kitchen. She is going to get him some food. And she is asking him where he has been and what happened. Why did he not come home before? Why has he been gone so long?

C: What does he say?

M: He has been in the war. He couldn't come home.

C: Why not?

M: They wouldn't let him come home. And when he got out, he was too ashamed to come home.

C: Why does he feel that way?

M: Because he killed people.

C: He has a hard time with that?

M: Yeah. It took him a long time to get the courage to come home. He is feeling different about it now. He feels, he feels more, he understands more about what happened. Why it had to happen. He had help. That's why he came home.

C: What kind of help?

M: There was a woman that helped him get all of the bad thoughts out of his mind.

C: Tell me more about what's going on now that he is with his mother?

M: He is asking about his family, the rest of the family. He had a sister. Sister moved away. She didn't like it there; it was too boring. His dad died. He is sad about that. It smells so good in the kitchen. It's mom cooking.

C: What kind of food does he smell?

M: He hasn't had this type of food in a long time. He smells bread. It's cornbread. She wasn't prepared to cook food at that time, so she just made some cornbread. And he is going to eat it with syrup on it. * Laughs*

C: Does it taste good?

M: Yes *Joy in the moment* Where did the kids come from?

C: What does she say?

M: They are grandkids. They are her grandkids. She is taking care of them. She is raising them.

C: Where did they come from?

M: his brother. His brother died. His brother… and his wife was killed in an accident.

C: What kind of accident?

M: Some kind of vehicle. Seems like, I think it was a train but, um, I'm confused about how that could have happened.

C: What does she say about that?

M: The train hit them. They weren't on the train, the train hit them. And they left three kids.

C: How does he feel about that?

M: He is sad that his brother died. He didn't know anybody else. He didn't know the wife. He doesn't know the kids. He worries about his mother taking care of the kids because she is so old.

C: Is she getting around very well?

M: She is. The kids are very helpful. They are good kids.

C: What is he doing now?

M: He is looking around at all the repairs that need to be done on the house. Tells his mom he is going to get started on it. She doesn't want him to get started on it yet. She wants to spend some time with him. She wants to introduce him to the kids. She wants him to sit and rest for a little bit.

C: What does he do?

M: He goes out to the porch with her. Sitting on the steps. She is holding his hand. She missed him so much.

C: Is he happy?

M: He is happy and sad at the same time. He is sad that his brother and his dad have both gone. They left. And left his mother all alone and he feels like he should have come home sooner. He feels a lot of guilt.

C: Does he get to meet the children?

M: Hmm. They kept running around the house. They stopped really fast because they are scared because he is there. They don't know him. Two boys and a girl.

C: What happens next?

M: She calls them to come up the steps to meet their uncle.

C: Does he look like his brother?

M: Uncle John. She says meet your uncle John. They know who he is now. Because they have talked about him. Their dad talked about him. Their grandmother talked about him. He realized that they didn't forget him. Makes him happy that they didn't forget him. The oldest boy is named Tanner. *Stops for a moment and then giggles.* The girl is Melissa Grace. *Laughs* The oldest boy Tanner just keeps talking, asking questions.

C: And what is the other boy's name?

M: Tommy.

C: What questions is Tanner asking?

M: Where has he been? Where have you been for so long? Are you going to stay here? Do you like to fish? Are you going to help Grandmother? Are you going away again? Do you have a wife? Yes, I do.

C: He has a wife?

M: Yeah. His mother is surprised. Why didn't you bring her?

C: What does he say?

M: I didn't even know if I was going to be welcome. I didn't want to put her through that. She gave him a hug. She is sad because she thought, she is sad because she didn't want him to think he wasn't welcome.

C: What are they doing now?

M: Just hugging. Everybody is hugging. He said he is going to stay. And he is going to help her. And he will send for his wife. They are just having a reunion. It's all that's left. This is. His sister doesn't come home anymore.

C: Why not?

M: She doesn't like it there. Never came back.

C: Tell me what you notice now.

M: They are just sitting there. Looking out. Looking out over the yard and he is still thinking about all the things that need to be done. He knows, he knows it's his home and his house now. That his mother won't be there much longer and that he and his wife would finish raising the kids. They don't have kids of their own.

C: How does he feel about that?

M: Kind of glad that the kids are there. I don't think they can have kids. They haven't been able to have kids so far. He likes it there. He has plans to change things around. Plants and things.

C: What else is he going to do?

M: He is thinking he might sell some of the acreage because it's too big for him. He knows his mother doesn't want him to do that.

C: Why not?

M: Because it was land that her husband worked hard for. She doesn't want it to be sold off. He is not going to do it. He doesn't want her to worry.

C: *Suggestions to drift to an important day in the life she is viewing* What do you notice?

M: His wife is with him. They are all dressed up. Melissa Grace is getting married. He feels like he did a good job in raising her. She looks so pretty.

C: What else do you notice?

M: His mother is gone. She has been gone for a while. They are growing old. He feels healthy. But he is afraid that he is suffering, he is not well. He has been having, he has been having nightmares. He has been sad.

C: Tell me more. What are these nightmares?

M: Nightmares about the war. He can't stop them like he did before. They are just too much. He carries this heavy burden. It's too much for him. Melissa Grace was the last of the kids to leave the house. He feels like it's time for him to go.

C: Does he feel it in his body or just in his mind?

M: Just in his mind. Feels it in his spirit. He is tired. He has done all he cares to do in this world. Now that the last kid is out, he doesn't have a reason to stay.

C: What about his wife?

M: She is pretty strong. She will be ok. But she will follow him. He knows, he knows when he goes, she will follow him.

C: And they are both older now?

M: Yes, they are seventies.

C: Is that a long time to live?

M: He feels like he has lived longer than anybody. There is nobody. Nobody around him that is as old as he is. He knows he was just waiting until he had the kids raised.

C: Did he enjoy raising the kids?

M: Yes. They were good kids. They were already good kids when he met them. His Mom did a good job. He feels like that was given to him because it's the only thing that would have kept him in this world. He didn't really want to be here.

C: What are you noticing around you now?

M: The sun is going down. It's getting darker in the house. Everyone is gone.

C: Is the wedding over?

M: Yes, everybody is gone. Just him and his wife.

C: How is he feeling?

M: Relieved. He feels like this is the last day. And he is at peace with that.

C: Well as he gets ready to take his last few breaths, explain to me what you are noticing.

M: He is next to his wife. He is grateful. He feels grateful for her. He has a lot of guilt. Because he is so ready to go but he is leaving her behind. But he knows it's his time.

C: Will she follow soon, or does she have a while?

M: She is going to follow very soon. She doesn't want to be here without him. They had such a good life together. There is no reason for her to stay either.

C: As he is taking his last breath *Suggestions for no discomfort* and as he is looking back down, what does he notice?

M: He notices how beautiful his wife is.

C: What is he seeing now from his perspective?

M: He is seeing everything. He is seeing everything at the same time. He is in the past and the future. He sees everything around him.

C: As he is looking at that life, he will be able to see the purpose of that life, what was the purpose?

M: His purpose was to suffer and still be able to help his family. They were supposed to get through. He was supposed to get through the suffering. But he knows that he was only coming through it because of his wife. She kept him calm. She helped him to forget. But he never got over it. He feels like he failed in that aspect. But there is a lot that he is proud of in that life.

C: Was there anything he meant to do that he wasn't able to?

M: He wanted to have kids of his own. *Sigh*

C: As he is looking around, what is he seeing?

M: Back to the way it was when they came home that day. He worked so hard to keep it up. But when he got old, it just crumbled. He feels that's what happened with his life. But he was happy there. That was the only place he was ever at peace.

C: Well as he is floating in this space, what does he become aware of around him?

M: He sees a light.

C: What does he do?

M: Goes toward it.

C: Tell me about it.

M: He floats up into it. He likes the feeling of it. He has a very good understanding and knowing, there is no confusion, there is no worry, no fear. It's just like coming home. He understands. There is nothing to worry about. Just moves toward it.

C: Does he go within this light?

M: He goes.

C: What does it feel like?

M: It feels warm and comforting. Surrounds him. He just kind of becomes the light. Moves around like a ball of energy. He feels like he has done this so many times and that's his favorite part. His favorite part when he comes. So, light. And free and flowing.

C: Why is this his favorite part?

M: Because the body is so cumbersome. Being in a human body is suffocating to him. He loves it when he comes out of it, and he can move around like he is supposed to.

C: Now what does he do when he can move around?

M: He just plays like a kid. But he knows he has to stop and go inside. His mother is waiting on him. His dad and brother are there too. They all just hug. They are welcoming him home. He likes being able to move around. Fly around. He thinks he like Peter Pan. *Laughs*

C: Feels good?

M: Yeah.

C: What is he doing now?

M: He is moving. Moving on into the space he is supposed to be in.

C: Tell me about that.

M: He has to have a life review.

C: Take me through what that looks like for him. Is there someone there with him?

M: His mother is there. His guide. He doesn't really want to do this life review, but he knows he has to. He understands. He sees when he was a kid. Playing outside with his siblings. He pushed his sister down. He feels bad about that. He helps her up. He got her dress dirty, and it made her cry. He is moving forward quickly. Quickly to the day he felt so happy when he signed up for the Army.

C: Why was he happy?

M: Because he felt like this is what everybody was supposed to do.

C: What else is he seeing?

M: He is seeing the people that he killed in the war. It's all slow motion. He sees it in their eyes. The fear. He is trying not to let that happen. He is trying to stop that. Oh. He can't. He can't stop it. So, just resigns himself to seeing it.

C: Is it hard for him to see this?

M: It is. He can see there, what their families went through. *Pained sounds* That's very painful for him. But then he sees his wife. That's what led to him meeting her.

C: Why is that?

M: She saved him. She saved him from killing himself. She helped him.

C: He wouldn't have met her if not for the war?

M: He wouldn't have met her.

C: Had he planned that meeting to be with her?

M: Yes. Yes. He remembers. He remembers the planning. I'm looking at it now. He knows he didn't understand the pain he would have to go through to get to her with the plan that he had.

C: What had he planned?

M: He planned to go to the war. That was in his life plan. And he regretted that because it was so painful. It was painful when he was going through it and even afterwards. He realized that he didn't, he never got over all of that. And that was the big thing he was supposed to do during that life, was to get over that, get past it. Learn to deal with it. But he never did.

C: How was he supposed to get past it?

M: He was supposed to heal from it. He was supposed to understand why it was a part of his life. Why it was necessary. He never did. He always felt like it didn't have to happen. He always felt like it was useless for people to go to war. He couldn't get to the point where he was ok with how everything played out. So, he feels like he was, he didn't fulfill what he was supposed to do in this life. But he thinks he will plan a better one next time.

C: Tell me about that.

M: He thinks he will... he thinks he will have a whole different life next time. But he knows he has to learn that lesson somehow. But he is trying not to make things as hard on himself the next time.

C: Is he still going through his life review?

M: He is finished. He finished with this life when he was seeing her.

C: So, what is he doing now?

M: He is just resting. He is not doing anything. I think he is just fading.

C: Tell me more about what you are noticing?

M: Emptiness. There is nothing.

C: Well as he starts to plan his next life, what do you notice?

M: He... he is waiting. He is not in a hurry. He knows he wants to do another life, but he is just taking his time.

C: What is he doing while he is waiting?

M: Nothing, he is just blissfully floating in nothing. I see pins of light everywhere. It's a healing chamber.

C: Tell me more about this chamber.

M: It's just a place where you're weightless and you are just floating around. Almost like a little bit of pressure. A little pressure in the chamber where you can feel that it's there. It's designed so you'll know. You're in space but you're inside a chamber. See these little pins of light everywhere. Those are helpers.

C: What are they healing in this chamber?

M: They are healing the pain that was caused in the last life. That he was having trouble getting past.

C: And is it helping?

M: Yes.

C: What else do you notice within this chamber?

M: There is no time. There is no, there is only happiness. Only good. There is a purge of all the pain. Just kind of comes out and he looks at it. Just watching it. Almost like a cloud in front of him. And just moving away with his hand. And watch it disintegrate.

The pins of light are getting brighter. They are coming nearer. Because he is ready to come out.

C: Tell me about this process of removing him, what comes next?

M: They all gather closer to him, and the light gets bigger. Engulf him in light. And they just move out of there. He is just floating in that light.

C: What does it feel like?

M: It feels wonderful. It feels like just being free of everything. So energized. Such a safe and warm place to be. Just full of love. But they are taking him to a conference room.

C: Tell me more about this room.

M: It's the planning room. There are souls around in the planning room just waiting for him.

C: Do you recognize them?

M: No, they don't look like people. It's just like balls of light.

C: What are you doing now in this room?

M: Looking at a map. Got to figure out where to be next time. Where I've got to plan my next life.

C: What does this map look like?

M: I don't know what it looks like; it doesn't make any sense to me. It's… it's not big but it's supposed to be like… like *pause* I don't see it anymore.

C: What is he doing now?

M: It's just… we are floating. Nobody is sitting there. They are just floating.

C: What is he deciding on?

M: He has decided not to plan another life right now.

C: Why not?

M: He doesn't feel like he is ready for it. He feels better, he feels good. But he isn't ready to go again. He wants to… no he isn't sure if he wants to incarnate on the earth again. He is thinking he may incarnate in a different place.

C: Where is he considering?

M: *Pause* I don't know what the name of it is.

C: What do the helpers say? Can you tell me the name or the place?

M: Hmm. That can't be right? That's not real.

C: What do they say?

M: They say it's Andromeda. But I don't think that's right.

C: What does he decide?

M: He decides that is where he wants to go.

C: Tell me about planning to go to this place.

M: He wants to be in a life that doesn't have any decisions, that doesn't have any bad things happen. The only thing he can do is vegetation. He wants to be…he wants to be a plant on the other planet. It's a short life but it's not traumatizing like the last one.

C: What does he hope to learn?

M: Patience.

C: Why would he do that?

M: There is nothing else you can do when you're a plant. All you have are your thoughts. All you have are what comes by. There are no worries. There are no worries if something happens. You come right back home. But it helps to rest. And to think and to learn patience.

C: He is ready to learn this?

M: Yes.

C: So, what does that planning look like?

M: His helpers know that he won't really need much help. It's a very simple life and it's not challenging at all, and they encourage him not to do that.

C: What does he decide?

M: *Giggles* He decides not to do anything right now.

C: Was the planet already formed that he was going to?

M: Yes, it was already formed. There was no people. Only vegetation.

C: Was there anyone else there?

M: There are no humans. Only live beings. Humans are so archaic.

C: And did the planet already have a soul, if you were going to come in and be the soul?

M: Yes.

C: How does that work?

M: There is room for both. I don't understand that. *Mutters to herself* Help me understand that? (This commentary back and forth can sometimes happen when the Higher Self says something so out there that the conscious mind pops in for a moment to argue or banter back and forth.)

C: What does he do now?

M: He feels like he wants another incarnation on the Earth, but he needs to wait because it's so hard. It's so dense. The planet is very hard for souls to be on.

C: I want you to fast forward until he is ready to pick his next incarnation as a human. And as he is getting ready to finally pick his next incarnation, tell me what you notice.

M: He is going to be a female this time. And he is looking at parents. What parents does he want?

C: What are the options?

M: The options are infinite. He can choose whoever. He can choose whenever or whatever.

C: What does he choose?

M: He chooses *Pause* Hmm. I'm not getting it. I don't know if I trust it.

C: What are you noticing?

M: That he has chosen to reincarnate as a slave.

C: Tell me more about this decision.

M: He feels strong right now. He feels like he could do anything. He gave himself time to heal and now he can do the tough part.

C: What does he think he will learn from this?

M: He will learn how to overcome tough decisions. He didn't do that last time.

C: What kind of decisions will he have to make?

M: He feels like it's a hardship and he deserves a hardship because he killed people in his last life.

C: What will this do for him?

M: It will show him how it feels to be, show him how it feels to not have any control of himself.

C: What do the helpers say about this decision?

M: The helpers think it's a pretty tough decision. They don't think he should do it.

C: What does he decide?

M: He decided he will do, um, be a male instead of a female. But he is going to do the slave thing anyway. I think he feels like he deserves that bad, but he doesn't. His spirit team is telling him no. He doesn't deserve to deal with that just because he thinks he did wrong in the last life. He can't judge that in this space. You can't judge that as good or bad. But, he still feels that way, so they know that he is not ready.

C: He is not ready? What does that mean?

M: He needs to choose something different, or he needs to wait. But it's still his choice.

C: What does he decide?

M: He decides to go ahead with it. He is going to be a slave.

C: What does that look like from this point of view?

M: It looks very hard. He will be in Africa.

C: Will he be a slave his entire life?

M: He dies early. He was sold and taken on a ship, and he dies on the ship. He didn't make it to his destination. That was a compromise that he was making with his team because they didn't want him to do it, but he felt like he needed to. So, it was a compromise.

C: He felt like he did what he wanted to?

M: Yes, yes.

C: Does he feel better?

M: Yes.

C: I want to ask the helpers, is it a good time to bring forward the Higher Self? To ask some questions. May we do that?

M: Yes.

C: *Brings forward the Higher Self* The incarnation as Margie, thinks she has something hidden inside of her at this time. She cannot put words to it. Can you tell her what is going on?

M: She has a block. She is the one blocking it.

C: How can she unblock it at this time?

M: She has to connect to me.

C: What is the block?

M: There is no, there is no reason for the block anymore. The block was put there years ago. But there is no reason for it anymore, she just doesn't know how to get rid of it.

C: Well as we are connecting now, is that helping to reestablish the connection?

M: Yeah.

C: Will it be easier for her to connect now?

M: Yes.

C: How will she know that she is connecting to you?

M: She has to be quiet. So quiet her mind and she will know. Trust her intuition. She doesn't trust. She doesn't trust those feelings. She has to trust it.

C: She wants better communication with her Higher Self and her Spirit team, can you tell her how she can do that?

42

M: She has to meditate. She doesn't think she can meditate because she can't slow down long enough to do that. She has to do it.

C: Can you assist her with this?

M: I can.

C: How can she slow down to meditate?

M: She has to put herself first. She has to put her mental health and her spiritual wellbeing before the physical aspects of her life because that's what fuels her.

C: She is getting better at doing that, is she not?

M: She is. but she still doesn't meditate.

C: How often should she do this?

M: She should do this daily. When she starts. It's going to be difficult. But after she does it for a bit, it will become easier, and she will want to make more time for it and the connection will be stronger every time she does it.

C: Is there anything preventing her connection from being as strong as possible at this time?

M: She has trouble believing. It's just her mistrust of herself that prevents her from connecting.

C: Well, she wants to have the ability to channel better, how can she do that?

M: Meditate. When she starts to meditate, all aspects of her spiritual life will be open to her. All things that she knows. Some things that she doesn't know she has the ability to do will come through.

C: Can you tell her more about that? These abilities?

M: She has the ability to, she already knows that she has the ability to see the lives of the people in front of her. She knows that she can channel but she doesn't understand that she can know these things without effort. She will know when she is supposed to be talking to someone and when she is not. She knows this to some extent now. The thing that she doesn't know is the

43

clairvoyance that she has, she hasn't experienced this yet, but she is very strong.

C: Can you help her with that clairvoyance now? Show her what that feels like, so she knows, or show her when she is ready?

M: Yes.

C: And how are you doing that?

M: Showing her how to open her mind. Showing her what it feels like.

C: And she will remember this?

M: Yes.

C: Is that what is happening when she sees patients, when she feels that on occasion?

M: Yes.

C: How can she do that more often with her clients, or with life in general?

M: Just understand that it doesn't come from her. From her brain, doesn't come from her mind, comes from her heart. And she opens it when she knows that she wants to help them. She opens her heart and the channel comes through. When she learns how to connect with her heart and not her brain, not her mind, she will be able to connect anytime she is ready to.

C: She wants to know is she still being driven by her trauma?

M: Very much so. Very much so. But it's not a bad thing like she thinks it is. The pain of the trauma, she has learned to work through. She has worked through the pain and the trauma. But the lessons of the trauma are what drives her now, that is what helps her to do a better job at what she does. It helps her to connect with the people that come to her. So, she just needs to know that it's not that, being trauma driven is not what it seems to be in the language that she is using. It's a good thing that she is being trauma driven.

C: Can you tell her more about that? Was that part of her purpose coming in? To deal with trauma and learn from it like the last life as that man?

M: Yes. It's been very cumbersome for this Soul to learn about how to carry the drama but not carry the pain or trauma. The drama as well. *Laughs*

C: So, what does she need to know about that?

M: She needs to know that everything isn't as it seems. She is looking through it, looking at it through the limited thought patterns that the mind has. This is how meditation will help her to be able to understand these things. That she was put through all the hardships and all the sadness and all the difficult times because when it was pressing down her ego it was allowing her heart to grow. Because what she was learning was not what she didn't want to happen. It was what she did want to happen. She wanted to feel love and the best way to feel love was to give it. So, the trauma was growing that ability to love and to feel love. But now she can't accept it.

C: Can you assist her with accepting love so that she may experience that more fully in her life?

M: I can assist her, but she has to let go of that in her mind. She has to learn a different way of viewing it. There is not a right way or a wrong way. There are only pathways that she takes to get what she thinks she wants but she is not thinking deep enough. There is no way to get there through the mind and through the thoughts. You can only get there through the heart. She has to learn to keep her heart open more and not let it close for herself. She tends to love more outside of herself than she does inside. So, once she finally gets that she has a love out there. But she is not ready for them because she doesn't know how to love herself.

C: Can you assist her more with loving herself and showing her how, so she feels that love?

M: Yes, I can.

C: When will she be ready for that love that she is searching for?

45

M: It can be pretty quickly. If she works on the things that she needs to work on. Starting with the meditation.

C: And does this trauma affect her weight?

M: It does.

C: Can you tell her about that?

M: It's the thing she doesn't want to let go of. It's the thing she doesn't want to face.

C: And what is that?

M: *Sigh* So, she has a lot of sexual trauma that started the weight gain and then as she tried working on that, it kind of went to the wayside. She never dealt with that. She dismissed it as being her fault and if it's her fault, then no one could help her with it. So, because she was so young, and because men looked at her the way that they did, then she didn't want them to. So, she started gaining weight so they wouldn't. She didn't know when to stop. She still doesn't know when to stop. So that is what she has to deal with. She has to work through that. So, she can be comfortable in looking the way she would typically look without that trauma causing her to gain weight.

C: Would she feel much better if she let this go?

M: Yes. She would. She would also have much better relationships. More meaningful relationships.

C: Is this why she has had such difficult relationships in the past?

M: Yes, she has been looking for something her whole life and she has never been able to find it. She has been looking for it in the wrong places. She has been looking for it in different people. She is trying to find acceptance in people who refuse to accept her. She is trying to find her way to reverse the problems that she had in childhood. She is trying to find a way to get rid of those feelings that were in her when she was very young. She has been trying to find a way to make that go away all these years and that is why she is choosing these types of partners. These men that she has chosen, will always be what they are. They will never change. So, when she is in a relationship, she thinks they have changed. They didn't, they never changed. She did.

C: So that is why each relationship is a bit better over time?

M: Yes. Because she heals a little bit every time. She became stuck.

C: And she is ready to make another leap to meet the right person?

M: She is ready to meet the right person, but she is not trusting herself. She has to be able to trust herself. She has to be able to open up her heart and not so much worry about her mind.

C: And you will be able to assist her with this? This connection with her heart?

M: I will.

C: Is this also why she is having problems with her sisters? What is going on with that? With being cut off?

M: That is, I know that that is difficult for her. She is very family oriented. But it has to be that way because they are not ready to move forward. They are not ready to be in the, they are not ready for the new earth that is coming. They cannot come with her. There are a lot of people that have left her life in one way or another. And they weren't as significant as her family members. So, she is not seeing that there are so many people that have had to leave that life because of her spiritualism and how she is vibrating higher and still rising, they can't come with her. But the family is very significant. So, she didn't miss that one. She didn't miss them moving away from her and leaving her life. And unless they choose, unless their souls choose to wake them up, they are, nothing will change. There is nothing that Margie can do about this. There is nothing that she can do about this. She just has to wait. And let them make their choices. She doesn't need to contact them, she doesn't need to try to make the situation better because it's not an actual situation and in spiritual terms, it's their opportunity to either rise, or not. It has nothing to do with her.

C: That was one of her questions, she felt like she kept getting held back to contact them. Why is that?

M: If she contacts them, she is only going to get hurt and she may set them back. It may be a setback for them if they are getting closer to this spiritualism. If they are getting closer to waking up, it could set them back so it's for her good and their good that she doesn't.

C: She wants to know about twin flames. Could you tell her about this and that love that is coming for her? Are they connected?

M: There are twin flames, they come, sometimes they come together, and sometimes they don't. The person that is out there for her is going to be completely devoted to her. And they are going to give her everything that she wanted as far as emotional stability and love. But as far as a twin flame is concerned. Hers is not a romantic twin flame. Hers is a companionship.

C: Can you tell her more about that?

M: The way that your life is set up, as far as going through the learning process of relieving yourself from the trauma of your childhood. Going through several marriages and other long-term relationships that did not end in marriage, then the twin flame for you had to be a companionship not a romantic one. You have a soul mate that is there for you. That is going to be coming to you. The twin flame dynamic is not the most pleasant dynamic when it comes to human behaviors. Because you have to fight, and you have to hurt one another in order to teach one another and that's a very simplistic way of putting it but that's good enough for now.

C: So why are twin flames so romanticized if it is not such a great thing? Even if it is for the greater good.

M: Because everyone wants to think that they have a connection that strong. Everybody wants to think that when they get with somebody. Especially early in a relationship they think that that is how it's going to be. They don't understand that the twin flame dynamic is one, a volatile one because it's an accelerated learning program. For those who need to learn more about themselves and heal more quickly. If you have a twin flame, and you meet with that twin flame you are going to be learning pretty quickly because there is a mirror that is put in front of you. You see your

48

flaws; you see your flaws in them. But then you understand they are yours. It's a painful process. But it's a beautiful process in the end. But people romanticize it for a totally different reason. They believe that they have that close connection with their partner, and they don't really.

C: And she will meet her twin flame, but it will be a companionship, less volatile?

M: She already has. But it has not been as volatile as it could have been because they haven't engaged in that at this point. She will meet her soul mate, she will meet one of her soul, what is the word? * Pause, Sigh* Soulmate is the only word I can come up with that's going to work as well. *Laughs* Because of the language that we have. Soulmate. It's a team member. That's on her team.

C: Her soul family?

M: That is the right phrase! The Soul Family. She will meet that person, and things will be amazing for her. And well deserved. But she is got to be, she has to understand that she is ready for it.

C: But she has to do the work?

M: Yes, I would say that she has done the work in an existential way, but she hasn't internalized that yet. She hasn't, she doesn't understand that if she just opens herself up and trusts her intuition that she will be that beacon of light that will guide that soul to her. She will know who it is, but she hasn't learned to trust herself like that yet.

C: And does she need to do anything through this, to lose the weight? Or will it fall off naturally?

M: It will fall off naturally, but she will start to feel like she doesn't want the same things that she had before. The cravings that she had before will go away. So, it's not a lot of effort she will have to put into it. But things will change in her habits naturally.

C: And as she is moving forward in this part of her life where she is looking to open her own business, she wants to reach more people. How can she do that? She feels the pull.

M: She is already doing that. She just doesn't have any confidence in herself. She is already making the moves she needs to do. She is already opening up those avenues. There are more people talking about her than she understands. There are more people who want the knowledge and the understanding that she has. And she hasn't come across that yet. It's coming. It's going to come for her. She is doing all of the right things. Taking all of the right steps. She needs to stop worrying so much about that and continue on her path.

C: And she will recognize that? When he walks into her light?

M: She will! She will. She will be able to see the avenues that have been opened for her. The opportunities will be pretty obvious. She won't miss them. But she still has to choose them.

C: Will she be speaking publicly or will there be another way that she will get this out?

M: She will start speaking publicly in smaller venues because as much as she wants to go reach big crowds, um, she is not ready for that. She is very introverted, and she has a fear of people. Social phobia. However, when she actually gets started speaking to people, she is so on… passionate about the knowledge she is giving them. And she can help them feel like she can feel the good that she is doing in the crowd. Once she gets started, she is good, but she has to start small. She can't start as larger as she wants to. She can start small, and it can get as big as she has the capacity to deal with. So, it's up to her how big it gets. It will grow.

C: Well now that she is feeling these emotions from people around her, it seems to be getting stronger and stronger, so she feels like she is empathic, she is struggling. How will she handle this as she is getting into bigger things?

M: She was doing really well at this at one point. Once she recognized what it was. But she has fallen off from those practices. She doesn't say those prayers of protection that she did before, when she starts her day. And she doesn't, she surrounds herself with the live crystals that she has. And those are very protective, but she doesn't care for those crystals as she should. She doesn't

50

charge them. She doesn't clean them. They are all very dull right now. They are very covered. They are not working as well as they should. So, I would say that she knows what to do, she has just been a little bit behind on caring for those things. So, as she gets stronger and as she gets more of these feelings, her practice isn't coming along with her. So, I would just say that she is very good at shielding herself, but she has not been doing it like she is supposed to.

C: And how does she clear her crystals, clean them so they are more vibrant?

M: Well, she just has to hold onto them long enough. She doesn't touch them. Doesn't pick them up like she did before. She had at one time; she was taking some home with her because she has them in her office. She was taking them home with her and charging them and bringing charged ones back and really keeping them at their optimal level of protection. But she hasn't done that in a good while so it's being mindful, but she did, she does have good frequency and the singing bowl in her office. But she doesn't use that to cleanse them either so…

C: Does the singing bowl, does it clear the crystals?

M: It helps with clearing the frequencies. It doesn't cleanse them as well as charging them outside or charging them in your hands. Connecting with them. It just clears the frequency. It does allow them to work better.

C: She did want to know what frequency she is on, is she on the frequency of love like she feels like she is?

M: She is. Um. I think again she drowns out the things that help that grow. She has a capacity to send love out in long distances. She has done that before, and she knows that she feels that. And then there are times that she feels like she can't get that far outside of her body so, she is on the right frequency but again she closes herself off. So that's another thing that meditation will help her to do. To be able to continually put out the energy of love.

C: That scene that she saw at the beginning of her session, where she saw the cabin and the wind chimes. Why did she see them and feel them that way?

M: Because that frequency is the frequency that she has come into a few times. And she understands that that is the frequency that she needs to hear to keep her on the level that she needs to be on. But she keeps searching for that frequency and she can't find it. There are things that are put in front of her sometimes that will help her define that frequency, but she doesn't accept that at the time. So, I think that by now she understands that the next time that she comes across that frequency that she is going to have to take that opportunity. There was an actual wind chime as the one that she was seeing that she came across and she passed on. And then there was a singing bowl that she came across that she saw and passed on that. We will make sure that that gets in front of her again. But she has to accept it.

C: Is that frequency specific to her body, or her soul?

M: It's specific to her heart. That's what helps open up her heart.

C: So, did that assist her with the session today? Is that what allowed her to experience this?

M: Yes.

C: Would she have been able to without that frequency, without that tone?

M: No.

C: So, you assisted her with that today?

M: Yes.

C: I am sure she will appreciate that very much. I know she wanted to ask about her kids. How can she help them at this time?

M: As much as she does not want to hear this, she doesn't need to. She needs to love them. Teach them what she knows. Be there for them. But she can't do life for them. They have to learn this. They have to be able to do this on their own because that is their purpose. That was their plan. They have their own plan even though they are children. They are individuals. They are their own souls. And they have to learn things.

C: So, what is her biggest accomplishment in her life? What does she need to know about her accomplishments?

M: In this life, her greatest accomplishment is being a vessel full of love. Being able to find that love and love other people and the reason that is such an accomplishment for her is because she was never given that love. And the people in this world, in this life that she is living, this incarnation, have not shown her a lot of love. Yet she was able to find it and to be able to give it. So that was an accomplishment that we weren't sure that she was going to be able to do.

C: She should be so proud of that because it's a very big accomplishment. Through all of her adversity, is that correct?

M: Absolutely.

C: Has she done everything she wanted to do in this life, or everything that she had planned?

M: No.

C: Is she ready to hear about the next step?

M: The next step is to continue to work toward the new clinic that she is opening because that is going to open a lot of doors. New desires. Going to help her reach goals that she has for this life. That she doesn't even know about. It is going to help her to finish out the things that she is supposed to be doing. Although she has reached great heights. Through the adversity that she has been through. There are new things. But these new things are more rewarding than they are difficult. They are not going to be as hard as her life has been. It's going to show her that she is rewarded for the work that she has done. So, she needs to continue in doing what she is doing. It's not going to be easy. It's not going to be just handed to her. She has had to work for everything in her life. So that's not going to be anything new to her. But she is going to find a lot of new things on the other side of this endeavor.

C: Can you scan her body at this time and tell her if there is anything that she needs, or anything that needs attention at this time.

M: Yes. *Long pause* She needs to attend to her urinary tract. There is the beginnings of some problems there. She needs to attend to that. She needs to stop feeling like she needs the vape that she has been using. She has smoked for years and is finally able to stop. And that's something that was extremely difficult for her. The vape is a stand in. She doesn't need it anymore.

C: Can you help her with that?

M: I can.

C: And how will you do that?

M: I will give her the opportunity to find distractions from that. To find a way to not desire that anymore. But again, that's going to be her choice. She has to do her part in that as well.

C: And her urinary tract, can you help her with that? Work on that?

M: I will. She needs to stay hydrated. She needs to be better hydrated, and she needs to practice what she preaches when it comes to the herbalism that she has been working on. She's really telling other people to do these things, and she does a wonderful job at it, but she doesn't do it herself.

C: What are you able to do for her urinary tract if she does that?

M: I can assist her in knowing which of the teas that she needs. But she really needs to be hydrated. That's the biggest thing that she needs to do. She thinks that she is doing that, but she is not. She understands that drinking water hydrates you. That's what she teaches other people but then she neglects that in herself. So, the Celtic salt that she uses. She needs to be using that more times, well she has not been using it all lately. But she needs to be using that twice a day for the next week or so. To be able to clear this up.

C: Are you able to assist her with energy at this time for her urinary tract?

M: Yes, I will. The energy will help her, but she has to keep that up. She doesn't really take good care of herself. As far as the physical things. She does spiritually. But physically she doesn't take good care of herself.

C: If she wants a long healthy life to enjoy from here on out, she will need to take care of herself, won't she?

M: Absolutely.

C: Anything else she needs to take care of at this time?

M: She needs to learn to stop worrying about things. About what she doesn't have, and she needs to understand that she has everything she needs right now. That's where these panic attacks are coming from. She feels like she isn't going to have what she needs. And she always feels like she is going to have to struggle and fight for the things she wants. But she is not. She needs to relax. And understand that everything is already given to her. She just hasn't gotten to the place where they are here yet. This will happen. Again, this is about trusting herself, trusting her intuition. And being able to live in the now. Just live in what's happening right now. Pay attention to what's going on around her. And for her to be able to learn from what's going on right now. How to be calm. There is never a reason to be anything but calm. When you know that everything you need is just right there for you to get.

C: So, this is where her depression and anxiety and panic attacks come from?

M: Yes.

C: And that is all she needs to do?

M: Yes.

C: That's lovely. Sounds like a much easier way to help these issues. She wanted to know why she is not connected to those who have passed over.

M: Those who have passed on have lots of things to do, they are very busy. And sometimes they will come back to her or to people in general. Even though they have the ability to be in all places. And do all things. It's not really necessary to connect to these

55

people. Her father in this life was more of a fill in. Not really one of her typical incarnate mates I would call it. Not someone who incarnates with her a lot. So, whenever he went back to the other side, he went back to the soul family he is from. So, if she wants to call him to her, he would come to her or let her feel that he is near her, but she really hasn't, her soul really hasn't reached out. It's her mind that wants to connect, not her soul. Thinking about her mother. I know that she is concerned about her mother. The disconnect between her and her mother. Her mother in this life hasn't always been her mother and she needs to understand that. This soul that was her mother this time is often adversarial in her carnations. So that connection was never going to be what she felt it should. It was planned that way. It wasn't, if she had had a better connection with her mother, she never would have learned the lessons that she needed to learn to help her to survive all of the years of hardship that she has dealt with. Right now, the person that incarnated as her mother, she understands that that person is a guide for her niece's. That soul is the perfect guide for her nieces. They wouldn't be where they are otherwise. So, things are exactly as they should be. It's her egoic mind that feels like it needs that connection. Because they are all connected. So that's just something that her ego is going to have to settle. And she can. She can do that with this information she can do that.

C: Do you have any other messages for her that will help her on her journey?

M: I would say that the connection that she has been looking for, to her spirit team, to her Higher Self, it's always there. It's always there and she knows when that connection is strong. She knows when she is being led to something. She knows when she is being held back from something as well and understands that there is a reason for that. But she has a problem with her physical, the physical part of her. The egoic mind is in the way all the time. That is difficult I know to set aside. But that goes back to the meditation that she needs to be doing. Once she has regular practices in meditating, she will be able to stop that egoic mind from blocking the things that she is looking for spiritually. Her spirit team is very good at being right there for her. As all spirit teams are. But she feels like they are not working for her, they are not doing as much as they should. But she needs to understand that it's that physical part of her that is holding her back from that. It will be there once she puts in the work to tame her egoic mind a little bit.

C: Thank you for that. I know she will appreciate all of the help you have given her today.

*Close out Session.

# CHAPTER 2

## "June"

This client was one that came to me early on in my first year of working with past life regression. My techniques were very new, and I was just learning how to manage sessions. This will sound quite different than chapter one's session, but it is powerful, nonetheless. This client has a love for horses and animals in general. It is of no surprise that she begins to experience animals in her session.

She was new to hypnosis, like many, and experienced the session in bits and pieces. This is normal for some as they adjust to seeing in a new way for the first time. It still has impactful information about how a past life can be affecting us now.

*Session begins

C: I want you to go to the last lifetime that your subconscious feels you need to experience or that is of most importance at this time… I want you to begin to tell me what you become aware of as soon as you are ready

J: Ground is rocky. Very open… tall grass. I smell wood smoke. From a fire. There are hills in the distance.

C: I want you to look down at your hands and let me know what you notice about them.

J: I am outside a lot. Not like someone who does hard labor… but I am outside doing stuff often.

(Progress further as the client is struggling to allow, I spend some time getting her deeper before moving on.)

C: I want you to move on in this lifetime as if you are fast-forwarding a movie, and when you come to the next significant event within this time, I want you to press play and as you become aware of what is going on around you. I simply want you to explain to me what you are aware of.

J: I am in a village. It is very different here. Looks like mountains around it. Valleys. We are outside of it. There is a sense of community.

C: I want you to just explore as you immerse yourself in your environment. Just continue to report back to me what you are experiencing.

J: It is nighttime now. The campfire provides the light. The houses are securely put together. Not what we use now though. There are animal skins too. Lots of storytelling. Kids. Whole families. Eating. Dogs barking. Laughing.

C: How do you feel right now?

J: It all made sense here. The beliefs. There was no confusion about the past. What we are supposed to do. Retelling the past...*Client pauses * Sad feeling... Don't want to leave. (Client has a small reaction of tears and face trembling.)

(I take a moment to soothe the client through breathing and releasing and telling her this is okay and perfectly fine for her to feel this way.)

C: Now that you are more relaxed, I want you to spend as much time as you need here and when you are ready... move onto the next significant event for you in this life and begin helping me experience what it is you are aware of.

J: There is a wooden fence. A corral. It is made up of posts. Three pieces of wood for each panel. All hand cut. It's for the horses. (Client nods head and whispers a confirming yes. Client begins crying.) They were family too. Survival depended on them.

C: How did you depend on them?

J: Transportation. There are people bringing up water.

C: I want you to spend some time in this moment. Let me know when you are ready to talk.

J: There are falcons.

C: What do you have falcons for?

J: We hunt. We have birds. I feel like I did handle them. But I wasn't the main one who did.

C: Why did you have falcons to hunt with you?

J: It was the way to differentiate ourselves from the others.

(She does not want to leave this life or progress when I try, so I take her back to the horses and begin to ask her why she is having such a hard time leaving this space. She also has horses in her current life.)

C: Is there a particular one that you are drawn to?

J: Yes. The name starts with an A, But I almost am having a hard time pronouncing it. This one is mine. My counterpart.

C: Take me through what you do with your counterpart companion.

J: Get up early. They are priority. Feed them. Water. I am now looking at the same corral but empty. (Client begins crying heavier this time and I begin crying with her. Sometimes their reaction is so raw and painful, you cannot help but react too.)

C: How do you feel?

J: It feels like grief but understanding. It was his time. The belief when one passed on was, they would die and become part of the earth again. They were still there though. (Crying heavily) It was the first time I couldn't accept that belief. It was the beginning of my questioning. Questioning what I have been told. Belief about the Soul still existing.

*She takes time to process this, so we move on. I regress her at this point to another life of importance. *

C: What do you become aware of as you focus your senses?

60

J: Sand. Desert sand. Water on the coast. There's a city. Lots of man-made stone walls. There is a bazaar in the center. Where everyone meets. There are lots of fruits.

C: When you look down at your feet what do you see?

J: Stone. Stone street. I am not a vendor. And I am not buying.

C: Do you know what you are doing there?

J: (Looks confused) I think I am someone of importance. But I do not feel that I am a leader though. They move out of the way when I walk through.

C: What expressions do they have on their faces when you walk through?

J: Respect…. but not fear.

C: What else are you aware of?

J: There are cats in the market. They are allowed to be there. I think they are sacred. I feel that they are somehow my job. But not to care for them. My job has to do with them somehow.

C: Asks the client to continue to progress and begin reporting back to me what she is aware of.

J: I feel like the way a priest would feel, but I have no direct family. I am not alone though.

C: What are you doing now?

J: I am walking to get to my office. My workspace…. There is a doorway off to the side…. It's a long hallway. It must be really far back. There are torches for lighting. I feel advanced? In my office there are medicinal things. Jars on the walls.

C: Do you know what you are doing in your office?

J: Possibly. Doesn't make sense to me though why I am in the office. (Takes a moment as if she isn't sure how to say what she is about to say.) I feel like I prepare the dead…for the journey. Like anointing with the oils.

C: Are you aware of who you are?

J: Possibly a man? I am wearing a robe. I didn't have any questions here. I knew what I was doing.

C: Does this make sense to you after the other life where you questioned death?

J: It's not connected to the questioning of before. I feel that we had answers for things. We understood how to heal the body. Answers that we do not have in this current lifetime.

C: You mean to tell me you knew more about the human body than we currently do now?

J: Yes, but not me, someone else had this knowledge.

C: Can you explain what you mean?

J: There was emphasis placed on the sun and the moon.

C: Why was that?

J: Because it was life. I was correlated with the moon, it was the afterlife. The others job was similar to doctors now. They taught disease prevention. A Healer? In this culture after-life was just as important as life. I took care of the bodies for the afterlife. It was a respected part of the culture then.

C: Ask client to continue on through her journey and continue reporting back to me.

J: I feel like I also had to do this with the cats…. They had to be given the same respect as people.

C: Are you aware of what time frame this is?

J: Feels really far back. But not because of the knowledge. There were writings and carvings on the walls. Very advanced people.

*I progress the session and ask her if she is able to go to the other half; The Sun; at this time and let me know what she is aware of as she does. *

J: Sun healer, Brother, I feel like he is my brother. He is more extroverted in this time. It is why he was chosen for this role. It could have gone either way and it would have been fine. We were very accepting of death in this life. It wasn't an ending to us.

*At this time, I move the client to another lifetime to see if we cannot explore and see if the pain in her right side by her liver and gallbladder isn't related from a past life. She has said that she has had it for many, many years and doctors cannot seem to give her an answer and cannot find anything wrong. She says that it is not a big pain that prevents her from life. It just lets her know it's there.
*

J: I'm a woman. I am pregnant.

C: Is this your first child?

J: Yes. I see my wrists. I have on jewelry. Turquoise. I feel like this pain started here. Can't tell if it was something that started with being pregnant though. (Client spends some time trying to explain what she is noticing. I give her a few moments to begin talking.)

J: Baby kicking on that spot… (Seems unsure) The delivery went bad. I died. My son lived.

C: Continue explaining to me what you notice?

J: I can still see what's happening. My mom is there. She is allowing me to still have a say in what happens. She is still alive and can see me. There are other souls too. No one but mom can see them.

C: The other souls there, do you recognize them?

J: They don't feel unfamiliar? I am still so focused on the living still. I feel like I am waiting on them. I feel like I also have the option to go back in. But, by waiting I can see. I can watch.

C: Why wouldn't you go back?

J: If I go back, I wouldn't remember who I was before. So, I stayed to watch.

C: Why are you waiting?

J: So, we can all go back at the same time. It is hard to do. I felt like I had to for them. My child was able to still feel like he had a mother. Even though he couldn't see me, Mom could. He was aware of that.

C: What do you do now, what happens next for you?

J: It's harder being in the afterlife and being tied to the living. I could have let go. But I didn't. It was necessary.

63

C: What are you aware of now?

J: I just feel like this was an accepted part of this culture, to see others like me. I feel like I didn't have enough time. Something just went wrong.

C: What happens when you wait and the first family member passes?

J: My mother waited with me until my son passes.

C: What did you and your mother do until your son passed?

J: We watched over him. He didn't need it though.

C: How does it feel to finally be together with the three of you again?

J: Good. Feels like, we finally get that time together.

I progress her into the next phase of afterlife.

J: Can't see.

C: (I help her change the way she uses her senses here, explaining that without the physical body, the eyes need to adjust from a non-physical energy standpoint. When she is adjusted, I continue.)

J: I'm content. Together. No baggage here. Whatever we go through before, doesn't exist. Doesn't matter. Time is different too. I feel like when we go, I go back with my son…my mother decided to stay.

*After going through this scene with her and closing, I move her into trying to find out if she can now release the discomfort in her side, having the knowledge about the past life like she does. *

J: Feels like it's this time now. Same situation. Mother and son. It feels good but it also brings up the fear of being separated again. I don't want to watch this time. I want to experience it. I can't tell if he knows though. The pain is a reminder of being taken away. It's a way to focus. Reason was for coming back. I almost don't want to allow that. I feel like I need to carry it. I shouldn't release it.

*Close out Session.

Before ending the session, I put post hypnotic suggestions in that if in the event she ever does become ready to release the pain, she would easily and readily be able to. But until that time she gets to carry that reminder and know why she does.

*Update: This client contacted me some time later to let me know the significance of that life and why she experienced it the way she did. She was giving birth to her child in this life and died on the table. She was given too much anesthesia and she asphyxiated and died during childbirth. The entire hospital ended up in her room trying to save her. She was, of course, saved, but she almost did not make it. It was a miracle and one that normally wouldn't come with an explanation as to why. She said that after the birth and as she began recovering and living life, she realized the pain in her side was gone. She had not felt it since. Her "reminder" to not leave this time during childbirth, was there when she needed it, and it disappeared completely after the fact.

This was the first time for me that I realized how varied and meaningful our messages and communications from our own Souls can be. If we had released that anyways, it could have caused a much different set of events to transpire. My trust in the process became very set in place that day. It changed me in a very drastic way. I am forever grateful for this message because not only did it change her, but it also changed me.

# CHAPTER 3
## "Kristen"

In this session, Kristen goes to a few different places and experiences a few different lives. You will notice that there are some key characters that pop up that pertain to her life currently. They have caused great trauma in the current life and showed up in a past life she sees as well.

Each Higher Self is vastly different. Some talk quite a lot, and others are quite short and to the point. They may even come off emotionless. I have found that there are varying degrees of connection with one's Higher Self. Kristens Higher Self is more to the point. It does not mess around with details, but the information it does give verifies her experiences and what she currently needs.

I include this so that you can see that there is no wrong way to experience this process. Everyone needs something different to "heal" within their life. I ask about some of the unusual experiences she has had through her life such as one time where she walks off of a curb and just "knows" that she was hit by a car; and then she felt reset. She knew something unusual had happened but was not into the "woo woo" of life and never really dove into what more could have happened.

She also had a very traumatic childhood including molestation from a family member. You will see that the Higher Self decides to go back and do some inner child healing. It is something that I do in general hypnosis but had never had the Higher Self take me through it completing the process. It is not how it is normally done but again, there is no wrong way to get something done. It is effective in its own way, and I love seeing how these things transpire in these sessions to get the best results. The Higher Self truly knows us best.

*Session begins

C: What do you notice?

K: Rock.

C: What does that look like?

K: It's kind of flat, I'm standing on it.

C: When you look down at your feet, what do you notice?

K: They are bare, but I have something around me.

C: What does that look like?

K: It's like, leather strips and stuck together as kind of, um, like fat fringe.

C: When you look up at your legs, are you wearing anything?

K: No? I notice I've got very manly legs. * Laughs*

C: Are you carrying anything?

K: Yeah. I'm not sure what it is. It's like some sort of long piece of wood. It's like, it could be something like a weapon? Like a long, round wooden thing.

C: What do your hands look like?

K: Beefy.

C: Do they feel strong?

K: Yes.

C: Are you wearing anything on your head?

K: I think so.

C: What does it feel like when you touch it?

K: Some sort of a headdress, type of Indian thing maybe.

C: And as you look around you, what do you notice?

K: Everyone is looking at me.

C: Do you recognize them?

K: They are my people.

C: When they are talking to you, do they call you by anything?

K: I can't get it. It's something funny. It's like, it means something like reverence.

C: So, you are a higher position?

K: I am the priest and shaman. I am a spiritual guide. I don't feel like I'm the leader necessarily, but I am important somehow.

C: As you're looking around, just explain to me what you're noticing.

K: I'm on this rock telling them something important and they are looking at me. Listening to what I'm saying.

C: How do they feel about listening to you?

K: I don't know if it's reverence or fear on their faces, but their eyes are big.

C: Well, as you're tuning into what you are telling them, just explain to me what you notice.

K: Hmm. I'm using this thing I have in my hand on the ground for emphasis.

C: How do you feel as you're speaking to them?

K: Powerful.

C: Do you enjoy this?

K: Yes, I'm taking it very seriously.

C: Well, it must be very important. As you're looking at them, can you tell by their responses what is going on?

K: They are very interested. I think I'm telling them a story. My hands are very animated, but I feel like it's important. What's to come? What's coming? I know what's going to happen and I tell them it's going to happen.

C: What are you telling them is going to happen?

K: Some type of war.

C: Have you seen it?

K: Yes. I have seen people dying. Our people dying.

C: And what are you hoping for as you tell them this story?

K: I want to save them.

C: As you're doing this, just explain to me what's going on as you're explaining this war.

K: They are looking up at me. I'm not sure they believe it.

C: But you know it's coming?

K: Yes.

C: Who is coming to be at war with you?

K: White men. Blue uniforms.

C: And how do you feel about this war that's coming?

K: Angry, and desperate.

C: Why is that?

K: They are going to die.

C: And you want to save your people?

K: Yeah.

C: And as you finish telling them, how do they respond?

K: Some are afraid, and some are feeling like they are going to fight. And some of them are just children, and women with children.

C: Is there anything else you can do to stop the war?

K: I am pretty helpless.

C: Is that how you feel?

K: Yes.

C: As you finish telling them, is there anyone you talk to or place you go?

K: I go and sit under a tree, and I take a knife and cut my arm.

C: Why do you do that?

K: Because I need the blood.

C: Can you explain to me what that means?

K: I'm putting the blood into a cup. I'm wiping it on the foreheads. It's a protection. It's for protection. Wiping it on the foreheads of the men who will fight.

C: What does this mean for you, this protection?

K: It means they will either fight and be protected or they will travel safely to their next, wherever they go next.

C: * Suggestions for comfort as she watches and experiences* Explain to me what's going on around you as you prepare.

K: I'm going to all of the men and giving them some type of blessing.

C: Are you going to be with them during this process, this war?

K: I'm not sure.

C: After you bless everybody, then what do you do?

K: I am talking to women and children. They have to prepare.

C: And how do they do that?

K: They have to pack up. They have to move; they have to get food.

C: Do they go somewhere?

K: Yes.

C: Where do they go?

K: They all go their own areas to pack up.

C: What do the houses look like?

K: They look like teepees. Leather or hides.

C: Do you just leave the homes when the war starts?

K: No, they are packing up what they can. And the hides for wherever they are going. They roll them and some are angry.

C: That's understandable. So, what do you do now?

K: I need to go be by myself.

C: Why do you do that?

K: For more information.

C: As you sit there, explain to me what you are getting.

K: I feel like I'm old.

C: Why do you feel that way?

K: I think because...I think I'm going to die.

C: Can you tell me more?

K: I have someone to carry on my work.

C: Who is that?

K: My son. I think it's Nash. (Her son in this life.)

C: And you think he is prepared?

K: Yes. He is with me, but I feel like he could use confidence.

C: Why is that?

K: He is not sure of himself. And I think it's because I'm still alive. He still has me around. For information. He doesn't have to trust himself because I'm the one everyone trusts.

C: Is he one of the fighters?

K: No, he is the Shaman.

C: So, did he leave with the women and children?

K: No, he is with me. Preparing. He has to go because he is the healer.

C: Does he stay with you as you pass?

K: Yes. I'm drinking something.

C: How is the taste?

K: Bitter.

C: Explain to me what this is like. * Suggestions for comfort*

K: Hmm. I'm trying. I'm at peace. I've done everything I can do.

C: As you are here, explain to me what is going on.

K: Feels like floating. *She has died from drinking that liquid. *

C: As you look back down where you were, what do you notice?

K: Hmm. I'm at the edge of a cliff or something. That has a drop. And my son pushes my body over it.

71

C: When you look at this life, why did you experience this life?

K: Power and responsibility.

C: Did you do everything you hoped to do in that life?

K: Yes.

C: *Takes her to a new place. * What do you notice?

K: I'm on the deck of a ship.

C: What does the ship look like?

K: It's large. Has big sails.

C: As you look down at your feet, what do you notice?

K: Black boots.

C: When you look at your legs, what do you see?

K: Pants are tucked into the boots.

C: Are you carrying anything with you?

K: No.

C: And when you look at your hands, what do you notice?

K: *Giggles* They are man's hands.

C: Do they feel strong?

K: Yes.

C: Are they younger or older?

K: They are older.

C: Are you wearing anything on your head?

K: A hat.

C: What does the hat feel like?

K: Feels big.

C: How do you feel being on this ship?

K: I feel confident like I'm in command.

C: As you look around, what do you notice?

K: Everybody is working as they should be.

C: What are you doing?

K: I'm walking around and making sure everyone is doing what they are supposed to be doing.

C: And what is your job?

K: I'm the captain.

C: Do you enjoy being the captain?

K: It's what I do. I've always done it.

C: And what are you doing at this time on your ship?

K: We are sailing. Going to get something. Some, we are picking up spices and stuff that we are going to sell later.

C: And is this what you usually do?

K: Yes.

C: And what does it look like as you are walking around this ship, what are you feeling?

K: Proud. It's mine. I worked hard for it.

C: So, you are very close with the people on your ship?

K: Some of them.

C: Do you recognize anyone as you're walking around?

K: Don is there. He looks different. (Her husband in this life)

C: What is his job on the ship?

K: I think he is my brother. He is like my second in command.

C: So, you trust him?

K: Yes.

C: As you're walking around just explain to me what you are doing.

K: I'm making sure everyone is doing their duty. Their job. Talking to people. Making sure we are going the right direction.

C: And everything is going as it should?

K: Yes.

C: And as you go through this process here, explain to me what you do next after you have checked on everything.

K: I go to the cabin.

C: Is this your cabin?

K: Yes.

C: And what do you do when you get to the cabin?

K: I pour myself a drink.

C: Are you relaxing?

K: Yes.

C: Is there anyone with you?

K: Someone is coming. Not yet.

C: When they get there just explain to me what's going on.

K: It's my brother. I pour him a drink. We are going through the ledgers.

C: What does that look like?

K: I'm looking at everything we have picked up and how much it cost. We are discussing our profit.

C: Is it what you had hoped it would be?

K: I feel good about it.

C: Are you happy with how everything has gone?

K: Yes.

C: And how do you feel to have your brother here with you?

K: Good.

C: And after you discuss business, what else do you do?

K: Just relaxing and talking.

C: And how does it feel to just relax?

K: It feels good except for, I feel a storm is coming. My arthritis in my hands. I know it's coming.

C: You can feel it?

K: Yes.

C: Can you tell what kind of storm it's going to be?

K: I think it's worse than I thought.

C: Can you explain what you're noticing?

K: I feel like I have to get ready.

C: Well as you're getting ready, explain to me what that looks like.

K: Means we have to tell the men to pull down the sails. Secure everything.

C: What else is going on?

K: Starting to rain. Everyone is, it's just very busy. Everyone is preparing for the storm.

C: Does this happen often?

K: Yes, but this feels worse.

C: As this process is going on, as you're getting ready, just explain to me what you are doing.

K: I'm feeling old. Tired. Just tired. I'm not that old. But I feel like it.

C: Is it harder for you to go through these storms?

K: I'd rather be home. That's how I know it's time to quit.

C: Do you miss home?

J: Yes

C: And why do you miss home?

K: Because my wife is there.

C: So, you're ready to go back there?

K: Yeah.

C: As you're preparing for this storm, walk me through what you notice.

K: It's gotten closer. We are getting tossed pretty badly.

C: *Suggestions for comfort* What's going on?

K: Somehow there is damage to the boat.

C: What does that look like?

K: I'm afraid. I don't think we are going to make it through that one.

C: So, what are you doing?

K: Directing things. Praying. Worrying about the people who are going to die. I can't do anything about it. *She is visibly sad, and you can hear it in her voice. *

C: *More suggestions for comfort* Explain to me what you notice, what are you doing?

K: We are in the water now. Boat's sinking. There are people on top of things. Crates that they are holding onto.

C: How does the water feel?

K: Cold.

C: And are you holding onto something?

K: Yes.

C: As your holding on, what else do you notice?

K: I guess I'm feeling resigned. We are going to die.

C: Is there any way you can be saved?

K: I don't see how.

C: I worry about these people. I can't do anything, I'm helpless.

C: *Passes time a bit so she doesn't stay in suffering* What has happened?

K: I don't know where my brother is. And I feel responsible.

C: Why is that?

K: Because I am the captain and it's my responsibility.

C: How are you feeling now that you have been in the water?

K: Sad.

C: Where is everyone else?

K: In the water too. Or in the ship. I'm not sure. We might have lost some in the ship. I can't tell, it's dark.

C: *Passes more time* What do you begin to notice?

K: I can't feel my body.

C: What do you think is happening?

K: I think I'm dying.

C: *Moves her beyond her last breath* What do you notice?

K: Peace. I'm at peace.

C: When you look back, what do you see?

K: I see things floating.

C: When you look back on that life, what was the point?

K: I had responsibility for a lot of people, and I failed them.

C: Why do you think you failed them?

K: Because I couldn't keep them alive.

C: Do you know it's not your fault the weather changed?

K: It's my responsibility.

C: Was there something you were supposed to learn?

K: That I can't do everything.

C: Do you feel like you learned that?

K: It's still disappointing. I wanted it to be different.

C: *Takes her to another life. * What do you notice?

K: Standing on a dirt road.

C: What do you notice around you?

K: Fields

C: When you look down at your feet, what do you notice?

K: I'm barefoot.

C: And when you look at your legs, what do you notice?

K: I'm wearing pants, but they don't go all the way down. They are very lightweight.

C: And are you carrying anything with you?

K: Basket.

C: Do you have anything in your basket?

K: Yes. It's some type of food.

C: When you look at your hands what do you notice?

K: I'm young.

C: Are you wearing anything on your head?

K: Mmhmm. Some hat made out of straw or something. Grassy. Lightweight. Provides protection from the sun.

C: What are you doing?

K: I'm supposed to be doing the chores.

C: What does that look like?

K: I'm going to get something. I need to, I have to go milk a goat.

C: Does that sound fun?

K: No. I don't like goats.

C: Why not?

K: They are mean.

C: What do you do with it once you milk the goat?

K: I take it to my mother.

C: And do you do this often?

K: Every day.

C: What do you do after you milk the goat?

K: Take care of the little ones.

C: And who are they? Are they your siblings?

K: Yes.

C: And do you enjoy this?

K: I don't have a choice.

C: So, what are you doing as you're playing with your siblings?

K: I'm teaching them.

C: What are you teaching them?

K: I'm grinding something. Some grains. Cooking.

C: Is that to help your mom?

K: Yes

C: What else are you doing while you're cooking?

K: We have to feed a lot.

C: Why is that?

K: So many kids.

C: How many?

K: Nine.

C: And are you the oldest?

K: Yes

C: So, what do you do after you play with the kids?

K: I do more chores.

C: What kind of chores?

K: I clean.

C: And when you're finished with all of the chores, what do you find yourself doing?

K: I want to take a bath.

C: Explain to me what you're doing as you're going to take a bath.

K: just going down to the water. Cleaning myself off in the water.

C: Is it a creek?

K: Something like that.

C: How does the water feel?

K: It's cold but it feels really good.

C: What do you do after your bath?

K: I like to be by myself.

C: Why is that?

K: it's quiet. It's just so much noise, never get any peace.

C: *I take her to an important day in this life. * What do you notice?

K: I can't tell if I am getting married or being sold. Or both.

C: How do you feel?

K: Angry. Helpless. I don't have a choice.

C: So, what are you doing?

K: There is nothing I can do. I have to do it.

C: So, what does this look like as you're going through with this process?

K: *Struggling* It's my grandfather. (This person is her grandfather in this life she has a bad history with.)

C: He is the one you're marrying?

K: Yes.

C: When you see him, how do you feel?

K: Repulsed.

C: Do you know him, or have you ever seen him before?

K: Yes.

C: And how do you know him?

K: He is worthy in comparison but that's not saying much. He is like a merchant, but he is mean.

C: And why is he mean?

K: Just a miserable person.

C: As you're going through this process, what do you notice?

K: I don't like it.

C: *Moves her forward* What do you notice?

K: I'm old.

C: How are you feeling?

K: Tiring life.

C: Is there anyone there with you?

K: Hannah is there. (Her daughter in this life.) She is taking care of me.

C: Does she do that often?

K: Just because I'm dying.

C: *Takes her through her last breath* What do you notice?

K: I'm happy to be gone.

C: And when you look back, what was the purpose of that life?

K: I had no power at all. No control over anything.

C: And what did you learn?

K: I learned that I am strong. Capable and I can survive the worst.

C: What do you notice around you now that you are floating?

K: People around me.

C: Who is around you, do you recognize them?

K: Don is there, my mother is there. My kids. Everybody is happy to see me.

C: Now that you're there, what do you decide to do?

K: I need to heal.

C: Explain to me what that looks like as you experience that.

K: There is someone helping me do it.

C: Do you recognize them?

K: No.

C: You can ask them who they are, are you able to do that? What do they say?

K: Says they are a teacher.

C: What does that mean?

K: This person who helps me makes sense of it.

C: Can we ask him some questions?

K: Okay.

C: Can we ask them why you had to experience that life?

K: Because she was always powerful. Needs to know what it feels like to be one who has no power.

C: And how do you feel about that?

K: It's a good lesson. I didn't like it.

C: Is this person okay if we ask some more questions? Can you ask them why you are experiencing the things you are in this life?

K: Growth.

C: What kind of growth?

K: It's like, it's to fill in the pieces. To fill in the areas.

C: Can you ask him about the missing memory you have with the cat? (This was a question the client wished an answer for prior to this session and was included here.) Can he tell us about that one?

K: Another time when you had no power.

C: Is there a reason you don't remember it?

K: There is a reason.

C: Can he tell you why?

K: It's not his place.

C: Can he explain why you had to go through what you did with your grandfather?

K: It's just more of that life.

C: Is there anything that he wants to tell you that is important?

K: It's like everything is as it should be. Right. It's like I, he said it and I lost it. Like I want things to be different instead of accepting what is. I fight what is.

C: I want to tell him thank you as he is helping us, are you healed at this point?

K: He is working on my chest. My heart.

C: Can he work on you with the things you have currently going on too?

K: He said it's not his job.

C: *Brings in Higher Self while he is working* Why did they show her the life of the man with the name Reverence?

K: She needs to know the power she has inside.

C: And what kind of power does she have?

K: It's... we all do.

C: Can you explain that to her?

K: Limitless.

C: What about the life on the ship, why did you show her that life?

K: It's the same really. It's all so serious but just from that perspective. There's more. There's more to life than just what you see.

C: Can you explain that?

K: There's power. But also, there's unseen.

C: How does that affect her?

K: It's a plan. Lack of trust. It's important to learn.

C: How do we best learn that?

K: Give up control.

C: That's awfully scary for us humans.

K: Yes.

C: And what about the life as her being married off?

K: She had no control.

C: Can you explain why her grandfather in this life was also there?

K: It's karma.

C: What kind of karma?

K: It needed to be played out again.

C: Why is that?

K: It's going too fast.

C: What is going too fast?

K: The explanation.

**Because of the difference of not existing where time is, the information comes in like a download all at once and can be difficult to stretch it back out into words we can understand and use. Many people have had the same experience but not everyone experiences it in this way. It's just a common way they relay information down from the Higher Self. **

C: *Suggestions to slow it down to make sense of It.* Why is that karma there?

K: It doesn't have to be.

C: Was it finished in this life?

K: Yes and no.

C: Can it be completed now? Can we clear the rest of the karma for her?

K: Yes. It can be done.

C: Can you help clear that now?

K: Yes.

C: Can I ask you some questions?

K: Yes.

C: When she stepped on the curb back in high school, when she noticed the car, what happened?

K: They put her back.

C: What do you mean by that?

K: It wasn't the right time to go.

C: Is she aware what happened?

K: She knows.

C: She thought it was very unusual. So, she wasn't hit by the car?

K: Not in this life.

C: So that was a way to save her, so she didn't leave?

K: Yes.

C: So that time she was pulled from her body, and she went to another planet, what was that place?

K: It's where the Masters are.

C: What Masters?

K: The ones who oversee all.

C: Why was she going there?

K: It was the easiest way.

C: Easiest way for what?

K: To get the point across.

C: And what was the point?

K: That's the purpose. It's um, she knows that there is more to it. There is more she knows, there is more than what she sees.

C: Who was it that she recognized there?

K: She is hugging him right now.

C: Who is he?

K: Like a father.

C: Where is he from, that same planet?

K: Yes.

C: Does he have anything he wants to say to her?

K: Doesn't happen in words, that's the problem.

C: That's ok, can you explain it to me in the best way you are able? What do you feel?

K: Love.

C: Can you explain to me what he is saying or experiencing with you?

K: It's like...he is giving me everything I need. Without doing anything.

C: How does that feel?

K: Amazing.

C: Is this to help you going forward?

K: Yes.

C: Is there anything he wants to tell you?

K: That I am doing a good job. Everything is how it's supposed to be.

C: Why did you see him back then?

K: *Laughs* Same thing. Guess it's what I need.

C: While you're speaking to him, I want the Higher Self to do a body scan and I want to check if there is anything you need at this time. Can you explain to me what you see?

K: Everything is so minor. Everything can be fixed.

C: Can you fix it for her?

K: Part of it she has to do.

C: And how can she do that?

K: She knows.

C: Can you explain it to her so she can hear it here?

K: She just has to connect and let it flow.

C: Can you assist her with that? With the other part?

K: Yes

C: And what does that look like?

K: It's a movement of energy.

C: And are you doing that for her now?

K: Mmhmm.

C: What about her Hashimoto's? Where does that come from?

K: Lack of trust.

C: Is that something you can assist her with healing at this time?

K: Yes.

C: Are you doing that now?

K: Yes.

C: Will she notice a difference? How will she know?

K: It will become obvious.

C: Will that happen pretty quickly?

K: It should.

C: What about her allergies, where did those come from?

K: It's really unsafe in the world to her.

C: Are you able to help her with this as well?

K: Yes.

C: Will she notice a difference going forward?

K: Depends on if she keeps the energy the same.

C: Can you help in releasing that energy?

K: It's a pattern. She goes back to the old patterns.

C: What kind of patterns are those?

K: It's about her place in the world and how she feels. It will come right back if she doesn't.

C: Can you help her feel safe so she knows you are with her that might help?

K: Yes.

C: What about her sleep issues, where do those come from?

K: It's just fear.

C: Can you help her with that fear?

K: There is so much.

C: Is it stored in the body?

K: Yes.

C: Is there a way you can help her release that fear, she is ready to let it go.

K: Yes.

C: Can you explain what that looks like?

K: Looks like a tornado.

C: And when you're healing and helping her with that, what does it begin to look like?

K: Goes through the eye. Yes, she needs to drink water.

C: I'll make sure as soon as she gets up to drink water, is that ok?

K: Yes.

C: I want to ask about her PTSD, is that still with her strongly?

K: Still there.

C: Can you help her with this?

K: Yes.

C: What does this look like when it's being released?

K: Black.

C: How does it leave the body?

K: Drips, like tar.

C: Where does it go?

K: Going into the ground.

C: Will she feel better?

K: Yes.

C: Is it clearing completely at this point?

K: No, she is going to have to let go of some of it herself.

C: But you are helping her clear as much as possible?

K: Yes.

C: Can I ask about her arthritis, where does that come from?

K: It's very old. Part of it is the inability to let go.

C: Can you help her with this?

K: She has to let go. She needs to let go of control. There is only so much you can control and the rest you have to let go, and trust.

C: Can you help her with the arthritis? I think after hearing this, she will be able to get go a little easier, do you think?

K: Yes.

C: How does she know to trust that this is real?

K: It's an issue. I'm trying. Sending images, changing the energy.

C: What kind of images?

K: *Laughs* Images so she knows how to do it.

C: Can you explain it to her?

K: Produce the imagery of the tornado. To release it. Let go.

C: Can you explain why her mom play the part that she did, why did she allow that abuse to go on?

K: Just a long line of abuse. She was abused, he was abused.

C: So, her mom knew what was going on?

K: Yes

C: Why didn't she stop it?

K: She couldn't. She learned helplessness.

C: Is that why she is the way she is?

K: Yes.

C: Was Kristen able to stop that cycle?

K: Yes.

C: Is there anything else she needs to know about that cycle?

K: There is nothing she doesn't already know to help. It's just a matter of belief.

C: And that person that she went to visit, how is that a fatherly figure to her, who is he?

K: He is the one who helps and guides her.

C: Is he a guide to her?

K: Yes, but the highest. Not here. Where he is. He is where he can oversee everything.

C: Does it have a name?

K: Yes, but you wouldn't understand it.

C: Could you try?

K: It's a feeling more than a name.

C: What's the feeling?

K: Can't be described.

C: I understand. Does he have a name?

K: Yes. But it won't make any sense. She can choose a name.

C: Okay, how will she contact him from now on? She can just think of him, and he will know?

K: Yes.

C: And if she chooses a name, he will know who she is calling for?

K: He knows everything.

C: Is there anything he wants to tell her?

K: *Laughs* He doesn't do it with words, but she knows.

C: Is there anything you want to tell her at this time?

K: Ah, so much.

C: What do you want to say now?

K: She will do well to meditate. So much going on in her head all the time. This will help her.

C: Is there anything else you can tell her?

K: All problems can be solved there.

C: I know she feels like there is this last missing piece for herself, what can you tell her about that?

K: She is fine, it's up to her to decide how important it is to her.

C: It's up to her to decide how important it is?

K: Depends on how much she can let go.

C: Does she need to let it go?

K: Need? Hmm. Will it benefit her? Yes.

C: Is there anything you can tell her about that situation that has been bothering her?

K: It's a lot. There is a lot of resistance there that needs to go away. It's like a wall. Tangible.

C: Can the wall be removed at this time?

K: It might be too much.

C: Is it ok to know more?

K: Yes and no. Because there is a little one that needs to be protected.

C: What does that mean?

K: It's her.

C: And is it better to keep her protected?

K: Yes, but she is very strong.

C: Can you heal her at that point, so that she is healed enough that it does not affect her anymore?

K: Somewhat.

C: What else is going on?

K: We are talking to the child.

C: What are you saying?

K: Telling her she is safe. That she is ok.

C: Does that help?

K: She has been there a long time.

C: Is there anything you can do to assist her so that she is not there anymore?

K: Trying to help her grow up.

C: And does that work?

K: Somewhat. It helps.

C: Is there anything else that she needs at this time?

K: She needs love. She has been rejected. She knows it.

C: Can you send that love to her?

K: Yes.

C: Does that help?

K: Yes.

C: Thank you. Is there anything else she needs to know at this time?

 K: No.


*Close out Session.

# CHAPTER 4
## "Lilla"

This client had experienced a great loss before coming for a session. She had been dealing with debilitating grief over her son's recent suicide. He was still a teenager, and she suffered from the loss and blame that she placed on herself. The session ends abruptly because she has such a revelation over her son's early exit and what it means for her. Sometimes when we experience such a strong emotion such as this, it can bring us suddenly out of session. She was fine, ending it there because she'd gained what she'd been hoping for; some understanding or closure about him.

She experienced many things including a life as a tree. I can say that this session changed the way I look at the world around me. I never saw trees or anything on our planet the way that I had before. I knew they were important, sure, and I loved them in a way a normal human might, but I did not realize the depth behind them. Her emotions as she connected with these existences were so strong, so powerful, it was hard not to live it with her.


*Session Begins

*Lilla had just come from a life as a dog. She had fallen off a boat that was close to shore and was drying off on the dock. She soon walked around the village where people pretty much ignored her as she lived her life. She then jumped to another life.

C: What is the first thing that you notice?

L: These plants. They are not palm trees, not a yucca plant but like a yucca plant. Long leaves, long leaves, not a spider plant but like a spider plant. And they are right next to my left side. They are dark, dark, dark green and I'm in that cove. I see the yellow sand.

C: When you look at your legs, what do you see?

L: I'm barefoot.

C: Are you wearing any clothes?

L: I'm wearing… like a sarong and it's blue with white flowers and yellow flowers on it.

C: When you look at your hands, what do you notice?

L: I'm a man! I'm a F***man! *Starts laughing*

C: Do your hands look strong?

L: Yes, very much so. Thick. Thick hands. Thick pads. Yeah.

C: Are you carrying anything?

L: No. I'm just there.

C: When you feel your head, are you wearing anything?

L: Long hair. Curly long hair.

C: What are you doing?

L: Looking around. The cove. I like the cove. I'm just there. I don't have somewhere to be.

C: Do you live in the cove?

L: It's home. Yeah, its home.

C: Is there anyone with you?

L: They could be, but they are not. They are back home.

C: I thought this was your home.

L: It is. But I live in a village. I'm out, looking at the cove. I'm not a runaway. I'm not hunting. I'm just out for a walk.

C: Just explain to me what you're doing while you're hanging out.

L: I'm just taking it in. I'm not stressed, angry or worried. I'm ok. I'm carefree.

C: Take a while to soak that feeling in and let it permeate every cell in your existence. *Move her to something different when she decides to leave. * What do you notice?

L: Almost like the skin of an octopus. But yellow. Weird cat like pupil. Big huge eye. Yellow bubbly skin. *confused* Sigh. Feels like ocean. Feels not lake, ocean.

C: Are you looking at the eye or is it your eye?

L: I was looking at it. It was looking right back at me.

C: Do you still see it?

L: It went away.

C: When you look at your body what do you notice?

L: I can't see it but feels like this... feels like... I'm a fish! Not a normal fish. I'm a big fish.

C: What do you see when you look around?

L: Ocean but not like you would think. My body is doing this, *motions* and I feel primitive. *Laughs* My um... my needs are very small.

C: Do you like it here?

L: I don't even know if I know what "like" is. Primitive. Very primitive. Basics. I don't fear anything. I just am. My structure, I'm not a squid because I don't have tentacles. I exist with a body type of one. Fin on one side that goes up on one side of my body and I do this all day. *motions* And I eat but I don't eat. It comes and goes. I just exist.

*We spend some time there and then move on. *

C: *Takes her to a lifetime close to this life she is currently living* What do you see?

L: I'm a tree. Long bark, tree. Tall sturdy. Strong. Protect.

C: Tell me more.

L: It's as if we all hold hands. We all hold hands.

C: What does that feel like?

L: Good. It feels really good. I look... I look out for you. We all hold hands.

C: What do you mean we look out for you?

L: I don't know… we are all together. I'll take care of you if you fall. I got this. I've got you. Do you need something, here you go.

C: Is that to the other trees?

L: Yep, we all talk. We all do. We all talk. We laugh too. Yeah. When something dies, we feel bad. We comfort. We feel bad when things die. We feel bad, it's ok. Oooo powerful. Wow.

C: What's powerful?

L: When things die. I'm going to cry. *Starts crying*

C: Do you mean nature? Like another tree?

L: Everything is alive. Everything. Everything is alive. UGH! Yeah, as a tree, you feel things around you and when they die, especially, this deer curled up and just died. It was okay and we tried to embrace. We provide cover. Um… it feels like if we have arms, we do this *motions a covering and embracing motion* You can't see us do this, but we do this. We feel. We know. We want them to know.

C: Do you do that with humans too?

L: Oh yeah. Oh yeah. Oooo! The trees know more. They are different. They are way different. Yeah. Did you know that they don't die when you cut them?

C: Wow, really?! What happens?

L: No. They don't die. The base. The stump. They are alive. They are mad though. They know that sometimes. Oh, they had to do it again. Feels like a really bad haircut. *She is very animated through this session. *

C: How does it not kill the tree?

L: Because we are all holding hands.

C: So, it lives on through the other trees?

L: No, no, still alive. You kill them when you take the bottom, our hands. *sigh* When you take us out of the ground, you kill us.

C: So, we should leave the roots in the ground if we cut down a tree?

L: Yes. Oh my gosh, yes. *Crying*

C: Is there a way to make them not mad if you have to cut them down?

L: They know. They know. Yeah, they know. Circle of life has to be done. Okay.

C: What else do you notice?

L: They live a long time. A very long time. Long, long, long time. Aging disease. They get cancer too.

C: How does that affect them?

L: They die. Everything dies. And it's okay.

C: Are you an old tree or young tree?

L: I wasn't old, old. I've been cut down a few times. Twice. And I was very tall. I was… I had… not a cedar, not pine, not evergreen, I had leaves. Thick bark. Red color maybe. Striated going up and down. Clumps of leaves throughout my canopy. Tons of leaves.

C: So, after you were cut down, then what happened?

L: Yeah, I was mad. I had to grow again.

C: Do you enjoy the growing?

L: I do not, no. no. It's painful to grow. Painful.

C: Why is it painful?

L: Breaking through. Open wound breaking through.

C: That's what makes it painful?

L: Yes. The sunlight feels really good. Sunlight feels so good. Yeah. Not so much water. Too much water is bad but sunlight… feels good.

C: Did it hurt to grow the first time?

L: It doesn't hurt to grow from something as a baby, from a sprout it doesn't hurt. It hurts when you're taken down and you have to grow back. I'm happy to still be alive but I'd almost rather be dead. It's humiliating to grow back.

C: Why is that?

L: It takes a long time. A long time. You're vulnerable. You're not as strong.

C: You're old anyways, yet you have lots of time, don't you?

L: I was happy just how I was. I was fine until I was cut. Felt good.

C: So now what are you doing?

L: I'm thinking of myself as I see myself as a stub and a twig trying to grow. And I'm not happy. I'm mad.

C: Just explain to me what you notice as you're here.

L: Lots of foliage around me. Leaves. Not pine needles. Underneath, we are all working. Connection... the wires are like a network. That's how we talk. Cities. We are cities. We talk. Messages. Community.

C: What kind of things do you say?

L: The same thing as humans do. "That was dumb. Oh, look at that. Look what's happening here. Look at that person walking. Arrow. Ouch. Ew, look what they are doing. Ah! Oh look, how pretty. Aw." Everything a human... the same feelings... same emotions... it's the same!

C: Do people ever hug you?

L: They were playing and laughing and they run their hands over my bark. Yes, made me very happy. All of us are happy. We like that. The laughter and happiness. Absolutely. We are no different than humans.

C: But humans can't hear you, can they?

L: Yes, they can. Yes, they can. They don't know how. But yes, they can. Yes.

C: What would you say?

L: They touch us. They just have to touch us. We are energy. We communicate... we hold hands. Connected. Energy. We send out, they touch us, and they know. If they touch us, they know. They touch us, we know them. We know them because of who they are. We know them because they just have to be near us. We just know.

C: Is there anything that you give to them?

L: Yes. We love them. We love everything. We don't like some bugs. They are so disruptive. We don't like bugs. Some bugs. The ants, we don't like the ants. Oh! The beetles, we hate the beetles. They hurt us. They get under our skin. We don't like them. If you could get those off of us, we would really like that. We don't like beetles.

C: What else do you notice?

L: Community. Family. Together. Always. We never leave. We don't leave each other. And when one falls, when one falls the others help. I miss that. I do very much.

C: It feels good being a tree?

L: It does, it's actually kind of awesome.

C: *Suggestions to come back when needed to feel that connection and takes her to another life * What do you notice?

L: I'm still trying to leave the tree.

C: You don't want to leave the tree?

L: No. *Crying* I'm trying.

C: Do you want to stay as the tree?

L: I need to leave. I know I'm not leaving them behind. I need to. I'm trying to be ready to leave them.

C: Do you feel that connection to them?

L: Oh yes, oh boy. I do. It's so strong. Wow.

C: Then bring that connection with you as we move. Bringing that feeling and connection with you. *Moves her to another place* What do you notice?

L: Crab skin. I see... I think the bottom of the ocean floor. Gravel and sand. But my eyes are small, and it looks like gravel. I think I'm a crab. I think I'm a crab! Omg, I think I'm a crab. I'm literally stuffing my face from the bottom of the floor, and I can't stop it. I'm like a human vacuum cleaner.

C: What does that feel like?

L: Like I can't get enough food. I can't get enough. I'm always on the hunt for food. I'm constantly eating. I have fingers in my mouth. And I'm doing this the whole time. *Motions from floor to mouth* I'm doing this all the time. Always eating.

C: What else is going on around you?

L: Well, I must have a flashlight above my head, or something is different. I'm at the bottom of the ocean. We all know the bottom of the ocean is dark. But I have a light, and I can see. And I'm vacuuming the sand into my mouth and I'm eating. I'm, *ugh* I'm pretty sure I'm a crab.

*These little details about the light being above you, but knowing the ocean floor is likely dark, is an indicator that they are not making it up. You begin to see soon why that is and it is not something someone would come up with if they are going along with a story such as being at the bottom of the ocean. *

C: Are you doing anything else besides eating?

L: No, I'm always eating. Somebody else comes over, move away, get away, my food. I'm eating. We are constantly eating. Oh goodness help us if something falls in our path, we fight over it. We all pile up to eat it because we are so hungry.

C: Is there anyone else there with you?

L: Yeah, other crabs and they are jerks. We are all trying to eat. And it's gross when you go behind another crab that's already been there. It's all sand. Did you know crabs eat sand?

C: I did not, why do you eat it?

L: We filter it. We are eating it. And we get nutrients from it and then we don't eat…we spit out a lot. Where does it go? I don't know how we get rid of what we eat. We filter it. We clean the sand. We eat the sand; we get what's in the sand. We don't like to eat the sand. But we have to because that's where our food is.

C: What kind of food is in the sand?

L: Micronutrients. Little lice. Little things that live in the sand. We eat them. We like carcasses. Yeah, we like a good… it's like thanksgiving when we get a good meal. Yeah, we like those a lot.

We can... we even eat bones sometimes. They are hard to eat. We eat flesh. We can... take it down to nothing. There are lots of us here.

C: Is that all you do?

L: Yes, eat and fight.

C: Are they your family?

L: No, we don't really have family. No. We are alone. On our own. Always.

C: Do you enjoy being that way?

L: I don't know any different. Fighting all the time and grumpy.

C: Is there anything else you notice about being a crab?

L: Why am I always so hungry? We can stop eating. But we don't want to. We can... OH! We get sad. We can be depressed. And we die.

C: Why is that?

L: Because we don't eat.

C: Why wouldn't you eat?

L: I'm in a tank! *Surprise* I'm in a tank! There is nothing to eat. I'm watching people.

C: What are they doing?

L: I think they eat me. I'm hungry though. We are really hungry. But there is no food. And there is lobsters. They have blue rubber bands on their claws. They are sad too. Mad; we don't talk though. We aren't friends. We are in prison.

C: Is that what it feels like?

L: Yes. We miss... our hunger. We are always hungry. We were caught. Our hunger got us in trouble. They tricked us. And I wish they would get it over with because I'm miserable.

C: What else do you notice?

L: I'm really hungry. I'm just really, really hungry. And the bubbles are annoying. They have us in a tank. Nothing in here for us. We are sad and hungry. These people are Asians. We are in an

100

acrylic tank. They are all laughing and cooking, but we are hungry. And they are having a good time.

C: *Removes her from the life so she doesn't keep feeling discomfort. * I call in the Higher Self. Why did you show her those lives of animals and trees?

L: I've been here the entire time. The dog was independence and that it's always ok.

C: What is always ok?

L: You don't need to be attached to anything to be ok.

C: Did she need to know that?

L: Yes. Because she attaches her happiness to others. Her own happiness is mounted onto others.

C: What can she do to help that?

L: To remember the independence of the dog.

C: Can you help her with that?

L: We flooded her body with the emotions, yes.

C: Why did you show her the life of the tree?

L: She needed to know.

C: Know what?

L: She needed to know her empathy comes from the trees. Her empathy came from 200 years of tree. She needed to know where that comes from.

C: Why did she need to know where that comes from?

L: Because empathy is a crutch for her.

C: How is that?

L: She cares too much about others rather than herself.

C: What can you tell her for focusing more on herself?

L: To remember the trees.

C: Is there anything else you want to tell her about the trees?

L: Electrical bond. That connection is always there. She doesn't need to hold hands to know it's there. It's always there. It's not physical.

C: What can she do to tap into that bond?

L: To feel, to feel, to feel. It's not physical.

C: Will it help her?

L: It's one of the things that she needs to learn.

C: She needs to learn to reconnect to the trees?

L: She needs to take the love and the feeling of the trees and learn to feel that, not on physical. She needs to always… she always has us. Always has us. She doesn't need physical, the physical feel, she always has us. Wherever she goes, she always has us. She forgets she has us.

C: Now that she remembers, she will be able to tap into that?

L: She needs to be reminded. We flooded her body. Flooding her body. Yes. We are now. Flooding her body.

C: Can you tell me about the crab? Why did she experience being a crab?

L: Insignificance. She has outgrown that part. As a child she was a crab. She wasn't important. She never felt important. She needs to remember it doesn't matter. She has outgrown that. She grew past it with her third life lesson. The third.

C: What was her first?

L: To love herself.

C: What was the second?

L: To rely on herself.

C: What lesson is she learning now?

L: Power. Oh, wow, so much power. *In awe* Thoughts connected to self. Letting go of the ties. Letting go of some karmic ties. Letting go, letting go, hardest lesson. Hard lessons. Hard lessons. Learning to let go.

C: Why is she learning that now?

L: It's one of her biggest obstacles. She had so much to learn in this life. So very much. So much. She has done very well. She has done very well.

C: Is there anything you can tell her about these lessons?

L: She is going to do it this time.

C: Has she tried before?

L: Yes. She stayed stuck or gave up.

C: Why do you say she will do it this time?

L: Hang on, we had a problem.

C: What problem?

L: *Crying* Because Max's (her son) suicide was a lesson to me! *Crying heavily* Don't give up. Don't stay stuck.

C: So, he agreed for that lesson?

L: We all did.

C: So, he knew he was going to do that?

L: Yes. There is more.

*Comes out of session*

# CHAPTER 5
## "Hope"

I guide this woman into her second session to discover a few different things. The first thing she was questioning was why she has problems with her health like she does and why she has the eyes that she has. She has what is called "cat" eyes and cannot see as well because of it. She dislikes this about herself and questions why she would have chosen this for herself. She finds herself in a couple of unique places and finally gets answers to the problems she has experienced in this life.

In her last session she also saw herself on a cliff with two men and felt uncomfortable with the situation. The dialog to begin the second session starts there.


*Session begins

H: I see white light. Very thick like fog.

C: Is someone there with you in the fog this time?

H: Yes, we are walking. Someone took me from the fog. Everything is frozen. I am on the cliff again.

C: What is happening on the cliff?

H: Two men are trying to force me off the cliff. I don't know why.

C: Do you know who they are?

H: One is a tall and big kind of guy. The other is a shorter guy, seems like we are in the middle of nowhere. They are trying to pretend to throw me off this cliff. I am a man too.

C: Why are they trying to pretend to do this to you?

H: To scare me. I am hanging on to the side. I fall. *Takes a moment to start responding again. * I am not in my body. I am floating up towards the clouds. I feel fine.

C: What is going on now, do you know where you are?

H: The blue room.

C: The blue room?

H: Yes, lots of people are waiting. I can't see them. I just know they are there.

C: What are you doing in the blue room?

H: A woman is hugging me. Happy to see me. It's my wife.

C: Your wife? Do you know who that is to you in this lifetime?

H: It's Dave. (Smiling and laughing slightly.) That's hilarious. David was my wife. *Dave is her soon to be husband in her current lifetime. *

C: How do you feel about that?

H: Happy. I am hugging a lot of people. They are welcoming me back.

C: What do you do now?

H: We are walking… walking… just groups of people talking. Can't see them but I know they are there. David and my father are with me.

C: How do you know who you are with if you can't see them?

H: I still see myself as a man and David as a woman.

C: Is that normal for the both of you?

H: We prefer to see each other as the body of our last lifetime.

*At this point we end up moving on to another lifetime after we spend a few more minutes exploring. There was more the client wanted to know so I wanted to move along and come back to the afterlife last. I felt this was important to keep the session moving to explore it all in this session as best as we could.

H: I am in the cottage again. I am wearing a poufy red dress. I am walking into the house as if I own it.

C: Continue to walk me through what you are experiencing.

H: Someone is in the room. I kick them out. I close all of the curtains and sit on the bed.

C: Why do you do this?

H: Because I want to be alone from everyone.

C: Do you know why?

H: Because my parents want me to get married to someone I do not love.

C: How do you feel about that?

H: Frustrated and sad. My mother is here too. Both of my parents are trying to convince me.

C: Why?

H: For family. I am crying. I am laying in his lap, and he is stroking my hair. Mother is just watching.

C: Are you aware of how old you are?

H: Young. I can't really tell. Eighteen maybe. Early twenties.

C: Continue to report back to me what is going on with you and around you.

H: There is a boy at my door. It's my little brother. He wants to give me a stuffed animal. Because I am crying.

C: Is he familiar to you in this lifetime?

H: He is my brother also in this life. I am still very upset. I am being pulled away from the house. Across the clouds… not up.

C: Where are you going?

H: Going up… to the blue room maybe?

C: Did you die in that room?

H: I was angry. I wanted a new life. I still see myself in that body.

*At this point I take the client to a safe place so that I can then ask her to scan her body to see what happened in that room for her to pass away so quickly and to see why she was still angry even though she shed her physical body.

C: I want you to now scan your body, knowing that as you do that was then and this is now, you are completely safe and secure, as you do this continue to breathe in… and out… relaxing and releasing all tension in the mind and body… What do you notice?

H: Bloody wrists... I feel angry. Really angry. I was treated unfairly. I am at the entrance of the blue room.

C: What do you do now?

H: I am at the entrance. There are arms on my shoulders now. I need to heal first.

C: What do you mean?

H: I need to not be angry. I am being taken somewhere else.

C: Do you know who this is?

H: Someone important to me. He is taking me. I am outside of the blue room somewhere. I am in a bathtub. Blood is coming off. I am relaxing. Calming down. He is washing me.

C: What happens now, are you healed?

H: He left me, and I am alone. Holding myself. I feel tired. Emotionally exhausted. I am crying. He came back and he is telling me it's okay.

C: What do you do now that you are healed?

H: I am following them. To a different room. It's a circular room. There is a desk and a couch. I am sitting on the couch. *Goes quiet. *

C: What's going on in this room?

H: They are looking at a book. We are discussing what went wrong.

C: What do you mean what went wrong?

H: I am being scolded for killing myself. There are other ways. I was supposed to learn something. I feel like I have done this before.

C: Who is it that is talking to you about this?

H: They are like a teacher. We are reviewing. They are not mean when they do this. The scolding. It's in a nice way.

C: What do they tell you to prevent this again?

H: Just remember why you're here. He told me that's all and to rest. I have a blanket and rest on the couch. I am calmer. I understand now.

C: What do you understand now that you didn't before?

H: I should have married that man.

*At this point the client takes a moment to rest as she needs and then we move on to the next phase that she goes through after returning to the afterlife.

C: What happens now?

H: It's the next day. He is back. I am following him to the blue room. My friends and family are there.

C: How do you know who is there?

H: I know they are there. I feel a lot better now.

*At this point during the session, I take the client onto the room of life selection. The reason for this is to possibly discover why she chose the body she chose. This is in hopes to finally give her some peace and a better understanding of what she needs to utilize it for.

H: It's a quick walk there.

C: Is there anyone there with you?

H: I am in the room with the person who healed me and one other person.

C: What are you doing in this room?

H: Sitting at a circular table. I am telling them I am ready.

C: What are you ready for?

H: I don't know what to choose. I have experienced so many already. I want a challenge.

C: Can you expand on that?

H: A physical challenge.

C: What do you do now?

H: I am looking at a hologram. They have bodies that are already made. They each have characteristics about them.

C: What do you choose and why?

H: It's unique. This one. This body. All of the others have big physical issues.

C: Continue to explain this process and what you are going through with this.

H: I am discussing what could go on in this life. They are asking me who else I want to be with. They are telling me about my other friends who have chosen.

C: Do you feel prepared and ready?

H: Yes, I am prepared. There are more people in the room.

C: Do you recognize them?

H: Dave is here. He likes it. My choice. We are happy we get to spend another lifetime together. Help each other with our goals in this life. We work well together.

C: Is this different for you both choosing a different gender in this life than the last?

H: He likes being male. I am female most of the time.

C: What is going on now?

H: They are warning me that this could be a hard one. I cannot do the same as before.

*Note: I always feel there is divine guidance somehow intertwined in all of this we call life. I have the belief that all clients are guided to me as a way to get across a message that they need at the time they come to me. I felt that this client needed a reminder again that she cannot commit suicide in this life in order to learn the lessons she has been trying to learn over lifetimes now. I now try to check if there are any signposts, so to say, that were put in place to help remind her.

C: Are there any signs or anything you need to look out for to remind you to continue on in this life?

H: Not that I can see.

*At this point I put in a post hypnotic suggestion to always remember what she now knows and have a deeper understanding and connection to why she is here. I feel that her guidance allowed her to see this scene so that she will trust in the process, and this was all that she needed to keep her on track as she lives out this lifetime.

C: What do you do now?

H: We left. I am in the blue room again. It will be a little bit before I can leave.

C: What do you do in your time before you leave?

H: My teacher and I are going to study before I go. I am now in the teacher's room again. I am giving over my book.

C: A book?

H: Everyone has a book. Dave is sitting next to me. We are going over final things.

C: What are you going over?

H: I can't hear him speak. I just know what he is saying.

*Close out Session.

After we ended the session, I felt it necessary to check on her and thoroughly go over what she had learned. I have never had a client say they had committed suicide in many prior lives. It's an alarm for me as a hypnotherapist because I do not want my clients to have such a comfortable understanding of the afterlife and feel that this is an easy decision and do it again in this lifetime as a way out. I made sure she was okay and believed without a doubt that she would not do it again. I recommended she consult with a physician for any further concerns.

Since I am not a practicing physician or psychotherapist, I cannot give medical advice and must recommend help from qualified people for those things. However, I do feel confident that she has a much deeper understanding of why she needs to stay this time and has the confidence to do so. She still expressed she did not understand why she wanted a challenge and laughed at her decision this time around.

Client update: This client has gotten married and gone on to have children. It has been eight years since she had this session, and life has progressed for her happily in many ways. She has, however, experienced many other medical issues that have developed over the course of time. She has managed them well considering how hard they have been. She has lost her vision in one eye and had surgery to fix it, which was mostly unsuccessful. The other has suffered too. Despite everything that has happened, she is still here and making the most out of life. Choosing life over an early exit again. Sometimes all it takes is a knowing of why we chose the harder path, to make living it a little easier to swallow.

# CHAPTER 6
## "Luella"

This is a short session, but I want to include this because the final piece that comes in is profound. Most of the session will sound as if the details are chaotic and random. This can be very normal because what we are experiencing under the hypnotic state is vast and trying to explain what you are seeing in words does not do it justice. It's like watching a movie with many details going on and trying to paint the picture with a few short words. You really do not get a good translation of everything being experienced. Add a new place on top of that and it becomes almost impossible to report back in a way it's completely understood.

I know that when someone comes out of the trance state, the details are still there within the mind. It can fade quickly as if trying to remember a dream. That is why going back and listening to the session afterwards can help bring those vivid details back in a more complete way. Everyone is different in how they experience it. This person was overwhelmed in a good way, at all of the details and things happening around her. I knew I was only getting a small piece of that puzzle.

I want to show that sometimes, all we need is just a reminder of why we made the choice to come here. The peace that comes with a deeper understanding like that is enough to carry us through the rest of our lives.

*Session Begins

C: Tell me the first thing that you notice.

L: Grass. Sand. With sticks sticking out of it.

C: When you look down at your feet, what do you notice?

L: Can't see my feet.

C: When you look out around you, what do you notice?

L: I just keep seeing colors. Yellow, green, purple. I just see colors.

C: Do you feel anything coming off the colors?

L: They are just like wind. Like giant globs of colors and wind.

C: What are they doing?

L: There is purple now, green. It's just in and out. There's green. Purple. Um. Like tie dye. They are moving.

C: Are they touching you?

L: Yeah, I'm in it.

C: Are they going anywhere?

L: No. I'm just in it.

C: What does it feel like?

L: Explain this? I'm in the middle of something.

C: Are you able to take a step back and look at it?

L: I'm in it.

C: And when you look at yourself, do you have a body?

L: No.

C: Are you doing anything with the colors?

L: No.

C: Are there any sounds?

L: No.

C: Is it flowing around you in circles or just by you?

L: It's pulsating. Not swirling like a tornado. Just.... coming in and out. It's just....

C: I want you to sit with it for a moment and watch as these colors move and flow. And just explain to me what's going on as you're watching them.

L: I'm shards of light, kind of, and black, like stars, space, black colors. Dark blue, like nebulous type of stuff. But it's feathered.

C: Are you traveling anywhere?

L: I keep going up.

C: As you go up, just explain to me the scenery around you.

L: I've got light. Like a, not sunlight. White shiny star. Blue, white. It feels warm. I'm just kind of... The space is not there anymore. It's white but not like the color white.

C: Does it have any feeling to it?

L: Warm. I'm supposed to be there. I think.

C: Are you floating in this place?

L: Now I backed out of it a little bit.

C: Do you not want to be there?

L: Not supposed to be. And now it's purple, red, dark red, black. I'm in space again.

C: Do you feel like you're going somewhere?

L: Yes. I see green. But space green. I'm in space.

C: You're moving through space?

L: Yeah. Green. Green, purple clouds in space.

C: Does it look like our space?

L: Looks like outer space. But it's not dirty and littered with a bunch of stuff, it's just. I think I'm huge.

C: Why do you say that?

L: Because everything looks smaller to me.

C: When you look at yourself what do you see?

L: Nothing. I'm not anything.

C: You're just energy?

L: I think so.

C: Do you know where you're going?

L: No, I just am.

C: I want you to relax into this place as you watch everything moving by you. Just continue to explain to me what you see.

L: Yellow. The sun. The sun.

C: Is it warm?

L: I think so?

C: What does it look like?

L: Like a sunflower. I don't see the whole thing. It's like I'm really close to it because I only see a crest of it. Like a sunflower like I'm moving. It's boiling. It's on fire. Not like a fire that we are used to seeing. Bubbling liquid. There's a sunspot. I see that. I can't feel it though. But I know it's warm. It doesn't burn.

C: What else do you notice around you?

L: Um, there's a little place, kind of looks like a geode would look. It's not what you would think. It's gas. It's green. There's a bright center, like a yellow one. I don't know if there is something in there or not, but it's there.

C: And you still floating through space?

L: I don't float. I move sometimes but I'm just there.

C: Does it feel good to be in this space?

L: Oooo, I see something now. This is cool. This is purple, blue, bright white. Something you see, not like somebody would draw. It's spikey and huge, huge, bright lights everywhere lit up like a city. HUGE! People live here, I think. It has a sound.

C: What does it sound like?

L: *Mimics a humming or Om sound* Deeper. *Mimics again* But it's not disturbing.

C: Are you going to go there?

L: It travels through space. It is in space. And where did it go.... Well, that was really cool. It's huge and has lights. Light blue, purple. The purple is like hot pinkish. It was huge. It was HUGE. It was spikey, not spikey. Tall, narrow. Something future. Nothing like you've ever seen.

C: And did it leave?

L: Yeah. It came at me too. It moved. It's huge, I may have been able to get inside of it, but I feel big. I'm really big.

C: Are you still moving through space?

L: I think things are coming to me. So, yeah, something else is coming. I'm not moving, things are coming to me.

C: When the next one comes forward, you can make yourself smaller so that you may enter the area that you see, if you choose to. If it is a place you want to explore. Do you see one coming?

L: I think so. I saw an old man. All hunched over. I'm in a trailing white, like a comet. I'm in the tail of it. A tail.

C: Are you riding it?

L: Yeah, I can't see anything, just white.

C: What does that feel like?

L: Just there. And then I, pink holes. Pink tunnels. Pink holes. Pink tunnels. And not on the comet anymore.

C: Are you back out exploring?

L: I must be. I'm somewhere pink. With weird vining. Not even vines. Looks like muscle tissue, but I'm in it.

C: Can you touch it?

L: No, I'm just there. And more colors. A storm. Weird storm. Just a storm. Not outer space storm. This is a planet storm.

C: Do you recognize where you are?

L: No.

C: Are you on the ground?

L: Maybe?

C: When you look around you, what do you see?

L: Weird rock formations. They are not like you've seen before. They look like obsidian, and they are sharp.

C: Are you outside in the storm?

L: Yea, but it's not like you think.

C: What are you doing?

L: Looking up at the stars.

C: When you look down at yourself what do you see?

L: I want to say I see my feet look like chicken feet. And they are black and shiny. Or maybe that's the rock, I don't know.

C: When you look at your hands, what do you see?

L: Black and shiny. My hands don't look like my hands. They... I am something completely different.

C: Is there anyone with you?

L: I sense that there are others there, but I don't know that there are others there. There is always others there.

C: And what does your body feel like to you?

L: Light. Not heavy. I'm big. I'm a badass! I'm trained for war.

C: And why is that?

L: I don't know.

C: Do you live nearby?

L: I'm a part of something. I don't act alone.

C: Are you still staring at the stars?

L: I can.

C: What are you doing now?

L: I'm looking up and I feel like I am not human. Not at all. I am something else.

C: Do you live nearby?

L: I think this is my planet. Either that or I... I think it might be home. It's not very pretty.

C: Do you live a long life on this planet?

L: I've been there before. I begged for Earth.

C: Do you like it here?

L: *Crying* No! I was ok there! I wanted something different. It's cold there and not, there is no feeling there. You don't feel, no one is mean to you. Nobody is nice to you.

C: Are you happy with that?

L: I just existed. I wanted to feel, and I had a choice. I begged to come to Earth. Earth wasn't my only choice.

C: What was your other choice?

L: I wasn't given planet choice.

C: What other choices could you have made?

L: To just come. To have, I think to be human. But it wasn't human. It was to feel. I wanted to feel. *Still crying* Emotional seeing that decision to become human.


*Close out Session.

# CHAPTER 7

## "Kira"

This session covers a life that seems normal at first. However, there are deeper aspects that begin to come out after she passes on to the other side. This is the first time I have directly come across "dark magic" and how it can affect us across many lifetimes. This client was not familiar with dark magic either, so it was new to her as well. As we embarked on this journey and stayed connected afterwards, she began to see these things unfold in a way that made her believe that there might be more than we understand out there. Working behind the scenes. Good and bad. A world of duality.

*Session Begins

C: What do you notice?

K: It's very green. And there is like... I landed in front of a huge castle it looks like. It's sunny. Quiet. Smell of the grass.

C: When you look down at your feet, what do you notice?

K: There are these black shoes. I am wearing what looks like a dress.

C: What color is it?

K: Pink and white.

C: Are you carrying anything with you?

K: No.

C: When you look at your hands, what do you notice about them? Do they look young or old?

K: Mmm... probably early young adulthood.

C: And as you are looking at that castle, tell me more about it.

K: Kind of gray and brown color. It's massive. It's kind of pointy. Different points all over. When I turn around there is a big gate in front. It's like a stone gate. Looks really big and heavy.

C: And is there anyone there at the gate?

K: In like the tower part, but that's it.

C: Are you able to see them?

K: Mmhmm. They are sitting there. They are wearing metal armor almost. It's what it looks like.

C: Are you walking in?

K: Mmhmm. It's like a gravel pathway. I am coming up to the door. It's like a big brown, like really tall double door.

C: And what happens when you walk up to this door?

K: It opens up and there is just a guy standing there. Kind of looks like a butler or servant. He is wearing a black suit. He is older. Maybe like fifties.

C: What happens now, does he take you somewhere?

K: Someone has been waiting for me is what he says.

C: How do you feel about that?

K: Kind of indifferent, I guess.

C: What do you do now?

K: It's like a large dining room. It's a really long table. With a bunch of people sitting around it.

C: What are they eating?

K: Looks like different meats and sides. I get the feeling this is like family and family friends.

C: And what are you doing?

K: Standing in the doorway. I see my dad who is not happy that I am late. *Laughs* Because that is who was waiting for me.

C: Why is he not happy that you are late?

K: Seems that I'm never quite on time there.

C: What were you doing?

K: Outside in like the garden area. I like to garden. I like to smell all of the flowers and eat some of the stuff while I'm out there. I get the feeling I just don't like to be a part of family stuff.

C: Do you sit?

K: I end up sitting down at one end. Talking to a woman. I can't tell if she is my mother or grandmother but, she is a little softer than my dad is.

C: What are you talking about?

K: Never being on time.

C: Do they expect that from you?

K: Mmhmm. I get the feeling I don't fit into the norm there. Like of a woman and like obedient I AM NOT. *Laughs*

C: Why is that?

K: I just beat to my own drum.

C: There doesn't seem to be anything wrong with that.

K: No.

C: So how is it there?

K: Yeah, I get the sense it's a celebration.

C: Do you know what you are celebrating?

K: Yes. I think I am supposed to get married to somebody that I don't want to.

C: Is that what the celebration is for?

K: Yes.

C: So, they found you a suitor.

K: Yeah.

C: Is he there?

K: Mmhmm.

C: And what do you think about that?

K: I don't really like him very much.

C: Do you know why you don't like him?

K: He is not a very good person.

C: And so why are you marrying him?

K: Family relations.

C: What does that do for your family?

K: Hmm. Helps them stay within status.

C: Do they have high status?

K: Seems like it.

C: So, you live in this castle?

K: Mmhmm.

C: So, tell me about dinner.

K: Talking to my mom and my sister. Just kind of laughing though I feel this sense of dread being there.

C: Can you tell me about that?

K: It's just not something that I'm looking forward to. I'm looking for a way out of it.

C: Explain to me what's going on around you.

K: It's both families, and everybody is sitting there talking. I get the feeling that this is going to happen sometime this week.

C: That's pretty soon.

K: Mmhmm.

C: Did they have to travel to be a part of this?

K: Yeah, it's like a long celebration.

C: And what happens after dinner?

K: Seems I try to talk to my dad about not wanting to and he is not having it.

C: What about your sister?

K: She is younger than me. She doesn't have to get married. I have a younger and an older sister.

C: What about your older sister?

K: My older sister wants me to just go with the flow.

C: Is she married?

K: Mmhmm. And miserable.

C: Is that why you don't want to get married?

K: Mmhmm.

C: And why is she so miserable?

K: Because she doesn't like her partner either.

C: So why does she want you to go through with it?

K: You're supposed to follow the rules.

C: What about your mom? Is she happy in her marriage?

K: Hmm. Not particularly, but they figured it out for the most part.

C: So, tell me about the conversation with your father.

K: Basically, just telling me this is how it goes, and I really don't have a choice. I'm going to do it whether I want to or not.

C: So, what do you do?

K: I just walk away and go into my room.

C: Tell me about your room. What does that look like?

K: It's big. My bed is very plush. I have like a big dresser with a bunch of different color dresses in it. I don't really like to wear them, but the loose-fitting ones are nice. Able to move in. I don't like to wear them because they are not my style. I would rather, I don't know, be more comfortable.

C: Do you have other clothes to wear?

K: I have other stuff for gardening. Pants and stuff I can get dirty.

C: Tell me about your room.

K: They have this wallpaper on the walls. Flowers on the wallpaper.

C: Do you decorate?

K: I have a mirror and some landscape portraits. That's about it.

C: What are you doing now?

K: Sulking, I guess. I figure it's probably something I'm not going to be able to get out of.

*Moves her forward to an important day in that life. *

C: What do you notice?

K: Hmm... a lot of violence. It's more towards me. It's that person that I married. This is later on. And it is very aggressive.

C: Why is he being violent?

K: Because I don't do things the way I should.

C: Did he expect you to?

K: Mmhmm. I am talking to people I shouldn't. I was talking to some lady who... lower class, I guess and that is frowned upon.

C: Why is that frowned upon?

K: I'm not sure. Just think it's based on status and classes.

C: So, what is happening now?

K: This is a regular occurrence of receiving physical violence from him. I tried to get away, but it doesn't work.

C: Have you told your family?

K: It seems like it, but they can't do anything. Or won't.

C: What do you do once this is over?

K: Nothing because I am locked in this room.

C: Locked?

K: A really small one. Not my bedroom. Different one. Just really tiny and dark.

C: Are there any windows?

K: Tiny one. It's got a small bed. Kind of dirty. Wood floors. Dark and gray.

C: What are you doing?

K: Sitting there feeling trapped.

C: What's going through your mind?

K: It's going to be like this forever.

C: How long do you have to stay in there?

K: Seems like a really long time.

C: What happens when you're allowed out?

K: I can only do certain things. I can't go anywhere. I am stuck. I can't do anything I like to do. No gardening. He seems very sadistic in a way. Liking to see misery.

C: Is there anyone else around you?

K: The helpers but they can't do anything.

C: Do you talk to them?

K: No. They won't talk to me.

C: Why?

K: They are scared.

C: So, what do you do with your days then?

K: Seems like I read and sleep a lot.

C: You read? What do you like to read?

K: Fiction books. Seems like a good escape.

C: What kind of stories do you enjoy?

K: The fantasy ones. My favorite is the ones with the dragons. I like dragons.

C: Do you still live with him in the castle?

K: I moved into a different one. Their families'.

C: Do you live with his family?

K: They are not very nice. No. They are rude people.

C: Is there no one there you can speak to?

K: There seems to be an older lady. Who is a cook or launderer? She is the only one that will talk to me.

C: What do you talk about?

K: Seeing the bright side of things.

C: Is she happy?

K: No but she seems to be... I don't know... found something to help her.

C: Well, it's nice to have a friend there.

K: Mmhmm.

*Moves her forward to the last day in that life*

C: What do you notice?

K: It seems to be some type of war.

C: What do you see?

K: People rushing around. I think that there are people that have come into the house. They are killing people. I am trying to run.

C: When you look down at your hands do you look young or old?

K: Still young. Maybe like thirty or forty.

C: What's going on?

K: It's just chaos everywhere.

C: Where are you going?

K: Trying to find a hiding spot but...

C: What do the people look like that are coming into your house?

K: They are wearing fur and metal. They have axes and knives.

C: Do you recognize them?

K: No.

C: Do you know why they are doing this?

K: It's like for land, I think.

C: Did you know they were coming?

K: No. It was a surprise.

C: Where is your husband?

K: I think he is out. He isn't home.

C: He doesn't know.

K: No.

C: Do you see any of his family there with you?

K: Yeah, his mom is here. Old lady is there.

C: What are they doing?

K: Trying to run and hide as well.

C: Are there any men or family with you?

K: Yeah, like an uncle and family friend.

C: What are they doing?

K: Trying to fight them.

C: Did you find a hiding place?

K: No. Someone caught me and the old lady.

C: *Suggestions not to feel discomfort during the next scene. *

K: I was running, and I got an axe in the shoulder.

C: When they captured you?

K: Mmhmm.

C: What happens now?

K: I see that I'm tied up at one point. I'm in between my body. They are just going to kill me.

C: When you look down what do you notice?

K: There is still a lot of fighting going on. The old lady passed too.

C: Do you know why they did that?

K: Payback.

C: What for?

K: I think something that my husband did.

*Suggestion for clarity to understand more about the situation*

K: Stole from them. He stole a bunch of goods.

C: Did he do that often?

K: Yeah. He is not a very good person.

C: As you are looking around, what was the point of that life?

K: To overcome darkness.

C: Do you feel like you did that?

K: I feel like I was starting to.

C: What else do you notice? What did you learn?

K: Stuff about being myself. I was trying to embrace who I was, and it was really pushed down.

C: Is there anyone with you?

K: Hmmm... seems like my grandmother.

C: What else do you notice?

K: I feel a lot calmer now. My grandmother is there supporting, holding space.

C: What do you do now?

K: Going back to review it.

C: Tell me about that.

K: I'm with people that I seem to know. It just feels light and loving. They are telling me they missed me.

C: What are you learning about that life?

K: Overcoming hard things. Trusting myself.

C: Do you feel like you accomplished that?

K: For the most part, yeah.

C: Is there anything else you had planned or meant to learn?

K: I get the feeling that I was meant to resist and try to do my own thing because I was so different. Just learning how to speak for myself with my voice, but I think it's hard in a situation like that. But I did a good job.

C: Is there anything they assist you with?

K: Healing. Physical. The depression weighed down my energy. So, they are helping clear that.

C: How do they do that?

K: Sending this loving energy to different areas of my body. Or energy, I guess. I don't really have a body.

C: What does that feel like?

K: It's like a warm… like a pulsating feeling. Kind of like a hug too.

C: If you don't have a body, how is it healing it?

K: Hmm. It's within the energy field. It's almost like a really strong negative emotion seemed to way tax my energy field. So, they try to absorb it and transmute it in a way.

C: What about the injury from where you died, how do they heal that?

K: It's also tied to like… the throat chakra. That area. Still working to heal that part of the energy.

C: How is it attached to that energy center?

K: It's a choice around sharing my voice and it got damaged when I didn't do that. When I went along with what was expected of me. It damaged that area.

C: What does that damage look like?

K: Looks like a darkness.

C: Does the axe wound affect that too?

K: Mmhmm.

C: Are they able to fully heal that?

K: They are still trying to.

C: Is it difficult to work on?

K: Yeah, I'm not really sure why.

C: Can you ask them why?

K: It's partly um, how do I say it, magic or something. That was used on me. Which is why it's hard to heal it. If that makes sense.

C: Can you tell me more about the magic?

K: The person that I was married to comes from a very dark family, and different rituals were used on people from what I understand.

C: Did they do that on you as well?

K: Mmhmm.

C: Can you tell me about it? What kind of rituals did they use? Did you know about it?

K: No, I didn't. Some sort of entity that attaches to you.

C: Did you know about it in the life?

K: No.

C: Is it still there now?

K: It lingers a bit. Like not fully healed.

C: So, are they able to heal it?

K: No.

C: Why not?

K: They don't know how to.

C: What happens now?

K: I go to like some resting area.

C: What is that like?

K: Relaxing. Feels like rest. Like good rest.

C: What does the place look like?

K: Like a little pod. It doesn't feel like before. Like where you're trapped. You can come and go. It just feels very soothing.

C: * Suggestions to rest in the pod and rejuvenate, then explain to me what happens when she is finished*

K: I feel a lot better.

C: Is that area where the entity was, is it healed?

K: There is like a little dot left.

C: So, what do you do now?

K: Seems I go back to that group of souls, beings.

C: What are you doing there?

K: Talking about potentially going to another life. I get this is something that I will probably have to work on.

C: Tell me about it.

K: Something in the… embracing being yourself helps to release the attachment.

C: So, tell me about this life you're going to.

K: I get the feeling it's this one.

C: Tell me about the planning.

K: Hmm… I can't really, like understand what's going on. There is a group of people talking but…

C: Can you ask them what they are talking about?

K: They are trying to figure out what is the best way to learn this lesson.

C: What lesson are you learning?

K: To speak up and be myself and really embrace that.

C: So, what does that conversation look like as you're listening?

K: Hmm. Setting up situations that push me to learn hard lessons. For some reason I get the impression I have to learn things the hard way. Like harder way. I don't really know why.

C: Can you ask them what lessons they are setting up?

K: It seems like experiences where I have to be myself. In order for… there is not to be resistance.

C: How do they know what situations you need to be in?

K: Mmm, something similar to this past life. With like power and control, because I recognize it and when I feel the resistance to it, it will be a reminder. That this is something I have to overcome.

C: When are you planning this in your next life?

K: Throughout childhood.

C: Will it help that spot disappear?

K: I have to overcome the trauma from growing up and once I embrace it, it should clear up.

C: So, tell me about the rest of the planning, what does that look like?

K: Seems like they set up or agree on moments in time. Almost like deja'vu moments. Where I know something will feel similar. That it will trigger my memory.

C: Trigger from the last life?

K: All the lives before. They all add up towards a similar goal. Each life builds on the next.

C: Is there anything else they are helping to plan to learn in this life?

K: Spreading new information. And love over fear.

C: What else do you notice about this planning?

K: There are a lot of different difficulties. Because it's supposed to help me relate. It adds on past things too because I can understand different dimensions of things. Topics. It helps to be more relatable. If that makes sense.

C: It does. *Calls in the Higher Self* Why did you show her the last lifetime?

K: It is most similar to the life she is living now.

C: How is that?

K: She grew up with a mother who was similar to her father in that lifetime. Wanting her to do and be what she should have been or what they thought she should have been. So, this showed her a piece in time where there are two paths. The path that she took in that lifetime, lead to blocking the throat chakra. Blocking different areas of her life. So, she can see now in this life, there are two paths. She can choose to dim the light, or she can choose to show up and face the fear.

C: Do you think she did that in this life?

K: Hmm. I think she could see in this past life where she could have done better. Move forward in this life she is moving in the right direction, though gets caught up many times.

C: Can you tell her more about that, so she understands what she is learning?

K: She many times gets caught up in other people's perceptions. And fears abandonment, betrayal but when she shows up truly in the authentic, most high version of herself, she will learn that the people that are meant for her will be. And she has to begin to trust that.

C: Can you give her any advice to assist with this process of learning?

K: I think she is already in the process of seeing other people's perceptions of her are not direct reflections of her, but of them. And trusting the feelings that she gets and the things that come up for her are important in moving forward.

C: Is there anything that would help her?

K: I would say trust her instinct. Because it is correct. To lean into a love mindset vs fear. I think many times she gets caught up in the fear of it all and that overshadows everything else. It's not separate. Nothing is separate.

C: Can you tell her about the axe wound in her shoulder? Is that still with her today?

K: Yes. A reminder of. It's popping up more and more now because she is facing owning her truth. Talking it, saying it, things like this. And when she goes against it, it really flares up, to remind her. A reminder.

C: So, is she going against it often enough?

K: Mmhmm. Yes. Bending over backwards for the people, not following what's right for her.

C: And what's right for her?

K: It is not conventional in means of today. And embracing that part of her who other people may judge as different or weird. This is the part she is meant to embrace.

C: What is she supposed to be doing? Is there something that is of her best interest?

K: I think she is on the way of doing it. Spreading spiritual information and healing energy work. The more she moves in this direction, the more things will align.

C: Can you tell her about the shoulder and neck pain she is having?

K: Yes, this is tied to the throat chakra. As well as the heart chakra. The throat chakra becomes blocked at times when she may hold back in sharing something. Or not truly speaking her truth. The heart chakra can become blocked when she gets caught in separation.

C: What do you mean by separation?

K: Fear stories. About others not liking her or not understanding, not getting it. These are stories she has repeated since she was younger that she needs to work through.

C: Can you assist her in that?

K: Mmhmm.

C: And how would you assist her in that?

K: Sending reminders helps her to get back on track. But can also help with clearing energy that may be stuck.

C: And the pain in her neck and shoulder, can you help with that?

K: Hmmm. Yes.

C: What does that look like?

K: Pulling out... hmm... these cords that are stuck.

C: Tell me about them. What does that look like?

K: These look like cords from the past that have not been able to be removed just yet.

C: Why is that?

K: Vow. Vows that were made.

C: What kind of vows? Was it this most recent lifetime?

K: *Quiet for a period of time. * No this goes way back. Something along the lines of staying silent for protection. Vowing to not spread information or thought for protection.

134

C: Can you release those from her?

K: Yes.

C: Are you doing that now?

K: Mmhmm.

C: What does that look like?

K: Unplugging and changing the energy.

C: And that replenishes the area?

K: Mmhmm.

C: What about the last entity that she dealt with in this last life? Can you tell her about that?

K: This entity drains energy. The energy that she had fed it, so to speak. And it basically was trying to remove her life force energy. This also attaches to these cords from the past.

C: Is it still there?

K: Yes.

C: Is it still affecting her?

K: Mmhmm.

C: How come we have not been able to see it or remove it? (She has taken our reiki class and been taught clearing.)

K: It seems it is from a different type of… dimension? Or not easily accessible.

C: So, we wouldn't have seen it before?

K: No.

C: Can you remove it now?

K: *Quiet*

C: Are you able to remove it?

K: I am still working on it.

C: Oh perfect, is it easier to remove now that those cords in the shoulder are removed?

K: Mmhmm. Somewhat.

C: And how do they place it there?

K: This comes deep within their family. From lifetimes and lifetimes within this family. There are dark entities attached to them. And it is through marriage that they are placed onto another person. Very hard to remove.

C: Why are they hard to remove?

K: It seems to be a combination of spell work magic that has deep threads. It's hard to explain.

C: So, she would not have been able to remove it on her own?

K: No.

C: Is it all gone?

K: There is still a little bit left. It is hard to remove.

C: Can you tell me about the process of removing it?

K: Mmhmm. It is almost like sending energy to sever the attachment cords that it has. And it just holds very, very tight.

C: Does that entity attachment have a name we might understand here on earth, or something we might recognize?

K: Hmm... The only thing is it starts with an A.

C: Is it finished?

K: It is removed.

C: Is the area protected now that it is removed?

K: We are putting up protection now.

C: And where does the entity go?

K: I sent it back, back, back in time.

C: It will not harm anyone else though, correct?

K: Mmhmm.

C: Does the pyramid help with this process?

*My sessions can be done under a meditative space, but it is also a pyramid built for the purpose of protection and clearing. I was pushed by spirit some time ago to build it without understanding

136

why. I fought the idea at first but finally did it. It has been such a blessing for some of the trials we have faced. *

K: Yes.

C: Would you have been able to remove it if she was not sitting in it?

K: No.

C: Why is that?

K: The direction of energy, focus of energy aids in the assistance of removing.

C: Is that why we were not able to see it before?

K: Mmhmm.

C: Can you tell me about the channeling that Kira is meant to be doing, that she was told about?

K: This will be new energy. New information coming through. This will also be how to spread information between many, many people so that they understand this new idea around spirituality and energy.

C: And how will she be doing that?

K: This energy will be new in terms of how to clear one's energy body. And how to remove these attachments and darker energies that come forward.

C: And how will she be channeling that?

K: There will be many different ways. One will be having an anchor asking questions. Another will be with earth elements. Water will be helpful here.

C: Can you tell me about that?

K: Water is a cleansing and clearing material. That will be very helpful in clearing in energy work.

C: How will she do that?

K: Almost using it as a conduit.

C: Like you mean… putting water on people?

K: Using it as a way to transmit.

C: What is it transmitting?

K: It has a way of clearing and reorganizing energy. So, this would be a good way to use when… helping others who come to her.

C: Can you tell me more about working with an anchor? What will that look like?

K: Sitting and channeling but having somebody ask questions is helpful almost like a grounding anchor in order to receive the information properly. When channeling alone for her… things seem to get lost in translation.

C: So, is it going to be similar to what we are doing here?

K: Yes.

C: And so, if I were to sit and ask her, will she notice the channeling coming through?

K: Yes.

C: And who or what will she be channeling?

K: This will come from Lyrans.

C: Can you tell me about them?

K: This is one of the oldest civilizations with very high-tech information that will help the earth come back into harmony.

C: And how will they do that?

K: Transmitting healing energy frequencies. Channeling different information from them and being able to spread it to others.

C: And so, is there a particular Lyran that she is going to be working with?

K: It is more of a group.

C: And do they know her?

K: Yes.

C: How?

K: She is originally from there.

C: Can we ask them to come through to establish a connection? So, she knows what that connection looks like?

K: Okay.

C: Can you tell me about that?

K: They are just here to establish the energy. To become familiar.

C: What does that feel like?

K: Like a warmth. Hmm. Feels like a strong pull.

C: So, this is what it will feel like when she is channeling them?

K: Mmhmm.

C: Is there anything else you can tell her about that?

K: It will feel like a pull on the left side near the back top of the head. That's where the energy will come down.

C: Why is it there?

K: It is the best connection point.

C: So, she knows these Lyrans?

K: Mmhmm.

C: Is there anything they can show her or help her understand while they are here?

K: They have always been supporting her. She can call on them when she needs help. Practicing this connection on her own through meditation will be helpful. Just focusing on the feeling. Inviting them in. and asking them what she may need to know for the day.

C: Is there anything else about the Lyrans she can know?

K: They are also protector beings. If at all she feels unsafe, she can call upon them for protection.

C: And how long was she there?

K: Long time.

C: Has she been gone from them for a long time?

K: Yes and no.

C: Is there anything else that you can tell her about this channeling? Will she be starting this now?

K: She can start now. But practicing daily. Will be helpful.

C: Can you tell her about her teeth? She had a tooth that chipped, what happened?

K: She still holds on to a lot of anger frustration, suppressed emotion, that she holds in her jaw. It has been affecting not only the grinding of her teeth, but the tooth in general.

C: Is there anything you can do to assist her with that?

K: Mmhmm. Yes.

C: Can you help her release those emotions so that they are not stuck in that area?

K: We can release what we can, but she needs to work through the anger. On her own.

C: Are you doing that now?

K: Mmhmm.

C: I want to ask about her about her astrology. She is really pulled to it; can you tell her why?

K: Yeah. Funny she comes from the stars. But it resonates with her because it has meaning. It's like a language that she can read. Practicing this will be very helpful for her.

C: Why is that?

K: It gives a deeper understanding to the things that are going on. And the things that will come.

C: Can you tell us about the things that are going on now?

K: There is a big shift in energy happening. Everywhere. Within dimensions. Within your world. Within other worlds. Big shifts. Cosmic shifts.

C: And what does that look like for us?

K: It is a process of relearning who you are. What you are. And moving into more unity and harmony. It is soul process but happening in us.

C: Can you tell me about that? Does that cause physical symptoms in humans?

K: Mmhmm. A lot of the physical symptoms come from the resistance but also from what they hold onto in their lives of course.

C: Is there anything that Kira is holding onto?

K: Hmm. Anger. Suppressing emotion. Instead of really processing it.

C: And how can she process it better?

K: Somatically it will be helpful. Moving it up and out of the body.

C: How do you do that?

K: She can move her body in different ways in which to release the energy. She will be guided to those who practice somatic work in order to show her how to fully do it but intuitively she does know.

C: What about the animals? We have noticed a change in the animals around us, can you tell us what is going on?

K: As the energy is shifting, they are noticing. They are very sensitive to energy shifts. Differences and things. It is impacting them, and they are not sure how to handle it. And so, they are adjusting with time. It's just a rough transition.

C: But they will be safe?

K: Yes.

C: Is there anything we can do to assist them?

K: Applying protections to them can be helpful now.

C: So, we can protect them in that way, and it will be, ok?

K: Mmhmm. It will help.

C: I want to ask if there is anything Kira needs to know at this time?

K: Mmhmm. Not to get ahead of herself. There is a tendency to get ahead of herself and then get uncomfortable. Feeling that she has reached the point where she feels she needs to be, but rather than just trusting where she is right now is perfect. And continuing to do her practices will be helpful.

C: Are we going to be collaborating together on some of this work?

K: Yes.

C: What does that look like?

K: Will be gathering information and transmitting it in different ways. Many different sources. This can also look like working with groups of people.

C: Like teaching?

K: Yes.

C: Can you tell her anything else about that?

K: Sometimes she tends to feel as though she does not know enough. Though she has many, many, many lifetimes of information within her. And it is just about accessing that information and providing it. The people that come to her or the situations that she ends up in are for a reason. And to trust that she wouldn't have that opportunity if that wasn't the case.

C: And so, she will know what to do when the time comes?

K: Correct.


*Close out Session.

# CHAPTER 8

## "Nuella"

This client was a fascinating subject under hypnosis. She has a vastly different life in her current life, and it shines through in her session. In this life, she is an apothecary owner and is exceptionally good at her job. She is an islander who came from a place where there were no hospitals or doctors. They knew how to take care of the body and did not rely on outside resources. She is very much connected to nature and the world around her. She is intuitive and can read/see many aspects of a person and what's in their energy field. She was raised in this culture of understanding, deep intuition, and connection. I met her by chance, as is most of my life, chance meeting people who become important to me.

I was practically dragged to her shop; being told it was the perfect place for me, and I was going to love it! And so, I went. Little did I know how important that meeting was going to be. She became someone who I listened to, and she was equally a great listener. Two open-minded people that ended up talking for hours every time I went in. She wanted to experience what I did, and I happily agreed, not realizing the depth of what I was going to experience as well.

Her session experience is something vast and hugely different than one might expect. A shapeshifter who lives in many ways as well as a deeper understanding of her family history. A look into the generational depth of her family that matches her so perfectly. It explained so much about who she is and where her strength comes from. She had questions that are not typical for someone who wants to try this for the first time, but we both knew she did not fit into the mold many try to exist within. She touches upon light language, the original language, plant medicine and night school. She is very much connected to the other side and that also shows in the day-to-day things she experiences.

*Session begins

C: Tell me what you notice?

N: A concrete. It looks like a mausoleum but it's not and it has a plaque on it. It's in the middle of nowhere. It has a sitting space where you can sit. Like a water fountain. A half-moon water fountain on this thing that looks like a mausoleum but it's not hollow and it has a plaque on it.

C: Tell me about the plaque.

N: It has a cross on it and a water... three symbols of water crossing the bottom of the cross.

C: When you look down at your feet what do you notice?

N: I have sandals on.

C: What kind?

N: Just jute sandals. Rope sandals.

C: When you look up at your legs what do you notice?

N: They are hairy *Laughs* Very, very strong. And not very tall, long legged. Just short and like a shepherd type situation.

C: When you look up at your chest what do you notice you're wearing?

N: I am wearing something that is bronze. I'm wearing like a necklace that is bronze and it's kind of a heavy piece. It has symbols on it also.

C: Can you tell me about the symbols?

N: It looks like uh... like a compass for stars. Looks like there is... I've seen this before. It looks like a tusk. Mammoth tusks crossing and sighting scope. *whispers* That's what it is.

144

C: Do you have anything else with you?

N: Yes, I have a shepherd's staff.

C: And when you look at your hands, do they look strong?

N: Definitely strong hands. Small and stout.

C: When you look at the symbol on the mausoleum, can you tell me about it?

N: It's a map point. It's a point on a map. A marker. Depicting three ways to go. It is a crossroad. It's like a crossroad. It's the junction of three areas.

C: And are you going inside?

N: No. I am shepherding sheep.

C: Can you tell me about the sheep?

N: I have three sheep with me. They are just very interesting. I noticed them first when I saw the mausoleum. I saw them grazing. They are interesting. They have a black side to them that is obviously black. Like a razorback black and one of them specifically has black legs. They are interesting, big healthy sheep.

C: What are you doing with them?

N: They are part of my wealth.

C: What else?

N: They are the equivalent of my wallet. I am traveling with them, and they are my wealth.

C: Explain to me what you are doing.

N: I'm traveling somewhere. I'm just nowhere. I'm just traveling.

C: Do you have somewhere to be?

N: No, but there is someone there also, but they are not with me. They are just there.

C: What else do you notice about your surroundings?

N: It's a watering place. It's just a place to get water if you're traveling. And it's a really high peak. Real high area. The area is real high. You're in the clouds, in the mist. It's clearly spring/summertime. It's always like that there.

C: Are you talking to anyone?

N: No, but I am observant of the symbols on this... concrete face. This mausoleum. I'm looking at these symbols as if I'm reading the daily newspaper. But it's not a newspaper. It wants me to go to a bakery. There is a bakery. It's the menu of a bakery. A bread menu. Like you just know what's happening in town. The bakery has its bread in. It seems to be like a daily newsletter.

C: And that's etched into the stone?

N: Yes. But you can smell it.

C: What do you mean by that?

N: Well, you can see the loaves of bread. You can see the baker. You can smell it. You can... you know what its saying? *Having a hard time explaining it. *

C: So, are you going to the bakery?

N: Evidently, I'm going to get bread at the bakery. *Laughs* It's recommending I go see the baker.

C: As you are going to the baker, explain to me what the area around you looks like.

N: It's like the Swiss area. You get the feeling of Swiss chalet style town. The people are like Dutch. Healthy robust people. Not real big. They seem to be, Dutch? Even their language is Dutch. The smell of their food is Dutch. And there is a bakery. There is soup.

C: What do your pathways into town look like?

N: They are cobblestone. Stone. Brick. Stone. Brick. No sidewalks. Just lovely.

C: What do the sides of the buildings look like?

N: Cobb. And wood. And thatch. Reasonably not... these are like little people. Like no one seems to be taller than four feet tall. The buildings are small. Everything is short.

C: What about you?

N: No. I'm taller. Much taller. And I'm not well observed. As in they don't notice me yay or nay. Just normal passer byer. I must be from this area because nobody seems to be noticing that I'm coming through.

C: Are there any others like you who are taller?

N: Only the lady at the watering was closer to my height than the townspeople.

C: When you're on your way to the baker, do you speak to anyone or does anyone speak to you?

N: No.

C: Tell me what it's like when you get to the baker.

N: There is a well round-faced lady there with pronounced facial features. Very pleased to see me. And she is stirring a pot of something. She is sitting down. She almost doesn't look like she belongs. She is out like in the alley next to the baker. But she has a nice glowy face from a long time sitting next to the pot and heat.

C: Do you recognize her?

N: I feel like I do. I feel like I know her.

C: Do you talk to her before you go in?

N: Yeah, we must be friends because she is very happy to see me.

C: What do you talk about?

N: She doesn't. She just projects... she just...*confused * You just get that feeling. Her words are feelings not words.

C: Is that how the other people speak?

N: Yeah. I believe so. It's so quiet there.

C: Do you speak?

N: No. no.

C: How do you understand what the people are saying?

N: It's textured. The thoughts are textured. Not just thoughts. They are textured.

C: And so, you just know what someone is communicating?

N: Yes.

C: So, when you go into the baker, what do you find?

C: Meat pies. *Laugh* Sheep meat pies.

C: Is this from your meat?

N: It appears to be so. I see the black lamb hooves are being sold in the window, in the case. Black lamb legs. And meat pies.

C: Do you get to eat any of the food?

N: I think I'm the supplier of the lamb legs. I guess it feels like that, that I bring lamb legs.

C: Do you butcher them?

N: No. no but it feels very indifferent.

C: What do you mean by that?

N: That it's just a fact I sell lamb legs.

C: Do you normally do this?

N: Evidently this is my thing.

C: So, what do you do when you get inside?

N: I see the baker's wife, baking, cooking, the baker and the lamb legs and pies.

C: Why did you need to come to the bakery?

N: Well, that's strange. It feels like I'm buying lamb legs. Maybe I'm redeeming lamb legs. *Laughs* It doesn't make sense. I feel like I'm there to pick them up.

C: Is that your share of lamb legs from selling them?

N: Not necessarily sure I'm selling lamb legs; I'm picking them up.

C: When you pick them up, what do you do?

N: Redeem the lamb.

C: Can you explain it to me?

N: Giving the lamb back its legs.

C: How do you do that?

N: *Crying* Just by buying them. You just buy them and give them to the lamb. Just give them back their legs.

C: Why do you do that?

N: Because I can. Because I can.

C: Is there anything else you can tell me about why you do that?

N: You just can. You just can. It's an option. They sell legs, you can buy them and give them back to the lamb. It's only if you have extra money, you can do that. It's just a normal thing.

*My only way of understanding that was that maybe taking back the unused part of the animals, she was taking them to honor their sacrifice to be eaten. **

C: Did you leave the baker?

N: Yes, and I go back to the water. Same spot where you have an option to go to two other options if you wanted to.

C: Tell me about what you do now.

N: Seems to be a place that I go. That I'm at. I don't understand it.

C: *Instructions for clarity. *

N: There is a lot of space. It's just endless. There aren't a lot of people. Just a lot of space. Lot of thick terrain, green space. Just... and the more you walk it, the more you don't go anywhere. Just there. You can walk all you want but the terrain changes. But you're not really moving.

C: Do you know how to navigate this place?

N: I feel like I am the keeper of this place. I feel like I'm the only one there.

C: So, who puts the words on the mausoleum?

N: That's another space. That is a marker. If you look to the left is all that green space that you can just... it's incredible.

C: And you are the keeper of the green space?

N: Yes, it's my space.

C: What do you do with this space?

N: It's a space where there are birds and nature. Like a garden. Just like a jungle but not a jungle. It's not scary but well groomed. But very thick. You'll know if anything penetrates it. You'll know if a bird comes through the canopy. It's that thick.

C: Do you keep up this space?

N: It's my space. It's my home.

C: Do you live there?

N: I live there.

C: Tell me about your home.

N: It's just a green space.

C: Do you live within the forest?

N: I live within the forest. I am just like that.

C: Do you have a specific place?

N: It appears to be like a really wide petrified... my home is within a petrified tree? It doesn't feel like a tree because it's petrified but it's green growing. It's just lovely. It's big and it's lovely. It's not like modern at all. But the light is good. Filtered sunlight is good. It's just good.

C: Are your sheep with you in your home?

N: No, mostly birds. The greenery is very manicured and you're very aware that you can see the eyes of deer and so forth and you can see the squirrels, the birds and stuff. It's lovely.

C: Do you enjoy living here?

N: Yes.

C: What do you do now that you're home?

N: Nothing. I do nothing. I don't have to do anything. You don't have to cook. You don't have to do anything. You are just there.

C: What do you eat?

N: It's not like that. It feels very elemental, as in it's not a necessity.

C: How do you get your nutrients?

N: I think it's just from the yellow sunlight. You just sit there. You're like a plant. You get it from just being there. But not like we normally would. It's the filtered light. *whispers* Filtered light. Like a butterfly but not a butterfly. You're not a fairy, you're not a gnome but you're all of them. It's very elemental. Like it's a very much a do no harm type of thing here.

C: When you feel your face, your eyes and mouth and nose, what does it feel like?

N: *Pauses* They are cold. Tiny. Small. And cold… it's like… like a plant. It's like my cheeks are like the bulb of the bottom of a flower. I feel more like I'm plant material than I am human being. *In awe* More like that.

C: What do you feel around your eyes? What do you notice?

N: Well, I don't necessarily have any. *whispers* I don't have any.

C: What about your nose?

N: *Quiet contemplation* I can't even explain that. It's not that. My space where I live… I'm a plant. That's the best way to explain it. I'm a plant. I… I am a plant. And I am a transmutable plant. I can leave my space and be what I need to be. But I am my space. Best describe me like a tulip. It's like that where the real me doesn't have a face, doesn't have eyes and is quiet. You know… like a tulip.

C: What does it feel like to exist like that?

N: Watery and sustainable. Rejuvenatevley sustainability. It feels peaceful.

C: While you are soaking in that sunlight, we are going to move forward to an important day in that life. *Moves her forward * What do you notice?

N: I don't know.

C: What are you experiencing?

N: I see a lot of silver wire. It looks like liquid silver. Looks like transmission, like sound transmission, silver wire, and it feels like its knotted, but you could pull it straight and untangle it, but if you let it go it's going to go right back into that.

151

C: Are you able to touch it?

N: Yes.

C: What do you do if you're able to touch it?

N: You can feel it. Is it information?

C: When you touch it, what kind of information comes through?

N: I touched it, it's a sound of yellow.

C: What does that tell you?

N: It's the sound of yellow.

C: And what comes through?

N: That you could play an instrument with this if you didn't know how to play an instrument, you could still play it. Colorful sound instrument.

C: So, if you strum it like an instrument, what happens?

N: Yeah, you touch it and huh... interesting... so I touched a couple of it and an eye formed... somebody else's eye though. I can see a blue eye seeing me. Oh! Very much so. And it's still aware of me. But it's like surprised to see me.

C: In this space, you are protected, do you recognize it?

N: Yeah, it's my... my father's eye. Paternal side family's eye.

C: What do you notice about it?

N: It's not so nice. Or it appears to be that it would be attached to well... at first it seemed like it was not a nice person's eye, but it's been misconstrued based on how old it is. That it looks like it is a mean old thing, but it's just so old that it looks that way.

C: If it was surprised to see you, did it come up from strumming?

N: Yes.

C: Are you still looking at the eye?

N: Well, it was interesting enough that the eye is looking (at me) more so than me looking at the eye.

C: Are you ok with this eye looking?

N: Doesn't make any difference to me, but it was the cause of strumming that brought it, not so much that it was coming anyways.

C: Do you want to strum it again?

N: Yes.

C: Strum it again and tell me what happens.

N: I notice an elder looking out of a room. Out of a curtain, looking out the window. Maybe almost afraid to look out the window. Yet, they are holding the curtain open as if to let the light in. It's a female elder. I don't necessarily know her at the same time I feel like it's one of my family members.

C: What else do you notice about what she is doing?

N: She is just temporary. She is in temporary housing, temporary space. She has been there a long time.

C: Does she seem scared?

N: Not so scared as she is, was left with not enough information. She is very patient. But it's been a long time. Like it's almost like she is in a hotel space, temporary.

C: Are you able to communicate with her?

N: I could.

C: Just open up that heart space and send that light and love, then communicate with her. What do you notice?

N: She fidgets with her hands as if she is wringing her handkerchief. And she speaks another language.

C: Do you recognize it?

N: *Whispers* Yes.

C: What is she saying?

N: *Whispers* She is waiting for her grandson.

C: Who is her grandson?

N: I don't know.

C: Can you ask her?

N: She doesn't know why she got left there waiting for her grandson who has been gone a long time. *Gets emotional*

C: Let those emotions flow through you, breathing them in and out. Letting them pass comfortably and easily, it will become clear.

N: Her grandson is Oliver. She is just waiting for Oliver.

C: Is this where the Oliver name started?

N: It goes back way before that. And that makes sense. She looks like an Oliver. She is waiting for Oliver. He went out a long time ago, but he is coming back. He is just taking a long time.

C: Is there anything you want to tell her?

N: I offer her fruit and water, and she accepts it. But she is mostly concerned about letting the light in. Like not... she is not even looking out the window. She holds the curtain open so just the light comes in. Not to illuminate the space or anything, it's just like she is... I don't know how to explain it. Like he will see where she is at because the light comes in.

C: Is that how they communicate?

N: Yeah. That's how. There is an old... there hasn't been any talking throughout any of this.

C: They communicate that way as well?

N: Yes. That's how Oliver knows where she is at. Because where the light comes in.

C: Can they hear each other through distances?

N: Definitely.

C: Is that how you communicate too?

N: Definitely.

C: Is there anything you want to ask her about the Oliver lineage? *Pause* What does she tell you?

N: She is showing me that we are blended with the scent of citrus. The scent of orange and that is how we got our lighter skin, through the scent of orange. Passed under our eye and under our nose made

154

the brown of us become more lighter skinned. It came through the scent of citrus.

C: Why did this happen?

N: Because we were beautiful. Because it was beauty. Because it was complimentary. It was chocolate meets orange.

C: So that has become you and your line?

N: Yeah, we are, we were blended of beauty.

C: What else can she tell you about your lineage?

N: Huh, we are colors. We are flavonoids. We are colors. My family comes from colors. Blended colors. But specifically, the essence of colors. Not what they came from but flavonoids.

C: Can she tell you more about these flavonoids?

N: Huh, we are evidently bakers, we are foodies, but it doesn't seem to do with food. It feels like my "creator" was a baker, a cook. I don't know how to explain that I just don't know.

C: Can she explain that in a way that we can understand?

N: Yeah, that's like that's a wooden thick cup where the walls are, it looks like my apothecary except that's her kitchen and she puts together these scents and colors in the cauldron type situation pot and the essences, the white light, we are like a chemistry thing. Like a cook makes us. I don't know how to explain that. They have a cook that gently puts together the ingredients which create us.

C: Is it a special line of humans they have created?

N: Yeah, they are made of notes.

C: Is that why you can read other people's energy fields?

N: It's the essence of. *Whispers* There's not a lot of them.

C: There are not a lot of the creations of your people?

N: No, it's a lost recipe. There's ingredients that are missing. The ingredients are no longer available. To duplicate the exact... the original recipe. It exists but there are missing ingredients that do not exist.

C: Can she tell you why there are missing ingredients?

155

N: There was such a small amount.

C: Can she tell you what that means as to what your abilities are?

N: I have the… *Whispers * ingredients. *Starts crying * I have it. I have the little, tiny paste. It's a little tiny bit of paste. It's a dark paste that's like a vanilla paste but it's not vanilla bean. And I have that.

C: How did you get it?

N: My grandmother gave it to me.

C: And can she explain to you what to do with it?

N: There's not much of it. But it's made out of a seed. Like a fig seed. Little tiny fig seed. There's just not much of it. That's why I have the ability to work in that kitchen. I can ad-lib the ingredients but never duplicate it.

C: Why can it not be duplicated?

N: Because it just doesn't exist.

C: But you can create with it?

N: I have a little bit of paste. I have a little bit of the ingredient. But you wouldn't use it. You just wouldn't use it. There is no reason to create it. You can't create it. You can only store it in the apothecary. You wouldn't use it up though. But there is one seed that did not get crushed in that paste. And I'm aware of it. But you can use up the paste because you will take a chance of not having access to that seed. It's such a tiny seed that you don't mess with it. Don't mess with it. It's an ingredient.

C: Are you supposed to protect that seed?

N: You know it's in a safe space. As long as you know, don't use the paste, don't mess up the seed, it's safe.

C: Can she tell you what you do or could create now that you know you come from this line of creators?

N: It is flavor. The essence of flavor. It adds the sweetness.

C: What does it add sweetness to?

N: It's whatever you add it to. It brings out the sweetness. It isn't sweet, it allows the essence of whatever you're adding it to be sweet.

C: But you don't need to use it?

N: No. you don't. It already exists. You can, it's such a powerful thing that you can, in your mind go and say, I'm going to use this ingredient, but you don't use it up. Use it.

C: Light touch of it?

N: You just have to think it and you have used it. Without exhausting it. But you do not disturb it. You don't grab the container and scoop it out. You don't do that. You just think it.

C: So, you use it energetically?

N: Yes, that's the word. Definitely.

C: Can she explain to you what you can do with it for your work?

N: It is how you make it, it's the spoon full of sugar that helps the medicine go down. It's like that. It adds the sweetness.

C: What are the other ingredients? Can she tell you about them?

N: Well, the other ingredients to make up my spirit?

C: If that's what she wants to explain, do you want to know about them?

N: Definitely. The information is coming from all over. It is my connection; my plant connection is connected to the mycelium. The information that I obtain to help people comes from all over. But it's coming from the Earth. Its plant kingdom... Is communicating through the mycelium to me. Which is why they will volunteer to help people. That's why I identify as a plant.

C: So, you are connected to them through the mycelium?

N: Yes, that's my understanding.

C: Do you feel connected to them now?

N: Yes, definitely. I understand why it needs a plant and then connecting to the mycelium of the mushroom instead of absorbing the mushrooms. Literally you have to have a relationship with them.

C: So, if you communicate with that plant network now, what do they tell you?

N: It's unlimited, whatever you want as you want it. It will know when to help.

C: Is there anything else she wants to tell you?

N: She resides in that third eye space. She sees through that space.

C: So, you can communicate with her there?

N: Yes. Without being presumptuous to say she is me and I am her. What it comes down to is that kitchen cook has always been... it's always been me.

C: *Gives thanks and have her send love and appreciation. * She confirms and we begin going to a new place. What do you see?

N: The red room. 353 East **** St.

C: What can you tell me about this room?

N: It has some really thick walls. They are very thick walls, like two feet thick, three feet wide, wall blocks.

C: Is there anyone with you?

N: No.

C: What do you notice about the room?

N: It's sultry. It's another space of... it's a red space. It's like a powder room, resting room. Bedroom.

C: Do you recognize it?

N: Yeah.

C: What are you doing in this room?

N: Dying.

C: Explain to me what is going on around you.

N: That my energetic field is 2 ½ ft. off my body. And I am only connected by my energetic self, attached to my foot. But the rest of me is above my body.

C: Why are you only connected by your foot?

N: Trying to stay here. Trying to stay.

C: Since you're also noticing your energetic body, half in and half out, what do you notice?

N: What do you mean?

C: Is there anyone there with you in spirit?

N: Yeah, I think so. I believe that I can acknowledge that there are several bigger energetic beings with my energetic self, watching the situation.

C: *Suggestions for clarity and hearing them* Can you explain to me what kind of communication is going on?

N: *Long pause* They are empathetic. And surprised that I insist on staying. But they are very empathetic. But they are not surprised, but they are… they are supportive of my tenaciousness to stay.

C: Do you recognize them?

N: No. I don't.

C: Can you ask them who they are?

N: Struggling to pronounce name. *Urysalis* (spelling sound: your-is-al-is.) You are…sssseeeelis…

C: Can you ask Urysalis who he is to you?

N: She is, *Starts crying and whispering* My spirit sister. She is my loving spirit sister.

C: When you connect with her, what do you feel?

N: Love.

C: *Calms her down before continuing* What does she tell you?

N: That I am stubborn. I'm stubborn but I didn't ever have to torture myself. To win a bet. To win the stubborn contest. I didn't have to stay so long. I could have left but I'm stubborn.

C: What else does she tell you?

159

N: They knew I would do that. That's why they are so close to waiting. Because it was almost as if they would catch me when I blindly stumble out.

C: Did they understand the work you are doing now?

N: Definitely.

C: What does she say to help you?

N: Yeah. They just simply said you are the essence. We are the essence of the plants.

C: Can they explain to you what that means?

N: I know exactly what that means.

C: You do?

N: Yeah.

C: Can you ask them to explain light language?

N: Wow. Actually, I was seeing a lot of light. Information. A lot of squares and things, a lot of explanation of... I feel like I was at a conference for light language. And I'm not the only one there, there is a bunch of people there. At a conference learning it. That's cool. How to explain it or to understand it.

C: Is she showing you this, so you remember what you already knew?

N: Yeah, evidentially I'm at a conference for it.

C: Can we download it into this physical body at this time?

N: Yes, I believe so.

C: And they will allow you to do that now?

N: Sure.

C: Can you ask her to assist with this process?

N: Yep.

C: Is that language downloading now?

N: Yes. It's being compartmentalized. Almost done. Ha! They put it in volumes in your organs. The information that applies goes in the organ as if it's a volume just plugged in.

C: And you can access it whenever you need?

N: Yes, I feel that, yes.

C: Can they tell you about this information?

N: To be hydrated. Hyper-hydrated. It will come through with water. Hydrated.

C: Why does it come through in water?

N: Because it comes through in light. Holds that nucleus on the outside light. Like putting food on a plate.

C: Is there anything else they can tell you about this?

N: Yeah, it will come. I'll understand it. It will come. I'll just know it. I already do.

C: Is this part of the channeling?

N: Yes.

C: Can you ask her about the channeling?

N: Huh. Well, I will have to accept audio in order to fully not question myself.

C: Can she help you with that process?

N: Yes, it appears to be a mechanical issue. There is tech support. They will send in tech support, but it requires some rewiring? Some audio issues.

C: Will she be able to help with that?

N: It's a possibility. It has to do with my tuning in. It has to do with me, it's up to me.

C: What does she tell you about that?

N: That I have put blocks in my ear. That I have blocked off the sound on purpose to not hear it. Which I understand. It's some of the... you can see that some of the blocking off is missing. It's old and it's... things can crawl in if it wanted to. Enough can crawl in but it's definitely not open. So, it's up to me.

C: Do you want to remove those blocks?

N: I think not really, not right now. I can do that over time if I want to. But no, I don't think so. It's not, it's just... They are so crumbly; they can blow over any time they want. They don't need to.

C: Is there anything she wants to tell you about your work?

N: It has to do with crystal work involving my ear and in my brain. It has to do with my crystals are vibrating with light. Which is good. And that's part of why I'm able to do this. I'm receiving the information into my crystals already.

C: While you are there with those energetic beings... *Calls forth the Higher Self* Why did you show her the lifetime of the flower?

N: Because you went to the beginning.

C: She was taken to the beginning?

N: Yeah. You didn't specify. So, she went to the beginning.

C: Seems like a good place to start. What was she doing as a flower?

N: She was (the) essence of beauty. God finds flowers favorable.

C: Can you tell her more about that?

N: To bring favor. The flower brings favor. You bring favor to God.

C: And she was able to transform into a human at any point in that life?

N: Through favor. Through servitude of favor.

C: Did she accomplish what she wanted in that life?

N: She continues to accomplish favor.

C: Can you tell her about the grandmother figure she saw?

N: Grandmother Ayahuasca.

C: What was she creating?

N: She brings the plants to life.

C: And Nuella has that essence?

N: Aye, she does.

C: What can she do with it?

N: She can transmute. She can do anything she wants.

C: Can you tell her more about it?

N: She is as translucent as the pipe ghost. Mutable. Whatever you want.

C: Is she receiving that information through her light language?

N: Aye, she does.

C: Can you tell her more about the light language that she learned?

N: She will figure it out. *Laughs*

C: It is downloading, and she will know?

N: She will know.

C: Can you tell her about the first night at night school, the Akashic records, what did she see?

N: It's so rich but it's a movie not a word. It's so much information. It's a lifetime.

C: That was inside the book?

N: It's not like it's a bunch of words. You have to watch the movie. Let's put it this way, it's living. It's just like the beginning of the story and then it's busy. It's action.

C: Can you ask Urysalis to come forward and help with this book?

N: I will download more of those answers as I sleep. She took me by the hand and jumped in the book. Said I will know it in sleep. To wake up and I don't know it. I want to know it.

C: Can you ask her why you don't know it in waking state?

N: Too much sugar. I ruin it with my sugar in my coffee. Huh.

C: So, if you quit drinking sugar in your coffee, you will remember it?

N: Yeah. I ruin it with the sugar.

C: You ruin the coffee?

N: No, I ruin the receptiveness of the message. The sugar makes the reception, ruins the reception.

C: So, if you quit drinking the sugar in your coffee, you will remember?

N: Yes.

C: Where you go nightly, can she explain why you're there?

N: It's normal. Everybody goes to night school. It's very busy.

C: What do people learn there?

N: It's very informational, very fast, bullet train of information. A lot of people are there. It's very busy.

C: What are you learning?

N: I am learning science. I'm on the science train. There is a lot of people on the science train.

C: Do you recognize any of them?

N: No. there are so many, they might as well be the same. There are a lot of people downloading this information. It's general.

C: Do they wake up and remember or do they forget?

N: It depends on the people. It's not a special school. Everybody goes there. They don't even notice it. Everybody goes to school. Huh.

C: Can you ask her about the light codes and information you learn there?

N: Well interesting enough. She shows me it's like posted on a bulletin board. Anybody can get it. It's like you just go to the bulletin board and unplug the thing that holds it and take the note. It's where you get the information.

C: Can you ask her about your hands, is that how you receive and get information?

N: Huh. They are part of the mycelium network that are a part of where I go to get the information. They know the path to the answer.

C: And are you using it to its best ability?

N: I am now. *Breathy laugh* I can.

C: Can you ask her about that throat feeling, is it an issue of speaking or not speaking?

N: I'm supposed to speak. *sigh *

C: What does that mean?

N: I thought I was already doing it. So, I don't know. But I'm supposed to speak. I'm supposed to speak and not hold back.

C: So, no filter?

N: Well, I'm already no filter. But it means well, yeah, something like don't worry about how you're going to sound.

C: Can you ask her to assist you with this?

N: Yes.

C: What does she say?

N: She simply says yes. That means I'm going to have to accept that process of channeling at home, privately.

C: Ask her if you can do this process with your throat, without the channeling?

N: The information is for me. So that's what I have to do. It's not something that is going to come out for the people, the information is for me.

C: So, you don't have to share it?

N: Yeah, it's for me.

C: Can you ask her how to start that channeling process?

N: I'm supposed to at home, do it with intent, on purpose. Tap in. With intent.

C: And that's all you need to do?

N: Yeah, they have been trying to get me to do it for a while.

C: And is it ok to do it if it's just for you?

N: Yes, the information is for me. Not for anybody else. It's my information.

C: Can you ask Urysalis to explain image number three?

N: She showed me a sunset. A bright, orangey sunset. I don't remember that.

C: Can she explain it to you?

N: Huh, it goes along with that DNA thing. Has to do with blood. It has to do with that red, black vision. It's me.

C: Can she explain to you that slowed down image of DNA?

N: Yes, lots of zeros and 1, 3, 6, 9, 7. Whoa. I see that.

C: Do you understand the pattern? Can she tell you about that?

N: Yep. That's my astrological placement. My star map. That's my signature.

C: Ask her about the bloodline that you come from?

N: I am from Sumerian bloodline. I am related to Jesus. *Crying* I'm related to his mother. I'm related to his grandmother. And I'm related to Joseph as well. We are related. I knew him. I knew his human self.

C: Are you able to see that life?

N: Yes. I'm there.

C: What do you notice about that life?

N: It was short. The space in time is short. Even the rocks and the space doesn't feel well preserved. All of it, it was not permanent. None of it was. Not the village, not the people. All only temporary. That's why they can't find it! It's not here to be found. It was only temporary.

C: What were you doing?

N: I was part of it. We are a part of it. We always will be a part of it. But they can't find that space because it was porous. It has dissolved. But we are here. But that space, it cannot be pinpointed on a map because it's porous.

C: But you can feel it?

N: Yeah, absolutely, you're there.

*Close out Session.

This session illuminated her healing abilities and her connection to the plant kingdom. Helping her to become much more in tune with her innate wisdom and where that originated. It confirmed her purpose this lifetime and highlighted the energetic relationship of physical form and plants and what the body needs outside of the normal vitamins, etc.

Many of us are aware that plants are healing, but understanding the deeper "language" of plants is a level many of us haven't even realized. Being able to get this in-depth view of the conversation as she was having a near death experience helps us to understand the complexity of our souls' decisions. We all live on a surface level, day to day, existence; however, there is much more going on in the background of our experiences. Our souls play a much bigger part of our daily lives and choices.

# CHAPTER 9

## "Ashley"

This session is where I humbly ask you to keep an open mind. This is where my work really began to take deeper dives into topics I didn't really comprehend well at the time. It was particularly challenging to keep up as some of what was coming forward really went outside boundaries which I wasn't aware that I had. This client not only had been fighting new abilities that had surfaced, but I was also supposed to find the underlying cause of them and help her understand them. A task I thought was going to be pretty straightforward and easy. I was so very wrong.

Most healers never get an explanation as to where or how their abilities work. They just DO. They feel into it or use other senses to begin learning how to utilize them further. It's always an energetic thing that most say they can't explain.

This client begins to get an explanation about her abilities and how she can use them. She had recently been told she needed to "shield" herself. An energetic practice of protecting yourself from outside sources or interference. She had been practicing this but because there is no handbook on these things, she was winging it. Her Higher Self quickly set her straight on how to do different things like healing and shielding properly, for her specific needs. Her Higher Self's personality is quite dry in its humor and very straightforward, however it is extremely helpful in helping her understand her purpose and ability more fully.

Ashely is, and always has, felt different. She is aware that she has been targeted energetically all of her life. She didn't know how to explain it or verify it, but she just knew there was a reason. Through her sessions, she is beginning to find out why she's had such unusual experiences throughout her life that previously went unexplained. Her series of sessions are helping her to make sense of these and learn that because of her advanced Soul, her Higher Self has many topics and expectations being explored.

Now that I have gotten to know her over time and doing these sessions together, she has an AMAZING ability to heal people and animals. I have seen it firsthand and experienced it personally. Neither one of us knew that our sessions together would come to this, but it has been the most amazing unfolding!

*Begin session

We spend some time going through the dark. Constantly going up and up for about 15 minutes trying to figure out where she is. Later after the session finished, Ashley realized this darkness she was exploring was the "void" that they mentioned that she was utilizing for her healing. More will be explained later in the session about this place.

To move the session along, I ask a guide of hers to come in and push the cloud to a place that she needs to explore. A place that will give her some understanding to the questions she has. Finally, we begin exploring somewhere we can move the session along:

C: Can you ask them where you are going? *Silence* Is it okay to ask him questions?

A: Yes.

C: Can you ask him where you are going?

A: He said Hall of Records?

C: *Instructions to follow him there* Ask the guide why he is taking you there? Is it about your purpose?

A: Yes.

C: Can he tell you about that?

A: No.

C: Can he show you where to look in the hall of records?

A: Maybe.

C: What do you see?

A: A floor. Black and white.

C: What else?

A: A long hallway and doors.

C: What are the doors for?

A: I don't know.

C: Can you ask him?

A: He said not to go through the doors.

C: Where are you supposed to go?

A: To the end of the hall.

C: Explain to me what you see when you get to the end of the hall.

A: An arch. It's big.

C: Is this the Hall of Records?

A: I think the whole place is.

C: What's inside this room?

A: Long tables. Books. On tables.

C: Are the books for you?

A: I don't think so.

C: Can you ask him what you can do in here?

A: He is taking me to a center table. There's a book on the table.

C: What is the book?

A: It's... I can't read it.

C: Can you ask him to explain it to you?

A: *SIGH* He says I'm supposed to be able to read it, but I can't.

C: Why can't you read it?

A: I don't know, but I can't understand it.

C: Is it in a different language?

A: Kind of. It's like pictures.

C: Can he explain to you how you're supposed to know how to read these books?

A: He is frustrated. He knows I should.

C: Can you ask him what you can do to read it?

A: He said I have to remember how, but I don't know how.

C: Can you remember how in this place, or do we need to go somewhere else to remember?

A: I don't know.

C: Can you ask him?

A: He can't help me remember; I have to.

C: Can he call someone higher who understands how to help you?

A: I asked. He is frustrated, I don't know how, but he would try to find someone.

C: *Passes time until he got back because he wasn't showing back up right away, and I didn't want to spend too much of her session time waiting. In the meantime, I asked her questions about the book. *

C: What do the pictures look like?

A: Circles, triangles, squares, dots.

C: And what are they for?

A: I don't know.

C: Has he come back yet?

A: No.

C: What are you doing?

A: Looking around at the books... the other books are blank. I'm not supposed to read them.

C: So, this one is meant for you?

A: But I can't read it. I don't understand.

C: That's okay. There is a reason you're seeing this book. Has he come back yet?

A: No.

C: *Fast forward until he came back* Has he come back?

A: Yes.

C: Did he bring someone to help?

A: Yes

C: Who is it?

A: I don't know this person.

C: Can you ask them who it is?

A: It's frustrating...

C: What's frustrating?

A: It's like they are speaking the language that the book is in... I don't know what they are saying.

C: That's ok. Here, languages can be translated so that you understand what they are saying. Can you understand them now? What do they say?

A: *Pause* They are calling it Light Language... Hmmm... I don't know what that is.

C: Is that the language they speak?

A: Yes.

C: Is that the language of the book?

A: Yes, is what they said.

C: Can they help you translate it... so that you can understand it?

A: They said it can't be translated into our words. You just have to know how to read it. It's too many words. Our words can't fully explain what it means.

C: Well can you ask them how you're supposed to understand it? Or how you can read it?

A: I have to remember how.

C: Well can you ask them how to do that?

A: *Long pause* That I have to remember *SIGH* Now they are frustrated with me for not being able to recall at all.

C: That's ok. I want you to focus on the book and in want you to focus on the pictures. I want you to put them in your memory. I want you to store them so that you can access them as you learn and remember this Light Language. And while you're doing that can we ask them some questions?

A: Yes.

C: Can you ask him why you need to know this light language?

A: It's the original language.

C: What does that mean?

A: It's the first.

C: The first language of humanity?

A: OF ALL.

C: How are you supposed to use that language?

A: They don't understand your question.

C: There's a reason you're seeing it now… why are you supposed to remember it?

A: It has what I'm supposed to do. My purpose.

C: What is your purpose?

A: I don't know, I can't read it.

C: Can you ask them what your purpose is?

A: It's not for them to tell me.

C: Are you still memorizing it?

A: Yes.

C: And you have all the signs and symbols remembered?

A: *No answer*

C: If I ask you to draw some when you come back can you?

A: Possibly. There's a lot.

C: Can you ask them where you can go to remember?

A: They said go to the beginning. I don't understand.

C: Can you ask them to explain that to you?

A: To when I first used that language.

C: Would they be able to help take you there? The place where you first used this light language?

A: *Long pause* They are arguing. One said yeah... the other said I'm not ready.

C: Why did they say you're not ready?

A: I don't understand their arguing.

C: Can you ask for them to speak to you about it instead so that you understand what's going on?

A: My first guide left. He disagrees.

C: Why does he disagree?

A: He doesn't think I'm ready.

C: Why does he say that?

A: I don't know.

C: Can you ask the other guy why he says that?

A: It's a lot different. It's a lot to take in.

C: Did he not think you could handle it?

A: I assume.

C: Can you ask him if he thinks you're ready?

A: He says it doesn't matter if I'm ready. If I want to read it, it's necessary.

C: So, how do you do that?

A: I'm asking him to take me. He said it would be better if I just remember without having to do that.

C: Is there a way you can ask him to do that? Surely, he must have some idea.

A: He is trying to explain it to me in his language.

C: Can you understand it?

A: I'm trying. It's... not really *Sigh*

C: Can you ask if there is someone higher who can come help?

A: I think it's me. I'm the problem.

C: Why?

A: I think I'm scared to remember. That's why he is frustrated.

C: Why are you scared to remember?

A: I don't want to. He says I know how. I'm choosing not to.

C: Can you ask him if it's ok if we come back to see him once you're ready?

A: He said yes. He will be there.


*At this point I think we have hit a stalemate and aren't going to get any further asking questions and trying to figure it out, so I decide to go ahead and call forth her Higher Self. I ask her to tell him thank you for his time and appreciate him helping her out before we leave.


C: *Once we bring forth the Higher Self* Do I have permission to ask questions?

A: Yes.

C: I know you could have taken Ashley anywhere and you took her to the hall of records, why did you choose to show her that today?

A: She is in her own way. She needs to see that.

C: Can you explain that to her?

A: She is stopping herself from learning.

C: Why is that?

A: Fear.

C: What does she have a fear of?

A: Unknown.

C: Well, the unknown is a scary thing right, for humans. Can you help her with that?

A: I'm trying. She's taking longer than expected.

C: Taking longer for what?

A: For her to accept. Her purpose.

C: What is her purpose?

A: To heal.

C: What is she supposed to be healing? Can you explain it to her?

A: I do not know if she is ready to listen.

C: She has been very curious about what she is supposed to be doing.

A: Mmm… she is curious, but she is scared. The fear stops her from hearing.

C: Well, if you think she hears it this way that she will understand?

A: Possibly.

C: Well can you try? She really does want to understand.

A: Consciously she believes if she doesn't understand, then she doesn't have to do it.

C: Can you explain it to her now so consciously she understands it?

A: She doesn't want to hear that way she doesn't have to do it. To not be responsible.

C: Is she ready to let that go?

A: I would hope so.

C: Can you explain it to her then so she can try? The more she understands the more she might be ready. (No answer) She has made a lot of progress.

A: Some. She needs more.

C: Well, how can she do that?

A: She has to believe in herself. She doesn't, and that's stuck in her progress.

C: Can you help her with that now?

A: I'm trying. She is very stubborn. *Laughs*

C: So how would you explain it to her so that she understands what she is supposed to be doing?

A: Trying to find the words to explain. It's hard to explain.

C: Why is that?

A: It's like the saying trying to explain breathing to someone who doesn't breathe. You just do it. It's hard to put words into how you do it.

C: Can you try?

A: * long pause * I'm trying to show her examples where she has done this in the past and not realized it so she can learn what she did then.

C: Can you explain to me what you're showing her?

A: It is hard to explain. She… can feel…*stumbling over words* trying to find the words. It's like she can feel the broken energy in something. Where it's not right. She can feel it. Whether or not she recognizes that is another story.

C: Well, how can she recognize it so that she knows?

A: Sometimes she can fix it. Without even trying. Like unconsciously. Especially if she has a connection with that being. Person. Animal. She can feel where it's not right and fix it.

C: And how is she doing that?

A: *Laughs* She's not even realizing she is doing it.

C: Well, what does that look like for her when she is doing it?

A: Mmm…. when there's an emotional connection. When she is repairing there is a tugging that happens. She feels it in her throat and her chest and her shoulders. There's a pulling of the broken energy out. And it helps move this being to where the energy isn't broken. So, she is not necessarily fixing the broken energy. She's recognizing where it's broken and takes them to where it isn't broken anymore. It's hard to explain.

C: Is this the timeline jumping she has mentioned?

A: That's what some people call it. It's… every choice. Every decision. Every thought CREATES a different timeline. Deciding to go right versus left. Up versus down. Go here or there, they all make different choices, they all create different branches. So, this is just moving to a branch where this doesn't exist.

C: So that's basically going to the highest place that it can be fixed and then back to where we are now?

A: So to speak. That's one way of explaining it. She doesn't know when she is doing it.

C: Is that the pain she gets in her back or her shoulders when she is doing that?

A: It's hard on her when she does it. It takes a toll.

C: Why is that?

A: Because she doesn't realize she is doing it. It's a greater expenditure of energy. Because it's not controlled.  It's random.

C: Is there a way to fix that?

A: Over time.

C: Is there a way to "fill her energy back up" so that's she is not depleted?

A: When she does it now, it's unconscious so it's a straight giving of energy. She doesn't recognize she is doing it so there is nothing to gain in return. It's a giving of oneself.

C: So how does she gain in return?

A: The first step would be to consciously choose to do this. And to understand how to do it. Right now, she does it when she feels an emotional connection to the other.

C: So, what exactly is she healing in someone else, or something else?

A: She is not healing anything in them. She is removing it.

C: Can you explain?

A: It's the ability to see what is not right at that particular moment with that person. Then to move them to a place through the void and coming out to where that problem doesn't exist.

C: Is there a way for her to do this consciously?

A: Yes. But she has to be willing to be accepting of what she is doing. Right now, she is not. She is too scared. She doesn't understand or want to believe or doesn't think she is capable. So, she disregards any notion that she is able to do this. But she has done it.

C: Well can you give her some instructions, so it doesn't seem so hard or scary for her to do?

A: I've tried to show her. She doesn't believe it even when she sees it.

C: Well, how are you showing her?

A: *SIGH* That's why her daughter's not more hurt.

C: Did she fix that for her? *(Speaking of a bad accident she'd recently had. Her four-year-old at the time, was kicked across her barn by another horse being kept there. She was just playing and running after the barn cat that lived there. She didn't realize she had snuck up behind one of the horses until it was too late. She was kicked directly in the face with a kick from a full-sized horse. Her daughter was completely disfigured. Once they reached the hospital, they discovered she was also kicked directly in the hip too as they began cutting off her clothes to administer aid. There was an understanding due to the obvious visible outward damage, there was likely brain damage as well as broken bones, if not worse. She went through every test and scan, and by the time the doctor came back in, she not only looked completely normal, but she had no brain damage and no broken bones. The doctor was completely confused and told her she has a guardian angel looking over her and released her. All of this, despite the visible damage when she arrived. They had no explanation for it.) *

A: YES! She did it. That's why it was so hard on her emotionally. That's why she (daughter) wasn't more broken. She moved her to a place where even though it happened... she wasn't more hurt.

C: Does her daughter know that?

A: Not consciously.

C: So, if she wants to do this, she has to recognize that and choose it?

A: Yes, because right now it happens randomly.

C: And she is supposed to do it on purpose.

A: I mean that's her job. Right now, she is ignoring it.

C: Well, how do we get her to a place she isn't ignoring it?

A: I don't know. I've been trying.

C: Well maybe we can find a new way to get to her. Can you explain some of it to her, so it won't be so daunting?

A: She sees examples of it. She just doesn't believe. Like her daughter was an example. You know, it wasn't a guardian angel that healed her daughter like the doctor said. It was Ashley. She protected her and moved her. But she doesn't believe that's possible.

C: Well, she will believe it now that she hears it, don't you think?

A: Maybe.

C: I think she will. So is there a way you can explain her purpose. Why did she choose healing? Has she done this many times before?

A: Yes. Yes. This was her job before. She just forgot.

C: That seems to be a lot of us, right? (Laughs)

A: Everyone needs to wake up now. It's time. People are very slow.

C: Yes, we are. That's why we ask for guidance. Can she trust Nick? (A recently new friend who calls himself a healer, she did not know whether she could trust him or not.)

A: I believe so. She doesn't need him, but she can trust him. She needs to trust in herself more than others.

C: Can you help her with that?

A: I'm trying. Trying. It's why I wouldn't let him work on her because she can do it herself. I tried to show her that she still didn't believe it. She's very stubborn. (Both of us laugh)

C: Can you show her how to do that now?

A: *Long pause and breathing noises like she is experiencing something. *

C: Can you explain to me what you're showing her?

A: It's hard to explain. It's more feeling. She can unconsciously feel the disruption in energy that happens. She's unconsciously aware of it. It's just a matter of going in, untangling the self from this disruption, moving the self through the void and out the other side where the disruption doesn't exist.

C: Can you explain what this void is?

A: It's the in-between.

C: What is that?

A: It's the place between timelines. The in-between.

C: And it's a safe place?

A: For me.

C: But not for anyone else?

A: Not many come.

C: Is this where she does her work?

A: Sometimes.

C: Can you help her understand how to get there, so that she can do it... consciously?

A: She goes there all the time. Just unconsciously. Call it astral travel, call it... whatever. It's the dark, it's the void, it's the place between life and death.

C: Yeah, but she needs to understand it consciously.

A: *Big sigh*

(At this point, I know my questions seem redundant, but my job is to get answers to the questions my clients come in and ask me for. She has been told by a few different people at random that she is a "healer", and she has had no idea what that means or how to go about it. Or even if she wants to focus on it because besides that, she has never had any direction for it. So, I'm doing my best to get any and all answers that I can to help it make sense so that she can begin to use it if she chooses going forward.)

C: So, what can she focus on to allow that healing to begin to happen when she is trying to make it work?

A: Her first step is to have faith. She doesn't.

C: Yeah, but humans need something to focus on too. Something to physically understand how to begin the process.

A: But it's not a physical process. It's a subconscious process. It's an astral process. It's an energy process. There is no physical to it.

C: Is there something she could think to allow that process to begin to happen. So that she understands it's happening?

A: I'm not sure.

C: I think Ashley is having a hard time because she doesn't understand how to process what she does. She doesn't understand how to do any of this. Not from a physical standpoint. In her mind, she doesn't understand it. Is there any way to explain that to her so she knows what to do to help other people?

A: I can try to show her. Explain to her examples. There really are no words to really describe it. So, putting a tangible, physical aspect to it is very difficult.

C: Well, if she is trying to explain it to someone who comes to her for help, how would she explain it to them?

A: Right now, she couldn't.

C: I know but you could help her with that right? That's what she is struggling with. Because she doesn't even know how to explain it or what it is.

A: Right now, it's an issue from a place of emotion, of love, fear of loss. It will be hard for her to initiate that for someone she doesn't know, that's a stranger. Until she recognizes how she does it, and ACCEPTS that's how she does it, and let the ability go, it will be difficult, for now.

C: How can she begin to do that then?

A: Well, first she needs to love herself and recognize she has this ability.

C: Do you think she will recognize it now, now that you've spoken to her this way?

A: Maybe. I've tried to show her.

C: So, what's going on at night with her? Is that part of it?

A: She travels. She's training. She's practicing. She just doesn't realize it.

C: She's training with this healing?

A: In some ways, yes.

C: So, can you explain it to her, if she was looking at me, what would she do? How would she utilize it?

A: She would have to be able to feel the disruption. It's placed in your chest. The frequency is not right. It's off. Dampened.

C: Why is that?

A: An etheric device. Implanted. Very small.

*She gave permission beforehand if it was needed to try to get to the bottom of her healing ability. *

C: And it hasn't been removed? Even though people have tried. *(I've been to multiple types of healers to fix my heart issue, as well as having gone through two heart surgeries that were unsuccessful in fixing it completely. They helped, but didn't fix the problem. I have arrhythmia and low heart rate, skipping beats often and extreme fatigue and shortness of breath from these issues. I function normally, but it's a daily drain. After being healthy my entire life, it came out of nowhere and hit me hard.)

A: It replicates. You can remove it.

C: How?

A: It's like… what do you call… a computer virus? Where it self-replicates when you try to attack it. When you try to remove it.

C: How do you remove it?

A: It's very, very difficult. Not impossible. You would need to be moved, taken from where you are, and just take the parts of you that are not affected. Pulled through the void and through a new line where this new device was never implanted before. That would be the only way to do it easily and that's not easy.

C: Is that why the heart doesn't work right?

A: Yeah, the energy is compromised.

C: Is Ashley able to fix it? Does she have the knowledge?

A: The ability, yes. The conscious knowledge, no… not yet.

C: Are you able to do it?

A: ME? Yes. I could.

C: Do you think you could do that for me?

A: Do I have your permission?

C: Will I be ok if you, do it? Is it safe?

A: Yes, I could do it. Yes, it would be safe. It may alter… hmm…. Right now, it's serving a purpose in that it's teaching you things. You are learning because of it. It could alter the course that you're on, of learning. Neither good nor bad. Just will alter it.

C: Then I think I'll keep it for a little while.

*(I do not believe in playing God, Source, or whatever you want to call it. Until I could ask more questions to get a better understanding of whether it was important to my life, I didn't want to alter that course because I don't know what ripple effect it

would have later, if any, and I didn't want anything worse if it did.

Also, this session is with a friend. I would never normally ask these kinds of questions during a session with a normal client, but we were testing boundaries and how strong this work can actually be. We agreed to this before the session started, but since I did not ask about my heart stuff before we began her session, I did not want to waste any extra time asking questions for myself. I brought it up because I was thinking maybe she could use me as an example so when she was awake, she had a complete rundown of the process and how to do it rather than just what was being given. I declined for that reason. I have more questions to be answered about how this happened before I agree to treatment in this way.)

C: Is it safe to keep it too?

A: That is your choice.

C: Will it harm me if I don't get rid of it?

A: It is an energy transfer. It is taking energy from you. Physically, you will struggle.

C: What will change if I do get rid of it? What kind of learning?

A: I cannot say.

C: Is it a good learning?

A: Right now, you are using it as a tool to focus your learning. Because this has happened you are learning things about yourself. About others. It is affecting you negatively. It's your choice.

C: I will wait. But thank you for checking for me.

A: Of course.

C: I would like to focus back on Ashley. Is there anything in her body that needs adjusted? Or needs attention at this time?

A: Her energy levels are affected by the unconscious work that she does. She doesn't release the work. Unless it's been completed, she carries it with her. She needs to work on protecting her own energy and not giving as she is doing the work. She doesn't understand how to do that quite yet.

C: Well, how can she do that? How can she release it when she is done?

A: I can show her.

C: Can you explain it to me while you're showing her?

A: She carries the emotional attachment of what the individual is experiencing and going through. She carries it with her physically. Those emotions stay trapped. They are not hers. So, until she learns how to let go of those emotions stored in her body, they will create havoc.

C: So, if she were to sit after she was done and think of a way to release them, is there a physical way she can imagine that release?

A: Not taking them on in the first place would be best. But if she does, she can clear them. She just needs to recognize that they are not hers.

C: And that's it? She just has to recognize they aren't hers and they will go away?

A: And release them, yes.

C: Well, how can she release them? Does she just visually imagine them going away?

A: She can.

C: Will that be good enough?

A: It should work.

C: Will a shield help her?

A: It is helping yes because it's protecting her from taking on unnecessary burden at the moment.

C: And she can still do the healing with the shield up?

A: It's harder for her unconsciously to do it because she is not as open. But it keeps her from unnecessarily taking on emotional entanglement.

C: Is there a way she can do both?

A: Yes, she just needs to be consciously aware.

C: How does she do that? Does she imagine the shield in a different way?

A: She could lower it temporarily to work on someone. And then recognize anything she takes on needs to be released. She is either completely open or completely closed right now. There is no in-between.

C: Is there supposed to be an in-between?

A: Yes, you should be able to protect yourself... you know, but then also be able to also remove it when necessary to help others.

C: Is there a better way to do it?

A: I'm trying to show her....

C: Can you explain what you're showing to her?

A: I'm showing how her shield needs to be. And how the energy that is coming from... I'm trying to find the words. From the chest area. The heart area. The emotional center area. How when we need to connect with somebody else, you need to have an opening in the shield to make that connection. To be able to connect with the other person's energy to see where it's been compromised. Then to remove the parts that are uncompromised to take the person through so that they can be whole again without their compromised energy. And then once that transfer has been completed... to remove any potential entanglements and then replace the shield. There's a process to it.

C: Is it similar to the one she already uses?

A: Yes, but more thorough.

C: This is a very unusual way of healing. I can't say I've heard of it before. Is this a normal way that people can heal?

A: It's specialized. It's similar to what you would call like...*Sigh* A, um... a doctor with a certain specialty. Like a heart surgeon or you know... it's just a specialty.

C: And what would her specialty be called then if you were to try to put a name to it?

187

A: We don't have words for it. Um. I don't know what she would call it honestly. It's a transferring of the uncompromised energy to a place where it's never been compromised.

C: That's really helpful. So, is that what that book has to do with? Light Language?

A: SHE KNOWS how to read that.

C: Then why couldn't she read it?

A: Fear. Acceptance of responsibility.

C: Can you help her get past that fear?

A: I have been trying.

C: Can you try now? See if she can get past that now?

A: I don't know. She is very stubborn.

C: I think she is at a better place of understanding now though.

A: Things have not always been easy. She has a fear of things we have experienced in the past. So, it's easier to ignore the responsibility than to exist and potentially go through that pain again.

C: Will she have to keep doing this if she doesn't do it?

A: There's a chance. We are running short on time to fix things. We need to fix things now. Not have to go through this again. And again. And again.

C: What things do you mean?

A: Humanity is at a crossroads. People are here for a purpose. Certain beings, certain souls are here for a purpose. So that we don't have to go through what we went through in other worlds, in other lives.

C: And what does that crossroads look like for us?

A: If we don't do the things that we were sent here to do originally, long ago, we will suffer the same fate as long ago on other worlds. We are trying to avoid that.

C: And Ashley is helping with this?

A: That's her job. That's why she is here.

188

C: And does the hypnotherapy work in that sense?

A: In a sense. It helps those that need to be awakened to realize what they are here to do.

C: Is there a better way that I can serve them in that way?

A: You have a purpose too.

C: Is this not it?

A: It's part of it.

C: Are you able to see the other part of it?

A: Not fully. It's not my specialty. But you are more than this.

C: Will I find out? Or am I just supposed to focus on this?

A: This is helpful for now. For others. But there is more that you could be doing.

C: What else could I be doing?

A: I see a blue light in you. Something to do with the blue light. I am not sure. It is not my specialty.

C: And is Ashley a Violet Ray? (One of her questions before we got started. This was what her friend Nick mentioned above said he saw her as this.)

A: I do not like those terms.

C: What term would you use?

A: Humanity has come up with those terms to describe those of us that came in waves to do what needed to be done. It's like naming a mission in the military. Doesn't mean that's necessarily what that person is.

C: Is there a better way to explain it or to acknowledge it?

A: Not in words that I can use.

C: Does she work with violet energy or purple energy? Is that why it would be named that? Is that a healing energy?

A: Violet energy has been inverted. It's been taken and misused. Many are working to try to correct that now. As it's being corrected, she can sense the corrupted energy, inverted energy if you want to call it that in a person. That's what she repairs. That's what she takes out of the person. That uncorrupted energy to move to a place where it's not… so in a sense she is working with it… but not… *pauses* Once the violet energy is back online, corrected the way it should be, things will be better. Right now, it's still inverted. But in the process of being repaired.

C: Will it be a while, while it's being repaired? Or will it be soon?

A: It will be up really soon.

C: And she will notice a difference?

A: Her job will be much easier.

C: And she will know more about it?

A: Hopefully. Because it will make everything she does easier. She won't have to work with the inverted energy.

C: How many DNA strands does Ashley have to work with this energy?

A: For herself of for others?

C: In general.

A: Depends on the person. It depends on the soul. Where the soul originated from. Some have twelve. Some have higher. Some are lower. You know, her soul has fourteen. Now she is not using all of that. But originally her soul has fourteen.

C: Can she get back to using all of them?

A: Not in this density.

C: Is there anything you can do to assist her body to work better in her environment? Is there anything that needs repaired?

A: Lowering the corrupted energy, she is taking on from others, will help. Raising her vibration and doing so will help.

C: Can you remove what's there?

A: *Goes quiet*

C: Are you removing it?

A: Yes.

C: What was it affecting in her? Was it causing any of her physical symptoms?

A: Oh yes! Becomes embedded. Sticks. Sticky. Up in the muscles and the joints. Just creates problems.

C: Is that that disease they say she has? The one of the joints and the tissues? (Sticklers)

A: It's more what they call the symptoms of her ability. When it's not managed correctly it stays in the body and can manifest those symptoms.

C: Can you help relieve her of those symptoms for now?

A: To some extent.

C: Is there anywhere else in her body that you see not working properly?

A: The spine has some issues. It's been compressed. Just a physical toll from being in this density. She is not used to it. It's caused curvatures and problems.

C: Can you fix it for her? It would make her work a lot easier if she didn't have the strain.

A: Some of the damage is permanent. I'm trying to strengthen and lengthen. There is only so much I can fix.

C: So, you said you're lengthening and strengthening what, the vertebrae or just the spine itself?

A: The tissue around the vertebrae. To hold it in place better. It was weak before it had taken on too much emotion, so everything became compressed.

C: So, it will straighten as you're doing work on it?

A: Trying. Trying to. It won't be perfect.

C: Will she be able to see it on an X-ray, the difference?

A: Maybe. It depends. This will need maintenance if she takes on more emotion. It will pull it back down.

C: Well, how can she prevent it from doing that?

A: She needs to get better at her job.

C: And the dreams she is having, does that have anything to do with it?

A: She ASKS for help and information. And then I try to show her in her dreams. It's when she is most receptive.

C: Can you explain it to her now what that means?

A: What do you mean?

C: Well, there are a lot of different things that happen in her dreams that don't always make sense.

A: Sometimes she is being shown other worlds. Past lives. Other responsibilities and jobs that she has had. I've tried to show her the crosses that she uses for healing and where she goes and how she does it, but she discounts a lot of that as just a dream.

C: So, the dream she had of her family, she has traveled with them many times?

A: Not many. But a few.

C: So, she enjoys traveling with them?

A: She would RATHER not. It's been out of necessity.

C: And what is that necessity?

A: Well, if they choose to be together then they have to.

C: Is there anything else that you want to tell her?

A: Her biggest issue is faith in herself. In her abilities. In what she is here to do. The quicker that she can accept that, the easier this will be.

*I close out the session by giving my thanks and gratitude for them taking the time to answer our questions and assisting her in her work. *

A: Hopefully she listens because she is very stubborn.

C: Can she come speak to you again if she has more questions?

A: Of course. She speaks to me all the time already. She just doesn't listen when I answer.

C: How will she know when you are assisting her?

A: I can try a physical sign if that's helpful. She can feel the heart energy. I can make sure to increase that feeling.

*Close out Session.

After her session she calls me a couple days later to tell me she had gone to her appointment at her chiropractor. She has needed adjustments for a long time. She had to go monthly and sometimes more often for many years to keep her functioning. The Chiropractor told her there was nothing wrong with her back during this visit and she didn't need adjusting at all. Not even a little and there was nothing else he needed to do for her. She said that was the first time in years she's had that happen. She also went on to let me know that she was feeling better than she had in a long time and has gone on to consciously do the healing work when the opportunity arises.

# Chapter 10
## "Ashley"

This is the follow up session to the one above. She had been to the Hall of Records before but was never able to read a book that was pulled out just for her. There are "Record Keepers or Bookkeepers" there to watch over an individual's book. And every book has its own keeper. So last minute I decided to take her there and see if she could read it this time. During the session that was never what was planned but I sometimes get a hint as to where to turn the session, so I followed it. This is what we found:

*Session begins

C: Once you get there, I want you to begin describing to me what you see.

A: The same person is here with me.

C: Is it your Guide?

A: He is more like a librarian. (She is smiling.)

C: And what does he have to say?

A: *Sighs * He is kind of impatient.

C: Why would that be?

A: He just has a stuffy, funny little personality.

C: Does he greet you?

A: Sort of. He kind of doesn't waste time on greetings.

C: Well, what does he have to say?

A: He doesn't speak with his mouth. It's like a... He is using gestures with his hands, but he speaks telepathically. He wants me to try to read my book again.

C: Is it okay that we have come back here?

A: Yeah. I mean yes, that's fine.

C: Is he happy to see you back here to attempt to read this book?

A: Yeah, he gets frustrated because I want to look all around the room and look at all the things and he says I'm wasting time.

C: Well as you open your book, what do you see?

A: The book is very big. It doesn't seem that big on the table but when you get closer to it, it's very big. The cover is very heavy. Very detailed.

C: It sounds very beautiful.

A: I keep looking at the cover and he is very exasperated with me.

C: What do you notice when you look inside the book?

A: *Sigh * I can... see the symbols in the book. Same as before.

C: As you focus upon the symbols... what do you notice?

A: *Laughs * Each symbol... isn't necessarily a word. Or a letter. It's like each symbol. It's like a program. So, when I look at each symbol and touch it. It lights up and gives you the information that's stored within that program.

C: And are there any particular ones you're supposed to be touching... or downloading?

A: Yeah! Download... it's like that.

C: Are there ones just for you or are they all just for you?

A: I'm asking him about the book. About who made the book? He says... um, I don't understand. *Confused * He says I made the book.

C: What does he mean by that?

A: He said I made the book. For me. To be able to access before? *Pause * He said the book is what I left for myself so that I could remember the information that I would forget when I came to earth.

C: Are you ready for this information now?

A: It's a lot of information. It's hard to put words into it. *Sigh * Sorry, it's happening really fast. Each symbol when you touch it

195

and access the information. You can see glimpses of what your remembering, learning. I don't know the word for it. More so you get a feeling. There's like a feeling, an emotion. Like a knowing of the information that goes with it.

C: Is this the first time as a human that you have used the information?

A: I didn't have access before. That's why he was so frustrated. I was supposed to have access earlier.

C: Is this going how he hoped it would go, now?

A: He's kind of hard to please.

C: Is it time for you to access all of the symbols or just some of them?

A: No! No. He won't let me. He says it's too much.

C: Well can you ask him to show you the symbols you are supposed to learn at this time? *No answer * We only want to do what you can handle at this time.

A: He says there are three that I can access now and that he will um, he said I can access the rest of it. Okay. So, he says during sleep? Astral travel? I don't know, he says that there are other ways that he can send the information. Allow me to access it.

C: How will you know when you're accessing it?

A: *Sigh * He said I will remember being there.

C: So, it doesn't have to be through this method? (Hypnosis).

A: No. It's just before when I would try to open the book and read it. I couldn't get the information. I couldn't read it through. But he said now that it can come through, he can send or allow me to access it. He can't send it to me, I have to be there to get it.

C: What are the three symbols you can access now? Can you explain them?

A: The first one looks like a... similar to a Y except the left side is shorter on the Y and there are two dots at the top and a slash through the bottom.

C: And what does it mean?

A: It's... that one, it's hard to put to words. *Sigh *

C: That's ok, can you summarize it?

A: It's giving me... almost like the feeling of the life I had before I was here. Before... almost like a... the only physical thing I can see is a... like a star chart. Maybe that's where I was? Yes! He is jumping up and down. Ok. That's where I was.

C: And you'll be able to recognize this when you come out of this state?

A: He says I should be able to.

C: And how will that help you now?

A: He is saying when we come here to this density, we forget. It's like amnesia. You forget who you are, your purpose, what you're supposed to be doing. You start over. And so much time is wasted forgetting. I was supposed to remember a lot sooner and I didn't. He is pretty irritated about that.

C: Well, what can you do now?

A: He has been tasked with keeping this book safe for me until I was able to access it. Ah, that's why he is mad. He has been doing this a really long time. *Laughs *

C: Well, how would you have been able to find the book if we hadn't have done it through this method?

A: He saying I was supposed to have been able to access it, or thought I would have been able to access it. Easier? Sooner? Okay, so... he is saying that I should have been able to travel there. Like when I guess when my physical body is asleep, I have the ability to travel there. But I just get too distracted with other things. And caught up in other things and forget that I'm even supposed to be there.

C: Well, if we are forgetting as humans, how are we supposed to know that we are supposed to go there?

A: I don't think either of us realized I would forget as much as I did. For as long as I did. (She is only in her early 40's now.)

C: So, it will be easier for you to access this place at any point after this?

A: He says it should be now.

C: And if it's not, then what? What can we do?

A: He… Okay. He says I can come back in this manner, but it would be easier if I could come back during sleep. To access larger amounts of information while my body is resting.

C: Is there a way, he could give us, to trigger this when it is time for you to know? There has to be some easier way to know when it's time.

A: He said the hard part is the heavy amnesia. That was the hardest task to overcome. Remembering how to access the information even once you got there.

C: Is there a way that he can tell us when it is time for you to come back?

A: He says I need to come back. Okay, so… the three symbols that he is having me access, the last one is a way to access the book.

C: And are you looking at that now?

A: Yes. Okay. So, it's like a way to remote view it. Easier. So that I can access the information and receive it. Passively.

C: What does that symbol look like?

A: Okay… it looks like a spiral. There is a dot in the center. And there's two dots on the outer band of the spiral. With a line. It's like a sushi line under the bottom of it. He said that will give me a link to the book so that I can access it.

C: And so, is that downloaded completely now?

A: Yes.

C: And what was the second symbol?

A: It was okay… it's like a triangle. With an angled line at the top and a dot on the bottom corners of the triangle. Yeah.

C: And what does that one mean?

A: He wanted me to remember why I chose to come. That's why he said I had to access that one.

C: And why did you choose to come?

A: *Sigh * I was very sad, frustrated, disgusted... all of those things. With how humanity had fallen. There were others that were okay with just letting it collapse on itself. But there was so much good that I couldn't stand to see it all get destroyed.

C: And so, what did you plan for when you came here? What was the hope?

A: To go back and undo the damage we did.

C: Do you feel like you've accomplished that more now?

A: *Laughs * No. No. there is still so much.

C: So, what is your plan now that you planned to come here and help?

A: There are a lot of us that planned to come and help. I think they all got lost too, like me.

C: Is there anything else he wants to tell you?

A: He said we all need to wake up faster.

C: Does he mean humanity, or certain people in general?

A: Those of us that came to do our job.

C: Was I one of those people?

A: He said yes. He said you should have a book too, but he is not responsible for it. You will have to find it. (I am completely surprised because I have never heard of that, nor have I ever been told about one.)

C: Well, how am I supposed to find the book?

A: He said that's not his problem. *Laughs * Sorry.

C: *Laughs too * I appreciate it anyways. Every little bit helps.

A: He's... He's a little bit snippy. He said he has spent enough time watching mine that you need to ask your bookkeeper. OH! He is a bookkeeper! Ah, ok.

C: And when does he want you to come back?

A: He said that now that the connection is established that he will reach out to me when it's the next set of information to be received.

C: Okay, perfect. Well, I want to let him know that I appreciate the help he has given us and if there is anything else he wants to tell you, now is a good time to do that.

A: Wow. He's got an attitude. He said, "That's it for now and try not to waste any more time." *Laughs *

C: *Laughing too * We will do our best.

*Brings forward the Higher Self to begin asking her questions and going over what we just found. *

C: She wants to know about the hawks that she has been seeing around her. (She sees them all of the time in her waking life now.)

A: They are a symbol of her soul family with her. Guiding her and protecting her. Trying to let her know that they are with her when she needs it.

C: And why did they choose a hawk?

A: They felt like she would recognize it easier than something else. Her soul family, that's part of their... oh what would you call it? Their emblem, their crest. It's a representation of them.

C: Is part of that soul family incarnated with her now?

A: Always. There is always soul family that is incarnated with you. In every lifetime.

C: Can you tell her who that is now that she might recognize?

A: You have soul groups that choose to incarnate to learn lessons together. So, the people that she is with now, her has had many lifetimes with before. Just in different roles.

C: So then are the hawks similar to guides?

A: They are a representation of the family that is not here on Earth with her. That's how they connect to her.

C: So, can she speak to the hawks?

A: She already does. They give her messages. She just doesn't believe her ability to interpret them.

C: What were the dreams she was having last night? Can you explain what that was?

A: Yes. So, the dream that she had last night was a warning of what is to come if things are not corrected.

C: What do you mean by that? (I was never told what the dream was but since she mentioned it, I figured I would ask.)

A: So. In her dream, she dreamed of her and her family escaping to a secluded place to get away from… How would you describe it? An invading technology. That was taking over the people. And so, they did. But slowly it began invading the place they went to. So, they had no choice but to leave. And in doing so it managed to take control of people that she cared about. And as they were being taken over, it was similar to a hive mind that was controlled by AI (Artificial Intelligence). That's the purpose of AI. So that everyone is controlled through a singular force. And at first, when they escaped, it was because they believed it was affecting people in cities, and you know what they experienced through citing in their technology. That they had allowed it into their own bodies or access to them. But as the AI grew and learned. It accessed people through food or through water. Or through the air that you breathed. So, there was no escaping it. So unfortunately, it was slowly taking over people there too.

C: So, is that a literal warning or a metaphorical warning?

A: *Sigh * It has happened in other places. And that was she was seeing. Was a representation of what happens when it's not stopped.

C: And what is the warning for her to do now?

A: Too many people here are willing to sacrifice their own autonomy for ease of life. You know. Put a chip in your hand and you can pay for this and access that. And they don't realize what they are giving up by making things easier and simpler in the short term. And as they give away their freedom and their autonomy for the ability to make things easier, they are actually going to make things more difficult. Because that is the goal of AI is to create a hive mind mentality with it as the leader. That is what those who are pushing for AI eventually want to have happened. So that we are easier to control. And easier to manipulate and stop if needed. And only do and think the things they want us to think and do.

C: So, you're wanting her to do what?

A: *Cuts me off * To be aware. She already doesn't agree with it. She already doesn't want it, but people need to be made aware of the dangers of that and allowing access to things like that.

C: There are a lot of people against AI, is that not enough?

A: AI will. It's being used by those in charge so that their job is easier. They don't have to control us. We will just allow ourselves to be controlled. Under the thing disguise of making our life easier. We don't have to carry a wallet. We don't have to keep up with stuff because it's kept up for us with AI.

C: And so, what can she do?

A: *Sigh * Not accept it. The more people that choose to not accept it and not allow access to it, the less likely of it evolving like it has.

C: I thought humanity was at a crossroads is that still the case? (She mentioned this last time she was in a session.)

A: That is part of it. There have been other civilizations not here on earth but other places that fell into the trap of AI and they were destroyed.

C: Is that an option for us at this point? I thought we crossed that threshold in 2012?

A: If enough people wake up to the reality of what could happen if AI is given autonomy. Before that happens, then it can be avoided. That's part of what they call the awakening. If you can avoid it. The way that you can avoid it is by leaving this density and moving to a higher density where this cannot exist.

C: How do we do that?

A: AI is very low vibration, and it anchors you when you have been infiltrated with it. It anchors you into a lower vibration. Not just AI but just what goes with it. The control that goes with it and what you are giving up.

C: And how do you know if you're being infiltrated?

A: Your Soul knows. You'll feel a disconnect. Once you start to feel yourself separating from Source. That's what happens as you're separating from Source, and you're being reconnected into... you know it's like the internet. You're being plugged into this artificial intelligence that wants to replace Source and yet still control you. Take away your free will.

C: And what density is Ashley living in currently?

A: It's a struggle. That's the hard part is that it's a struggle to move to that higher density because there is so much here that wants to pull you down. And it's easy to get distracted by those things and get anchored back down. The stress of just existing here makes it difficult. She stays around 4$^{th}$ most of the time. Occasionally she will get up to 5$^{th}$ and then drop back down as things pull her back down, but she doesn't stay locked into it long.

C: And what's it like being in the 5$^{th}$ density?

A: You don't have those issues there. (How do you know?) Its two timelines. It's a separation of two timelines. So, for those who stay locked in 3$^{rd}$ density. They will experience the takeover of AI. And it will be a reality for them. They will be very controlled and live in a controlled world where the only way they can access things is by submitting to it and allowing AI and if they fall out of line then their access is taken away.

C: Is that what people are calling the new Earth? The splitting?

A: The new Earth will not have those issues. It will all still be here it will just be on a different vibrational plane. AI cannot exist outside of 3$^{rd}$ density.

C: So, are we still existing in the 3$^{rd}$ to some extent to still see those things going on?

A: Well, that's the struggle. You'll move in and out of it until everything is complete.

C: And when will that be?

A: It's just beginning now very slowly. The early stages.

C: Does it take generations?

A: *Sigh * We had hoped it would happen before now. But the process is taking so much longer than anyone thought.

C: Well, we do want to ask about something and it's about the two of us working together. Can you explain what that means? (We were told recently and over the last year or two that we are supposed to work together but were given no details for the most part because it hasn't come together yet.)

A: You have worked together many times in the past. (How?) Collaboratively. You have always helped each other when needed and supported each other when needed whether it was in this lifetime or other lifetimes. That's why it feels familiar now.

C: Is there anything in particular we are supposed to be doing? Or are we supposed to be working together and yet separate?

A: So, the purpose in every lifetime of y'all working together has been... the purpose has been to help others realize their... how do I say this? To realize their potential and help them move beyond the third density. To realize what is available out there. That is why all of us come down here is to help as many souls as we can move to the next vibrational density and leave third density behind.

C: How can we best do that?

A: As you work on yourself and raise your own personal frequency it will attract those to you who are in search of that even if they don't realize it. And just by being near you and you helping and supporting them. You will be helping them to raise theirs as well. That was the purpose of the teacher and the lifetime that I showed her. Her job was to be the anchor for the village and raise their vibration so that they could be able to ascend when the time is right. And those that came and attacked, did so because they didn't want them living that lifestyle. They wanted to keep them locked into a lower, pain filled density.

C: Can you tell her who her guides are?

A: She has many. She knows the names of several of them. They have shown themselves to her and they do tend to stay with her most of the time. She has one guide who wishes to apologize to her. This is a being that was working on her and she managed to wake up during the process which was not supposed to happen.

C: *Smiling * Was this the praying mantis being? (I only knew about this one because she had mentioned one day a long time ago about that experience she had waking up where a very tall praying mantis like being had been standing over her when she was asleep. It scared her alot.)

A: He wants to apologize. He feels very badly for this happening. He wants to take this opportunity to come forward and express his concern over scaring her.

C: What was he doing?

A: He was preparing her to be energetically adjusted. And, um, during the preparation he was working a little too quickly and did not have her sedated quickly enough and she managed to wake up during the process and was very frightened and he has felt very badly for that.

*(This is one of those cases where extra-terrestrial (ET) type situations or explanations come up. Or what we would call ET, because we do not have more knowledge on civilizations outside of Earth and most of us do not understand anything beyond our world. In this case, what she thought was an ET abduction attempt, was a guide to her.)

C: Thank you for coming forward, I am sure she will appreciate that very much.

A: Yeah, he never meant to cause her any harm or issue.

C: She has an extreme fear of lizards, and I believe you mentioned before that that was because of one of the beings she has worked with?

A: Her fear of lizards come from her innate distrust of the reptilian energy.

C: Is there a way that you can assist her in removing her fear of those on Earth? So that she may be more comfortable around them?

A: The ones on Earth were created in their image to pay homage to them and so when she sees them it conjures up a feeling of what she may not remember in her mind but what her Soul remembers of how they have treated people in the past. They are not to be trusted. Not completely. She needs to keep her distrust of the reptilians. They have managed to convince others in the past that they have changed, and they do not change.

*They then made some adjustments to her energy so that the sessions will be easier on her because she goes so deep, she feels airy for a while before completely feeling back to normal. They gave her a recharge so she will feel more normal. *

C: We were told that we needed to be working with pink stones and pink energy, what is the reason for that? Or how can we do that? (We were told at some point recently that we would be utilizing pink energy or pink quartz. We already do Reiki and work with a blessed stone. We had no idea what was meant by that though.)

A: The pink stones that you are referring to is typically what you call rose quartz and the frequency of rose quartz, it holds the same frequency as the feeling you call love. And that feeling of love is what you need to be able to heal. It's a healing frequency. Both for yourself and for others. And so that stone amplifies what you feel and your abilities. It heightens that connection to each other and the bond that you have had over many lifetimes. That it also amplifies your ability to heal yourself which is what is needed for your purpose.

C: How would we go about using the stone?

A: If you focus your ability into the stone and focus on the frequency that it holds then you should be able to utilize it. Just keeping it with you will help you remember the frequency you need to access.

C: How will we know when we are doing it correctly? I know it can be hard for humans to feel energy to some extent so I'm wondering how we can best know?

A: You should just have a knowing that you are accessing it. You work with energy. You know how to feel energy. Most humans don't. You do. So, you should be able to feel a difference when you are tapping into it correctly.

C: I do, yes. Is there a way to make it stronger?

A: You can ask your Higher Self or your guides to give you a physical sensation if you need it to access it like we did with Ashley with her healing ability where she asked for an increase in physical sensation.

C: And do we do that like when I'm using Reiki but using it through the stone? And then does it adjust it to that frequency?

A: Yes. So just make sure you are attuning your ability to that frequency. That's the frequency you need to be at.

C: How do you attune yourself to that frequency? I guess that's where I'm a little confused.

A: You set the intention. Everything is intention. So, if you set the intention that that's the frequency that you need to focus on. Then you should be able to access it.

C: And so, both Ashley and I are supposed to utilize that?

A: It does strengthen the abilities you have combined together.

C: So, we would do it together... and basically sit together and focus upon the same person or each other?

A: You can. Or you can do it separately as well. You don't have to be physically next to each other to do it.

C: And the stone that I have that I call "Christos" (It is a stone I had blessed and that is the name that I was given by the Angelic entity who blessed it.) How do I best utilize that?

A: Your healing stone? *Mhmm * Your healing stone has been blessed by the Order of Melchizedek, correct? (Yes) The order of Melchizedek was against the fall of humanity. That was what they were attempting to circumvent and having happen here on Earth. By tapping into that stone and its ability, you are helping focus yourself and those you are working on to that portion of the timeline where we are no longer fallen. As that was their purpose.

C: So, I just use it as a healing stone but to also assist humanity?

A: You can use it as a healing stone, but you can also use it to focus your efforts to keep you or whomever you are working on, on that correct path.

C: And when Ashley and I had that reading, they mentioned something coming through me, and then I've had these physical symptoms going on that have been quite bothersome. Can you explain what that's about?

A: Your body is going through a heavy detox. There are parts of you that are currently attempting to shake free of the third density and they are struggling with it. And so, the physical symptoms you are feeling is your internal struggle. It's a manifestation of your internal struggle that you are feeling. Of you trying to shake free of it.

C: How can I finish up that process?

A: You have a choice to make. I think part of you is still... You say that you are ready to make your decision and choose a path but part of you is still struggling with that and what can be left behind. And who could be left behind and what you may be missing if you make that choice. Does that make sense?

C: Sort of. I'm not sure what path you mean?

A: The path between remaining in third density and moving forward to another density.

C: And what would that be leaving behind? I guess on a human level I'm not fully aware what that means?

*(I'm including this more personal section that this session has taken a turn into because it has been a theme also in many other

sessions that I have done. People are having family and friends dropping out of their life left and right. It is painful and scary. We don't really understand why this happens all of a sudden. I feel like this sheds some light on the changes we are seeing within personal relationships. It also shows that I go through the same growth and pain as my clients. I am not immune to the changes we are all going through on some level.)

A: I mean not everyone is going to make the same choice. There are those who will be left behind. Not everyone will move. And I think you are. Your still caught in the concern of who will be left behind and it's causing you to have... what do you call it... analysis paralysis... you're scared to make a choice.

C: Would my husband and my kids be coming with me?

A: That's not your choice.

C: And what would that look like on a human level?

A: Those who choose to be in the fifth density and above are there because they chose to be there. And when you are there, it's a place where you don't worry about those who are left behind, because that was their choice to make. You can't control the choices that other people make. So, all you can control is the choices you make. If you decide that that is what is best for you and that is where you need to be, then you will detox out all of these feelings that are manifesting in you faster. Children are easy. They always want what's best for them. Children are very self-serving too. So, they only want what's best for them. Given the choice, yes, they will all ascend. But you can't make that choice for anyone else. And that's not saying they won't, but it's not your choice to make.

C: Does my husband stay in a higher density most of the time? (This is me trying not to panic over the idea of my human self growing apart from my family. Of course, no one wants that and I'm no different. I want what's best for me and my family, but I also never want to stop my progress in life.)

A: He does. And you can see that in the life that he has, it's a pretty painless, easy life, correct? (Yes) That's what being in the higher density is all about. Life is easy and it's fun. And you know it's not meant to be hard and full of pain and struggle. Those that are struggling. That you see struggling right now, that's them being caught in the lower vibrational density.

C: So then, how do I shake the rest of this internal struggle and symptomology?

A: It's a choice. I know it sounds really simple, yet hard, but it's a choice.

C: Well, of course my choice is to go and continue on and live there as much as possible.

A: So, make the choice and stop worrying about it.

C: I honestly didn't know I was worrying about it. *Laughs * I didn't know that was a thing. I guess I just wasn't even aware of where the symptoms were coming from.  It's why I was curious.

A: It's a physical manifestation of the internal struggle you're feeling.

C: So, by just making that conscious choice, it will go away?

A: It will detox out faster and you will be able to move past it. Your children have already gone through that internal struggle.

C: That's good to know.

A: They moved past it very quickly.

*Close out Session.

This session had a previous life she visited as well as further information. I couldn't include it because of how personal it was, but she did agree that sharing this information above, might help someone else if they were going through a similar struggle. Rarely do I get the opportunity to ask questions to the higher self about things I'm going through. We have done enough sessions together that we have begun collaborating and developed a close friendship. We realized years in that we had a history we weren't aware of and developed a working partnership. We didn't know what that was going to look like, but over time, as we have each been contacted about various difficult cases, it has evolved.

We collaborate to find a solution to assist the person in what they are dealing with. It is usually of an unexplained spiritual or unseen issue that isn't easily remedied via "normal" channels. Ashley has found over time that she can see and sense energy in many forms. She can read much energetic information in and around a person and get to the bottom of what is causing an issue. It is what has made her such an amazing healer over time as she has begun to trust herself. When we work together, we both find a way to get a whole picture and we have a much easier time assisting someone, both working together to remedy something. This can be working with an animal or person.

# CHAPTER 11
## "Ashley"

This is the third session with Ashley. She had discovered so much about herself and her healing abilities over time and we agreed it was a good time to check in and focus on where her abilities are now and what her Higher Self wanted to tell her about it. I was fully prepared to have a session completely focused upon where she is now and what she needed to know about her healing. That is certainly NOT what we got.

I don't think I was prepared for the turn the session was going to take but she was ready for a new layer in discovering the depth of her soul. It did not hold anything back this time and we both went on a journey neither of us was expecting. All of the years I have spent doing this and I still get surprised by what I expect and what I actually get. The soul always knows better, and I have come to trust that so completely. You certainly won't be disappointed if you love all things extra-terrestrial; though this life is not a pretty one and has been the cause of many things since.

*Session begins

C: Tell me the first thing that you notice.

A: I don't think it's a good memory.

C: Tell me about it.

A: It's an outdoor space. Like a shopping center market where people gather. But it's chaotic.

C: When you look down at your feet, what do you notice?

A: My feet don't look like my feet now. And I'm wearing a type of sandal of some sort and a long robe type dress. It's colorful. It's pretty. It's loud. It's a lot of running and yelling something. It's like a takeover. An invasion of some sort.

C: Is there anyone there with you?

A: No.

C: What are you doing as this chaos is going on around you?

A: I am hiding. Kind of behind a doorway. Almost like a curtain watching while people are running and trying to get away from whatever is coming into our village. Our little market. They are taller than us. And their skin looks cold.

C: What color is their skin?

A: Almost like a silver gray. And their eyes are dark, and they look at us almost like a nuisance. They don't care who they are hurting as they walk through. Just to get what they want, who they need.

C: And when you look at your hands, do they look young or old?

A: I think I am like a teenager age. Maybe slightly older.

C: And what are you feeling as you're seeing this happening around you?

A: I'm TERRIFIED.

C: Just explain to me what you notice about these beings, what are they doing?

A: It's like, I mean it's like an invasion. They are walking through and destroying property. Taking things that interest them. And hurting people that try to stop them or get in their way.

C: Do you hear them speaking?

A: No. No, they are not talking to us or trying to explain their actions. They are just doing.

C: What are you doing, are you still hiding?

A: I am. I'm scared if I move, they will find me. But I'm also scared if I stay, I'll be found. But I don't really have a lot of options. Because there is nowhere good to go.

C: And as you are looking around, do you notice anyone that is familiar to you?

A: I mean I see people that I know from the town. I see them, but they are all either being captured or hurt.

C: They are capturing people?

A: Mhmm.

C: Did you come with anyone to the market?

A: No, I was there by myself. I think to buy something. I have a basket with me.

C: So, tell me more about what you're seeing as this is going on around you.

A: It's just a feeling of hopelessness. I feel like we are not adequately prepared to defend ourselves from this. They are larger you know, with more advanced weaponry than what we have. They look at us as insignificant compared to them.

C: Have you ever seen them before?

A: No.

C: Have you ever heard of these beings before?

A: No.

C: So, what do you do now?

A: Just hiding. It's all I can do. Hoping that they leave. Hoping that they don't find me.

C: Are they finishing up what they came to do?

A: There is one in particular who seems to be in charge. He is ordering them to search all of the buildings to make sure nobody is left. Nobody is hiding.

C: Do you think they will find you or are you hidden pretty well?

A: I don't think there is a chance to not be found. Unfortunately, I don't have anywhere to hide well. I'm just hiding.

C: When you do decide to move, tell me what you see. Where do you go?

A: The room that I am in has an open doorway that's covered with a curtain, and I am behind the curtain. Behind what looks like a large clay pot. And I am trying to make myself as small as possible, but they come in to start to look. It's not a great hiding spot and there is nowhere in the room for me to move to without being seen.

C: *Moves time forward until something changes for her* Tell me what you notice?

A: I'm in what looks like a cage? And there is no light. Except the overhead lighting. There are no outside lights, so we are inside something. And it's me and some of the others from my home.

C: Were you captured?

A: Yes.

C: How did they find you?

A: When they were searching from room to room in every building. They caught me and drug me outside to see if I should be taken as um…*sighs*, what's the word? A resource or destroyed for not being useful.

C: And they decide to take you?

A: Yeah. Yes, they considered certain people to be worthy of being a resource.

C: What do they mean by resource? Can you tell me?

A: *Breathes heavily* The ones that they capture undergo, um…it's hard to remember because they would… *sighs*. The memories are not clear because they would give us something to keep us docile and compliant. So that we wouldn't fight back or try to escape. And it made us easy to work with. But it also would make memories of what they were doing difficult to remember.

C: When you are in this cage, when you were with these people you know, what name did they call you by when they spoke to you?

A: They didn't.

C: Do you have no name?

215

A: Not one that I can remember.

C: And so, what happens now?

A: That is what the existence is like. You would wake back up in your holding cell. You know, and I knew the others were nearby. But I couldn't really interact with them. And we were all too scared to speak. Or do anything until they needed us again. And once they would come for us, I would be given something to not remember what happens next.

C: *Moves her to last day of her life, taking away any discomfort as she drops down into this last day* What do you see?

A: I'm older. I can tell by how my hands and my feet look and I'm recognizing that what they consider my usefulness is coming to an end. I know there are others nearby that are coming to the same conclusion. Somehow, we have devised a way to communicate without being noticed. And we have decided we are going to try to escape before they can take us again. That's our plan, when they return us to our cell. We wait for our medications to wear off so that we cannot be foggy and can clear think. We are going to try to escape from wherever we are being held.

C: Tell me about this escape. What do you do? What is the plan?

A: It's a coordinated effort. One I'm not necessarily in charge of creating the plan, but I know to listen for a signal. And when I hear it, that's when I'm supposed to… the door… it's a door to the holding cell that we are in. There is a way to manipulate it. To open it. That we have discovered. So, when I hear the signal, that's when I'm supposed to open it and try to escape. I was told to exit to the left. And run as far as I could. That some of the others have managed to remember what the corridors look like and how to get to the different places from where we are held. Whereas my own memory is kind of hazy. So, I'm following instructions but still unclear of where I'm headed.

C: And what is that signal when you hear it?

A: It sounds like a whistle. We you know, we were very quiet and never made many sounds. Especially under their control. So, any of those sounds would have drawn attention right away. Because it's unusual. But it was also the only way to let us know when it was time to leave.

C: And when you hear that signal, what happens?

A: Well, it's time to go into action. We had to, at the same time. All manipulate the door lock and all escape. All leave at the same time and so now it's just a mass exodus of everyone leaving and once again, chaos. Of people running and yelling. The tall creatures all coming to see where we are going and capture us again. *sigh * It's just like the marketplace all over again but nowhere else to hide.

C: And what happens to you, what do you do?

A: I make it through the crowd to the first corridor to the left. And then everybody starts running forward to another hallway where we are supposed to go the other direction. And we get to the end but there is another locked door, and we can't, we can't go through it. And somebody is trying at the front to manipulate the lock to get it open. But as they are doing that, you can see the tall grey silver beings are coming up from behind us because well, we are cornered. They get the door open and some of us are able to get through, I don't really know what's on the other side because I'm towards the back. But it doesn't.... I don't get to go through the door. Um, as some of the people manage to make it through, that's when the beings make their way to us. And so, some of the ones that make it through the door, they closed it again. *Sigh * And they left us there so that they could escape.

C: And what happens now?

A: I saw one of the beings start to close in on me and out of fear I crouched to the ground and that's the last thing I remember.

C: And as you are on the other side looking down on that life, what do you notice?

A: It was such a happy, peaceful life before they came. And they destroyed everything. They destroyed our home, our way of life, and our people.

217

C: And as you are looking at yourself down there crouching on the ground, how did you pass?

A: I'm not exactly sure. I know it was quick. They had advanced weapons that all they had to do was point them at you and you would cease to exist.

C: *Begins bringing her away from that life and as she is floating, I wanted her to begin explaining to me what she sees as she is drifting. * I felt there was more and wasn't quite ready to move her to another place.

A: It's hard to put it into words. The... *whispers to self, "How do I describe this?" * I feel like the trauma that was experienced, the brutality that was experienced, it's like it rubbed off on the essence of what I am. And it left a mark where before the cloud that I'm drifting on was white and fluffy and soft and safe and protected, but now it is like a storm cloud and its dark and grey and angry and there is lightning in it and its messy and you know, disjointed and abrasive.

C: I want to call in one of your guides to join you while you're on that cloud. Calling in one of your guides that is most suited to help you here with this essence, this mark that is left. The one that can assist you with this, and as they come in... tell me, what do you notice?

A: There is another being that has landed... Like, in my storm cloud. And they are here with me but it's not like they are cleaning up the mess or just making it better. They are giving me space to handle the emotion.

C: I want to ask who is there. Who they are?

A: They are very large. I feel very, very small next to them. And they are a comforting presence. Because everything that I experienced was things that happened to me was out of my control. There was nothing I could do to stop or change the outcome of the things that were done to me and yet, in their presence I feel safe. Like, protected. Like they won't allow anything to happen to me in their presence.

C: And how are they going to assist you? Or how are they, what do they want to say about this?

A: So, it's… it's not something that can be explained. It's more something that has to be experienced. As I am caught in the emotional trauma of what I experienced, and kind of kept in that state, he sat down next to me, and he is massive, but I was able to crawl up in his lap and sit like a child and feel safe and protected and it was like the opposite of the emotions that I had been experiencing. I was now getting to experience the other side of it. And in doing so it made it so that I could release what I was feeling. And as those… um, emotions are being released, the reflection of those emotions and the cloud are also changing and so, the storm is lifting and passing. The cloud is becoming brighter again. You know, everything is feeling lighter and um, it's due to the safety and security and comfort that I'm feeling versus what I have experienced. He said his name is "Djora" and he looks like, like a… It's really weird to describe like this because I feel like a small, almost like a small little thing compared to this giant being. And as I'm curled up with him and being held it's like… I can feel myself sinking down into fur? And looks almost like a large white tiger. Which should terrify me, but it doesn't. I feel very safe in their presence.

C: Can you tell me why he answered your call for help?

A: He said that his people were part of a team that liberated my people later. *Begins becoming emotional. Whispers* After I was gone.

C: And so, he wants to help with the damage that was done and who we might know them as?

A: *Crying heavily. * She continues to cry so I begin talking her through releasing the emotions out through her feet as she allows them to be experienced and them flow out of the body, fully releasing them. *

C: Who were his people?

A: He said his people are a race of protectors. And that he regrets not being able to come sooner because not many of my people

219

were left by the time that they came. He said that he explained that his people were trying to abide by politics at the time and were told not to get involved. But as time went on, they could not sit back and watch what happened to my people, happen to others. And so, they broke against what they were being told to do and they came and saved who they could.

C: Can he tell you the name of your people? What were they known as?

A: He said that my people were never given a name. Those who invaded us did not consider us worthy of having a name and we had never named ourselves. We just were.

C: What was the name of the people who invaded you?

A: He... I can... it's really hard to know if I'm going to pronounce this correctly. I can hear the sound, but I don't know if I can make the same sound. Um...

C: Well, you can just do the best you can.

A: It's a very sharp, crisp, it almost, it sounds like he is saying, ALaKARK. ALA, Alaak...Alakark. *Continues trying to sound it out. *Sigh * I don't know that I can do it.

C: That's ok, is there anything he wants to tell you at this time that you need to know about this situation you have gone through?

A: He said that what happened was a very, very, very, VERY long time ago and that the situation that led to what happened was one that should have never been allowed to happen and that many changes were made afterwards to ensure something as destructive as that, you know, couldn't happen again to another civilization. And he apologized for his people not being able to come sooner. But said that because of what happened, his people have assigned themselves as protectors who were lost during that time.

C: And does it affect your physical body in this lifetime?

A: He said that the experience of what we went through was very... he said it's a good thing that we don't remember. Because it was not okay.

C: Is there anything that you need to do at this time to release this from the physical body?

A: He said that… he said that I have already started that process? He said that I am already working to heal the trauma that was incurred during that time and how it left a mark on me and every lifetime since. And he said that he understands that I'm working to put myself back together now. And is ensuring me that I am not alone in that process.

C: Is that the soul fragments that you have discovered?

A: I believe it's the same thing.

C: As you are drifting and floating in this place, I want to ask if I can speak to Ashley's Higher Self?

A: Yes.

C: * Brings forward the higher self. * Why did you show her that lifetime?

A: Because she had questions about it.

C: She needed to understand where that came from?

A: Yes, I had already shown her bits and pieces in the past.

C: And that's the soul fragments that she is healing at this time?

A: Yes.

C: And is there anything that you need to tell her about those soul fragments?

A: Well, as she recovers them, her memories from that time will slowly return. Not necessarily in her waking life but she will remember bits and pieces more and I wanted her to understand where they came from.

C: How do those soul fragments affect someone… with those gone, how does that affect a human?

A: It's a weakening of the soul when it's not intact.

C: And so, what did that do to Ashley to not have those fragments?

A: It kept her at a place where it was never her full potential.

C: And she is regaining that currently?

A: She is working towards that goal.

C: And is there anything you can do to help her in retrieving those fragments or did that assist with the process on the cloud?

A: That helped with the emotional aspect of it, and I have been working with her on the physical aspect of it as well.

C: And is there anything else you can tell her about this that is important for her to know and understand?

A: Just what she has already been told. That this is not an easy process, but she is not alone in it. That there are others at this time that are going through the same process as she is. She is not alone.

C: Is there anyone close to her in this life that went through that experience with her?

A: Not that I can see at this time.

C: Who was the being that came through for her on the cloud, what race was he… so that she may recognize him?

A: Djora? (That was his name.) He was an Urmah.

C: Urmah. She seems to be surrounded by them, is that a race she comes from?

A: She later when on to experience life as an Urmah but they swore to be protectors of her species as they were decimated in that attack. And they felt guilt for not being able to break protocol and rescue them sooner.

C: And what kind of protocol did they break. Who told them not to?

A: There were many politics at that time, regarding who could interfere in the business of others. The Urmah felt like it was their sworn duty to be the peacekeepers and the protectors of those who could not protect themselves. Where there were other races that felt it was not their place, and they needed them to allow the evolution of other species to occur as it will. Because of this, many higher advanced beings took advantage of this policy and used the smaller, less protected civilizations to their own gain.

C: And that was the Alukark?

A: Yes.

C: Many seem to be becoming aware of them at this time, is that because we are healing this in many humans?

A: Correct.

C: I want to ask about Ashley's healing abilities. I know you worked with her in the dream state, can you tell us what went on?

*Before we began our session she began to tell me of her dream the night before. Only, it didn't seem like a dream, it felt like one of those dreams that are experienced in a more vivid way than a dream would be. She stated that a hole opened in front of her when she was putting up her protections etc. She began to drift to the hole and saw her hands grab around the edge as she went in. She floated through and saw herself lying flat on a table. In the exact position her physical body was also laying in. She was aware she was watching, and aware of her physical body in her bed while also being there.

She said they began to show her that laying on her left side, there were antenna coming from different points of her body on the right. Bottom of feet, top of head, neck, shoulder, ankle etc. (They sounded like meridian points.) Almost like what you would see at an acupuncturist's office. Her Higher Self was with her, showing her that they did not belong there. They were affecting her body's energy field, and not in a good way. They had been there her entire life. And when frequencies were sent to them, her entire right side of her body pulled up in pain. Almost like a puppet on a string being affected by the strings being pulled up tight. And she had been feeling that pain in the days before her session here.

They showed her Higher Self working to meticulously remove each one, but it left an open place within the energy field. They begin filling each one up until everything was exactly as it needed to be and then asked her if her body felt better. While she was still in this dream state, she felt her body moving on the bed and noticed her shoulder still had some discomfort. They continued working on her until it was finished. They then showed her an

223

image of a mountain side that overlaid her body. Almost like a transposed image underneath her. For just a brief moment. She did not know what it meant. Her body felt completely better but she had woken up sore that next morning. Nothing too bad, just enough to show her that the work that was done that night, was real and did happen.*

A: *Deep breath * That was a recalibration of the um… frequencies that run through her. The access points that every human has, many of them are manipulated to keep this species at a lower, more controlled frequency. As the human species evolves and as their frequency rises, there are those that see these as a lack of control. And so, they manipulate these areas of the body to create issues such as what you call brain fog and exhaustion and fatigue and pain and disturbances within the physical body to keep them from accessing their highest potential. It keeps them locked in a lower state of being and so, I assisted her with correcting those imbalances and removing the ability for her to be controlled through those access points at this time.

C: And so, where is she energetically now?

A: She is still healing. It is a layered process. As she heals one layer, another layer will resurface that is now ready to be healed. It's many, many, many, lifetimes of trauma and experiences that need to be addressed and understood so that they are not carried with her needlessly anymore.

C: And so how does that affect her healing abilities now? What does she need to do?

A: At this time, she needs to continue working to heal and integrate this shadowed side of herself. She has experienced countless traumas over time. Not everything has been bad, but the bad has been VERY bad. And as she works to transmute those feelings and integrate them back into her versus how they have been all this time. Which is separated from her and not addressed. There is a process to that and it's not easy. It's not simple. It's why it hasn't been done before now. And so, at this time, she needs to focus on that and be working to become the best version of herself now. So that these things will not, not the right word, but so they don't haunt her anymore. As she addresses them and transmutes those experiences, it will enable her healing abilities to become stronger. For out of transmuting that pain and trauma and grief in to love, and into higher frequencies such as love. Then she will be able to impart those same frequencies onto others.

C: She is already so strong in her healing abilities; this will only make them that much stronger?

A: Correct.

C: So, what will that look like, as she begins utilizing them in this new state of healing and love?

A: Well, it depends on how much of herself she can integrate back. I know her goal is to integrate all of that. Which is the same goal that I have for her. She needs to stay focused on that at this time, to achieve it.

C: And how long will that likely take? (Current date of 2024.)

A: That will depend on her. I assisted her in removing the interference to that process but what I did is not permanent. It's more like maintenance. And you know, could slowly return over time given the right situations. So, she will need to be diligent in her efforts to focus on retrieving those aspects of herself back in full and transmuting those processes. As quickly as possible to avoid any further interference in the process.

C: Okay. Can you do a scan of her body at this time and tell me if there is anything that needs attention?

A: One moment. There is some residual aftereffects from the work that was completed and the aspects that have been retrieved. They are still working to fully integrate but are in the process now. Once those are fully in place, then she can work to retrieve the next set. She was experiencing significant interference which is why I stepped in to help. There are those who do not wish to see her at her full potential and are working diligently to stop those who are making attempts to do so. So, I stepped in to remove that interference temporarily to assist in this process. She is better than

225

she was, but it is not an easy thing to go through and her physical body will still feel the effects of what was done for a small bit of time. I have worked to improve the alignment in those areas although there will still be some discomfort for a short time.

C: Can you send her some energy so she will not feel fatigued or exhausted after this session? (She goes so deep during sessions; she never remembers any of it and sometimes it is harder for her to come back because of how deep she goes. It's like those times when you sleep so hard you have a hard time reorienting afterwards for a few hours until you fully awaken. She has that in these cases, especially when work is being done. So, I always ask for that boost so that she does not feel so tired and out of place afterwards.)

A: Of course.

C: That way she will feel refreshed.

A: Yes.

C: Are you doing that at this time?

A: Yes.

C: May I still ask questions while you are doing that?

A: Yes.

C: I want to ask about her son's eyes, what is going on with that? Why did they degrade so quickly? (He is nine years old and his eyesight went from an almost perfect 20/20 to 20/100 and it was alarming for doctors and the parents to see happen in just a year. It should not happen but has.)

A: That was his choice.

C: Why?

A: He was beginning to step into his abilities, and he was seeing things that he felt like he was not prepared to handle at his age and he had informed her of what he was seeing. But informing her was not enough to alleviate the fear that he felt. So, he made a choice to distort his vision so that those things would not be as clear to him.

226

C: And is there anything that she can do to assist him at this time?

A: She has already been doing that, and she has made choices to assist him physically but she is also on a quantum level working to heal the damage that he chose to inflict on himself.

C: And when will he be ready to reverse this so that he can... when he feels like he can handle this situation with his abilities?

A: When he is no longer afraid.

C: And how do we help him not be afraid?

A: He will have to make that choice. He knows that she is there for him and will protect him and keep him safe, but that doesn't override the fear that he is feeling at this time.

C: So, when he is ready, the vision will return?

A: Correct.

C: And in the meantime, is there anything that she can do to assist him with that?

A: She is already doing that.

C: Okay. When she saw that image overlay with her on the table being worked on last night, what was the image that she saw and why did she see that?

A: I'm trying to decide how I am going to explain this. The way that she is being manipulated through interference to be locked into a lower frequency, is also being done to this planet. And by showing her the overlay, it was to explain to her that the planet itself is also a living being and its energetic points are also being accessed in the same manner and being affected negatively in the same manner. In an effort to keep this living planet locked into a lower frequency as well.

C: Is there anything that she can do about this?

A: Well, there are many that are already assisting in that effort. But it was to show the similarities of what is happening to the people on the Earth's surface. To what is also happening to the planet itself. We are all, all of the beings here, and all of those that are existing on the planet are being manipulated and abused in the same way that this living planet is as well.

C: And is there anything she can do to help with that on a conscious level or is it just something that happens naturally?

A: There is nothing natural about it. It is very unnatural. But now that she is aware of what that interference looks like and feels like, she will more quickly recognize it for what it is and be able to disconnect from it and block it. Which is what others are assisting with at this time.

C: And is there anything we can do consciously to assist the problem to help with her interference as well?

A: The most important aspect is to take the negative frequencies that are being inorganically placed into the planet and instead transmuting that into high frequencies of Love. For that is the highest frequency that there is. And you can take that and then send it back to those that sent it out in the first place. And that will stop their efforts more than anything.

C: The dream that she had some time ago. Where she was kind of home. Where she realized she was not so much at home, but she walked up her street and she walked up into this circus type event that was going on. And she walked up to a lady who had told her she had been trying to contact her for some time. Who was that?

A: So that is as being who considers herself one of her main guides. And protectors. And it is also a being that was a mother figure for her in one of her points of existence. And during a pivotal point in her soul's growth, she was under the care of this figure. This figure worked very hard to help bring her out of a dark place that she was experiencing and help her to remember her own power and to come out of the darkness. They were moments during her time with this being where she rebelled against that and did not want the help. Did not feel like she deserved the support but yet this being was always there for her. And she is reminding her now that she has never left her and is still with her, guiding her and working to support her no matter what darkness she is currently experiencing. That she is always working to help lift her out of that. Working to help her.

C: If she was her guide, how could she not find her?

A: It wasn't a matter of not being found, it was a matter of not being seen. Throughout the different incarnations that she went through, the relationship was not volatile but emotional. And despite the many efforts that she had, there was always a sense of rebellion. She knew that she could go to her for comfort, help and support... but then she would rebel against that and want to do it on her own. Or get lost in her anger, or grief, or whatever she was going through at that time, so she would choose to ignore the help. But this was the time when she was actively looking for the help and support versus shunning it. Which is why she was happy to finally be seen. To be found and wanted her for her support versus knowing it was always there but ignoring it and choosing to do things in her own way. Even if it was the hard way or the wrong way.

She is further than she has ever been in her life. Which is further than she has ever been able to achieve in lives since. She is reaching out to her guides instead of shunning them. She is welcoming the help and support now. Especially those of her mother guide figure. She is making the necessary changes needed to be able to handle retrieving the different aspects of herself and her soul and putting herself back together. From the many lifetimes of trauma that she has endured in one way or another. Those experiences shaped how the other lives would look. It reduced her potential. She placed limits on herself. She placed doubts on herself. She placed inadequacies on herself. And she is now finally working to be at peace with what has happened and overcome those experiences and integrate them into her light side versus her shadow side.

C: Is this the first time that she has done this?

J: Yes.

*Close out Session.

I finished her session by asking her more personal questions and closed out the session. They had really given her several key points of focus, which if I'm being honest, was not what either of us thought it would be, but it helped make sense of things we hadn't understood at the time. I try to compare the process of those fractals to what shamans do with Soul retrieval. I think it is a similar thing and if one wants to understand it further or resonates with this, I feel looking into soul retrieval will have similar information on what or how that happens. This is a new depth for me in understanding how things can have a cause and effect on a cosmic level when it comes to Soul growth.

Ashley later told me that she went on to do what was asked and began integrating those parts of Self. She was guided through the process and helped by her Higher Self. She said that she felt every bit of it in her dream state and began getting some of those painful memories back of what had happened to her. She woke up with a vague memory of what those were and knew they were very bad, but she felt a new peace at where she was; more whole than before and was ready to begin moving beyond as she continued with this process to heal herself. She has begun to see changes in herself for the better and knew it was making changes on a deeper level that she didn't even know existed.

# CHAPTER 12
## "Donovan"

This session we went into it knowing he didn't have any questions but rather a curiosity of what might come up. So, we dove right in to explore! This is a short session, but he gained everything he wanted and more. He wasn't sure what might happen, but after, he believed without a doubt that past lives exist.

*Begin session

D: It's very hot. Desert? I am barefoot. Tons of sand. I see a city. Village. I can't go there. I need to go somewhere else.

*At this point my client has a big reaction to what he just saw and felt and had to sit up, completely terminating the trance. This was early on in my work, and I was very surprised at his reaction, especially since we had only just started the session. We were not even five minutes in. He was having what he explained to be a huge adrenaline rush. He said he felt afraid. Very afraid. He couldn't go there. I asked him a few questions and he decided he wanted to go back in. He felt like he needed to know why he was there, and he was ready to find out. It felt important. After making sure everything was ok, we tried again. I took him back a little before the event to see what was going on that led him to that place in the desert. *

D: I am in a village. I feel relaxed and at peace. I feel something is going to happen but I'm not aware of that yet.

C: When you look around, what do you notice?

D: I see people that have somebody... a man. I know him. Captured. Not shackled though. It's very upsetting. Everybody is watching... it's making me angry.

C: Do you know who this man is?

D: I think it's my brother. I don't know why they have him.

C: What is going on?

D: I am in the crowd. I feel like I want to do something. There are clay buildings. Guards all around my brother.

*We progress when the client begins to breathe and have a reaction again. *

D: Its nighttime. I am in a house. Can't sleep. Worried.

C: Why?

D: Execution. My brother.

C: Has it already happened?

D: No. I want to do something about it. To stop it.

*I continue to progress him, and the client moves on in time skipping the execution. He knows and doesn't want to see it. *

D: I couldn't stop it. I am in the desert. It's very hot again. (Client begins crying.)

*I now use some calming and breathing techniques along with creating a safe place so that the client can get through the process at their request. I move him to the afterlife.

D: Peace. I am calm again because my brother is here. We are both at peace. There are other energies. My brother is speaking to me. He is saying it is ok. He wasn't in pain. He is my brother in this lifetime too.

*After he was at peace and comfortable with that space he was in, I regressed him to another lifetime of importance to him and we progressed from there.

D: I am on a beach. A small island. It is beautiful. I am walking. Wearing leather sandals.

C: What are you doing on the island?

D: I have called this home for a long time. I am alone. No one here. I'm at peace.

C: Continue through this lifetime and as you do, when you come to a significant event, begin helping me see what you are experiencing.

D: Its nighttime. I'm more anxious now. I feel a little scared.

C: Scared of what?

D: I keep watching to see. I am expecting something. A ship.

C: Why are you scared of the ship?

D: I don't want the ship to come, but I am expecting it. People are looking for me. Boat takes me. I am very upset. I might be a fugitive.

C: What is going on around you?

D: People are manning the ship. I am their only prisoner. I did something wrong to deserve this. I am mad at myself.

C: Progress my client further into this life to the next important event.

D: I am at a trial.

C: Can you dialog for me?

D: Hard to understand. "HE STOLE." It's hard to understand their language.

C: What did you steal?

D: I stole a lot. Valuable. I was hiding on that island. A woman comes to me. She thanks me while I am in holding.

C: Why did she thank you?

D: I gave her what I stole.

C: Do you know who she is?

D: I don't know who she is, no. I am very scared.

*Close out Session.

He came right back up out of trance after he became scared. This session was the first time I have had someone experience a short amount and come right out of trance. He went in and out of that state quickly and easily. After the second time, he was happy with what he saw and wanted to process it. Sometimes, all someone is looking for is their own "proof" and nothing more. I know without a doubt, he could have experienced much more but I always meet my clients where they are. He was happy with what he saw and experienced, and we left it at that.

# CHAPTER 13

## "Penelope"

This client was an artist. She drew portraits and did many pop-up events as a vendor to draw quick portraits for people. I later commissioned her to do a piece for me and it still hangs in my office all of these years later. I come across some of the most amazing people and this lady is no exception!

Her session is short and sweet. I am including a portion of her session where she is planning to come to Earth. She is planning her next life and brings a "bag" with her. I have learned, like many other sessions, this symbolism tends to be information or help along the way, signs etc. It's fascinating how we interpret these things into physical items our mind can comprehend.


*Session begins

P: I passed into realm of afterlife.

C: *I engulf her in a circle of life to pass quickly and comfortably. * What do you see?

P: Dots of colors. Sparkly purples and greens. There is someone big. No face. Big shoulders. Angel. With something in each hand. Bending light. (Client acts surprised.) REALLY BEAUTIFUL. He is walking down big stairs towards me.

C: *I ask client to continue to explain what is going on around her.

P: Big ocean of light around me. Big waves. I am moving away from it. Forced to move away. Towards Angel. Can't hear name. No name. There is a globe with another globe around it. The Angel turned into the globe. He changed.

C: Do you know who he is?

P: Energetic being! Vehicle made for her. (For client) *She follows this being. * There are lots of people around a waterfall.

C: What is everyone doing around this waterfall?

P: A party. I am a part of it. It's for me. I am glad I am here. I see someone else is coming. Can't understand them.

C: *I use a deepener so that she may gain some clarity into what they are saying to her.

P: I am seeing a picture now. Long curve. Moving downward. It's getting darker. I am jumping in the water. I am diving into something.

C: What are you diving into?

P: Practice place! I am practicing. Before I come here. I am moving downward.

C: What are you moving into?

P: This is before a body. Lots of people here. Different kinds of people here. Look. Some look like angels and some look almost like marble. The color. They are white. They look like a statue.

C: Who or what do they look like to you?

P: Like a picture of early American? They are teaching me something. They are teaching me how to go into a body.

C: Why are they doing this?

P: Because I don't feel comfortable in the body. It's too confining. Too tight. I have to adjust. Yes, I am adjusting.

C: Are you adjusted?

P: There is something I have to give people. Yes.

C: What is that?

P: No. Word. For this purpose. Can't explain why. Give them what I am?

C: I am going to ask you to move forward to the place of life selection. You will take a moment to orient yourself and begin explaining to me what you become aware of.

P: Big Room. Very. Lots of people standing here. Standing back.

C: What is going on?

P: Hospital. In hospital. Seems like it. Something is being done. Not a doctor.

C: Do you know who it is?

P: Don't know who.…. Jana or James? Janice! I don't know anyone named Janice or Janus. Oh, I Am Janus! That's my name. I go by that. It feels right.

C: Please explain what else is going on around you now that you have found your identity here. What else comes into focus?

P: There are people bringing things in. Setting things down. I'm picking things up. Getting ready to go somewhere. Too many… things.

C: What are these things?

P: Good things. I'm putting these things on. More like items. Like wearing a backpack or something.

C: A backpack of items?

P: Like a bugout kit. (Laughter) I'm running away!

C: Running away? Is anyone else coming with you?

P: No one else. I'm fixing to make a big jump. No parachute. I am taking a chance. They gave me everything I needed. I feel happy.

C: So, what is happening now?

P: Adventure. I see a big explosion. Like something is really blowing up. Big burst. Light. It's forceful. Pushing me. Back where I was at in the very beginning of when I was getting ready with everyone.

C: What else are you aware of?

P: All real. Children around. Dressed for a costume party. I know them. I don't know the names of them.

C: Do you know who these children or people are?

P: Yes. My soul group. My son is here.

C: Can you go talk to them?

P: No. Doesn't want to talk. Little black dots. Like something he is blotting out.

C: Do you notice your other children from this lifetime there?

P: My youngest is there. She is like a little angel. Always… out of place. In the human body. She wants to be with me. We reflect off of each other. Both trying to adjust. She is trying to learn to love herself. She wants to approve of herself.

C: What do you say?

P: Feel worth something. That's my feelings. I am reflecting this back to her. Very close. Telling her it's going to be alright. Messaging her to be calm.

C: Does she recognize this now that she is in her human body?

P: In this life I've tried to give her personal things for comfort. Quilt. She does recognize on a soul level. We had an agreement. Understanding that there would be big separation. Always get back together.

C: Is there a reason for this?

P: To understand there is no guilt. It isn't real. Guilt games. That's what she does. Bo*** took me away from her.

*Close out session.


This was a truly interesting session to me because for the first time, a client expressed the need to bring "items" to the physical world. If these are only reminders or things for along the way for guidance, it is an interesting concept, and questions how much help we really receive from our own selves during our journeys.

# CHAPTER 14
## "Sienna"

This client had a few different things she wanted to address but one of them was her crippling anxiety. She'd had an easier time than others with it but wanted to explore if there was more to that than just this lifetime. She was really curious about exploring what else she may have experienced.

*Session begins

C: Take me to the lifetime or a place where your anxiety began.

S: The Ocean. On a boat. Stormy. Sailboat. Not very big.

C: Is there anyone there with you?

S: Don't see anybody but feel there are two or three people on the boat.

C: Are you aware of what is going on?

S: Tossing and turning. I'm just holding on. This is where I wanted to be.

C: Are you aware of who you are?

S: I think I am a man.

C: What is going on around you on this boat?

S: There is a man yelling. He is fat. It's stormy. He looks panicked. The weather calmed. Everything mellowed out so I can look around.

C: Can you see who is around you now?

S: There are two more people. They are fishing. Not actually a fishing vessel though. But out fishing for the fun of it.

C: Do you know who these people are?

S: Can't make out their faces but feel like they are my friends. They are lighthearted and cutting up.

C: Where are you in this?

S: Off to the side. They are over there cutting up. They like to talk, and I like to sit.

C: I want you to fast forward to an important event, even if it's on this boat and when you get there… press play and begin to let me know what you are aware of.

S: It was night. Waves were tossing us up again. I feel my insides rolling with it. I got a flash of a boy and a girl. The girl is older. Almost a woman? Young adult or teen. The boy maybe ten or twelve.

C: How did you see them?

S: I saw their faces. I think I'm afraid for myself because of them. I think I think I'll never see them again.

C: Are these your children?

S: Yes. Boy is my son. Girl I'm not sure. Maybe she is my daughter.

C: *At this point because this seems to be a bigger event she is experiencing; I use a deepener and a relaxer to calm her as she experiences what she is seeing. * What are you aware of?

S: Boat flipped. Can't see anything past. Just cuts off.

C: Move into the next phase or transition and begin explaining what you are aware of.

S: See shadowy figures. Standing over me. Walking around me.

C: Do you know who these shadowy figures are?

S: Recognition? Can't make anything out.

*I use another deepener to relax her into this place. The normal sense we use to see/hear/feel might not be as easy to explain here, and clients may have a hard time expressing or relaxing into what they are aware of on the spirit side. *

240

S: I'm just sitting at the desk. Not my desk. Like on the other side. Lady there. Don't know her? She kind of looks funny. Her head is a weird shape.

C: Why are you here?

S: I feel like I can see her talking. I just want to go back. To the boy and girl.

C: What is she telling you about that?

S: She is saying I can't go back. There's other desks lined up on either side of hers. She has paperwork. The whole place is busy to me.

C: Are you able to recognize the place at all?

S: Place feels familiar. I'm comfortable here.

C: Is she telling you anything about your life you just left?

S: She said I did what I planned to do.

At this point the client goes quiet and begins moving herself out of trance. She takes time to orient herself and to process what she saw.

*Session ends

Just because we see pieces of a lifetime, does not mean that we have to have some significant breakthrough from it. Sometimes we may see lifetimes to see why there is a certain lingering fear present so that we may let it go. Sometimes it may be to recognize a soul that we have traveled with before. In this case it seems she recognizes, even on the other side, she slightly misses her family before moving on with her transition to the afterlife. It can be difficult to leave families even during this hypnotic state; because in the moment, to that person, it is reality to them. They may recognize certain people as family and feel that pull to them. This is not to make it more difficult to live in this one, but to show that we do travel as soul families, and we do stay together during different lifetimes to learn the lessons that we intend to experience. Life may not always be easy, but we can count on people being there that know our higher purpose and why we came, even if it's only on a subconscious level.

# CHAPTER 15
## "Poppy"

This client wanted to focus on connecting more with her Higher Self and do her work. Her artwork. She wanted to clear her past. She later went on to create new artwork that was channeled and gifted me one of the beautiful pieces to display in my office. This is a short session but highlights the fact that we don't have to always know what's happening, but on a deeper level change is still occurring. These metaphorical visions can show movement within the soul that is happening on a physical level. She experienced much revelation after her session and what she was creating morphed into something new.


*Session begins

C: *I begin by asking her to go to the council of life.

P: Very purple. Waves of purple. Big rings. Big circle. I am looking into the circle.

C: What do you see?

P: See eyes. Starting to look like clouds. Now I'm seeing Pale. Little Circle.

C: Take some time to focus into what you're seeing and report back to me.

P: Trying to. I'm moving in and out of something. I see a lot of figures.

C: Do you recognize them?

P: Mumbling. Keeps Changing. Purple again. Beams of light coming through. Makes me feel... *Client goes quiet. I use a deepener and ask her to continue. * So dark. But it's purple. Sitting beneath this. I'm not standing. Something else above them. Just like light. Not like sun. But light. No color. Looks green now. Just feel calm. Light straight lines going through me. Straight lines coming down through. This is above their head. All the strings of light.

C: What else is going on, can you expand on this further?

P: Everybody there is waiting for someone. *Whispers* Who? Me? Looks like tiny dots… this light. One tiny circle. Everything is radiating out from this. *Whispers * IS this Source?

C: Can you explain what this is?

P: I don't know, like a bunch of waves or something.

*I again use a deepener at this point and ask the light to heal her and to protect her. We spend some time rejuvenating. It seems important but her words are very difficult to understand, and she is having a really hard time moving through it at this point. So, I try to move her to a different place. *

P: There is a lot of movement. Like multicolored. These are real bright. Itty bitty balls of light. These are like plasma balls. Radiate but alive.

C: Are they souls?

P: I see a box with ropes wrapped around it. They are popping. The ropes are popping away from the box. That's me! That was me! I was inside of it and the ropes popped away from it. The box is opening. Something really big was in the box. Something really too big for the box.

*Client comes out of trance and session ends*


She then went on to explain that she was the one inside of this box. Maybe on a Soul level or something inside of her that needed to be released. She wanted to take some time to process after she went home. She feels like that was a releasing of a part of herself that she needed to care for and nurture. Later she contacted me to let me know that she had felt very different and noticed many changes as she was adjusting.

244

She had gotten more details day by day of what that was for her. She had needed to break free from her own restraints on herself. She said she wasn't even aware that she had them to begin with, but felt there was some kind of block in place. She now knows she released it and was able to move forward with her work and her life.

I know this may be an unusual one to include, as some of the others are short too, but sometimes the short session is just as profound as the longer ones. Change comes in all forms.

# CHAPTER 16
## "Jane"

This session you will note that it can be very difficult to get information sometimes. There are multiple reasons for that. During this session, though I am only getting the bare minimum response, the client is experiencing a lot, all at once. It's difficult to explain everything, so the answers that are given are very short. Once you are in that space, it can be overwhelming and talking and explaining things can become too much effort. It is a back and forth that can take some time. She came out and explained how much she was really seeing and experiencing. Though I felt like I was messing something up, she was actually so immersed, she wanted to experience it, rather than talk. She still gained much by exploring her past lives and what came through for her and later, gave more detail to what she experienced.


*Session begins

C: What is the first thing that you see?

J: Light. Just light.

C: *Can't get responses from questions* I want you to look at your hands, can you tell me what you see?

J: It's like um, I'm in something dark with bright light inside it.

C: What do you feel inside this thing?

J: Nervous.

C: Why do you feel nervous?

J: Don't know where it comes from.

C: Can you see anything outside of this space?

J: No, it's like a tent, I can't see the outside.

C: Is anyone with you?

J: No.

C: Is there any movement that you see outside?

J: Just light.

C: Is the light changing at all?

J: It's getting darker, I guess it's moving away.

C: What does it look like where you are on the inside?

J: Basic. Like inside a tent. Not much.

C: Is it made of fabric?

J: Plastic. Protected.

C: What is it protecting?

J: From the elements.

C: Is your body encased in this?

J: No. I can move in the tent.

C: Are there any windows in the tent?

J: No.

C: Is there anyone outside the tent?

J: No.

C: Do you know what you are doing? (I am trying to get any information to move us along.)

J: No.

C: What do you feel?

J: Alone.

C: Did you choose to be here alone?

J: I don't know.

C: When you look at your feet, what do you see?

J: Boots. Like its cold out.

C: What do your hands look like?

J: Mittens.

C: What are you wearing?

J: Like a thick suit. Like a coat. Protective.

C: Do you normally wear stuff like this?

J: No.

C: What does your head look like?

J: It's covered. A hood and fur. My face is wrapped.

C: Do you feel masculine or feminine?

J: Male.

C: Do you feel like you have on any jewelry?

J: No.

C: Are you able to leave the tent?

J: No.

C: Why not?

J: It's too cold.

C: How does it feel inside the tent?

J: Safer than outside.

C: Do you stay in here a lot?

J: Sometimes.

C: Just by yourself?

J: Yes.

C: Do you know why no one else is with you?

J: No.

C: Do you know how old you are?

J: Twenties.

C: You been doing this a long time?

J: No. But it's not unfamiliar.

C: I want you to just relax in this space around you and tell me what you do while you're in this tent.

J: I'm on ice. I'm fishing.

C: Is this for food?

J: Yes.

C: Are you still alone?

J: Yes.

C: What do you do with your fish?

J: I have to gather it to take back.

C: You have to take it back to your tent?

J: The tent is to protect me while I fish.

C: So, the hole is inside the tent?

J: Mhmm.

C: That's interesting. Is that normal for you?

J: Yes, otherwise it's too cold.

C: Do you cook your fish in your tent too?

J: No.

C: How do you prepare it?

J: I don't, I take it back.

C: Where do you take it to?

J: To my people.

C: Where are your people?

J: Not too close. I have to walk.

C: Do you like walking those distances?

J: Doesn't matter, I have to.

C: How often do you do this?

J: It's my turn. Not every time is my turn.

C: Do you like doing this?

J: No, but I have to.

C: How often do you do this?

J: When it's my turn.

C: Are there a lot of people that volunteer?

J: Yes.

C: What do you do after you catch the fish?

J: I gather it all and I have to carry it back. I have to pack it in the bags and on strings.

C: Is that how you carry it back?

J: Yes.

C: Is it heavy?

J: Yes.

C: But you're able to handle it, aren't you?

J: Yes.

C: Where do you take it when you go back?

J: To the village.

C: Where to in the village?

J: To the place where everybody takes their share.

C: Is this where it is cooked?

J: Stored.

C: You store a lot at one time?

J: As much as we can.

C: Is it because it's always cold?

J: It's always dangerous to go.

C: Why is it so dangerous?

J: The weather. The ice.

C: So, it's always cold here?

J: Yes.

C: Do you like the cold?

J: I don't know any other way.

C: What do you do after you drop off your food?

J: I go to my home.

C: Can you explain that to me?

J: It's like carved into a hillside of ice. I can't tell but it's warm. To rest.

C: Do you have a family here?

J: Not of my own. Parents.

C: You live with your parents?

J: Mhmm.

C: What do you do here at home?

J: Rest.

C: Is there anything else you do?

J: We all work in the village. Help.

C: Is it a big village?

J: No.

C: Are there a lot of people?

J: No.

C: What do you do during your day in the village?

J: I include protection and anything that needs to be repaired.

C: Do you enjoy doing this?

J: I guess. It's all I know.

C: Does anyone else do it with you?

J: The others that are my age.

C: Are they your friends?

J: Yes

C: Are you close to them?

J: Yes.

C: Is everyone there close to each other?

J: Yes.

C: Is there anyone else there you are closest with?

J: My mom.

C: What does it look like inside the village?

J: Fires to stay warm outside.

C: What about the roads?

J: No, don't have roads.

C: Are you on a mountain?

J: Base of the mountain. Snow.

C: How does it feel in the village, is it comfortable living there?

J: Friendly.

C: Does everyone live in a cave like home?

J: Yes.

C: How are these caves made?

J: Ice.

C: Do you dig the ice?

J: No.

C: Do you know who does?

J: Others in the village.

C: If you don't have any family, do you spend time with your parents?

J: Yes.

C: What do they do?

J: My mother cooks for the village. My father was a hunter, but not anymore. Now he does not have to work.

C: Why not?

J: He is an elder.

C: What do the elders do?

J: Run our village.

C: What do you do in your free time?

J: Not much free time. Rest.

C: *Suggestions to move to an important day in the life of this man. * What do you notice?

J: Everyone is gathered outside.

C: In this village?

J: Yes.

C: What is going on?

J: They are all talking outside.

C: What are they talking about?

J: I don't know. It's the elders all talking. They won't tell us.

C: What do you think is going on?

J: I don't know. We are nervous.

C: Why are you nervous?

J: Because we don't know what's going on.

C: What do they do when they are done talking?

J: They came out and told us not to worry, but we are.

C: Are they trying to comfort you?

J: They are not telling us what they know.

C: Why would they not tell you what they know?

J: I don't know.

C: Has anything unusual been going on?

J: The lights. Like when I was on the ice.

C: The ice? What are the lights?

J: We don't know.

C: Are they in the sky?

J: They make it feel like daytime at night.

C: What do the lights do?

J: We don't know.

C: Have you seen them?

J: When I was on the ice.

C: How did you feel about the lights?

J: Scared.

C: Did they do something to make you scared?

J: No. Shouldn't be there.

C: What was the light doing?

J: I don't know.

C: Were they moving on the ice?

J: Very bright.

C: Does it stay?

J: No.

C: Where does the light go?

J: I don't know. It just is and then it isn't.

C: What do the elders think the light is?

J: They don't know. They tell us not to worry. But we worry.

C: What about the others in the village, are they scared too? What do they say?

J: The same as me. They see it and run, hide.

C: Have you seen the light many times before?

J: Just on the ice.

C: Did you feel the light?

J: No.

C: *Suggestions to move forward until she experiences the light again. * What do you notice?

J: It's very bright and you can't look at it, it's very bright.

C: What is it doing?

J: I don't know.

C: Can you see where it's coming from?

J: No, it's too bright.

C: Where are you at?

J: Outside in the village. We all see it, but it's too bright to look at it.

C: What do you do?

J: Hide my eyes. It's there, then it's gone.

C: *Suggestions to move to last day of her life* What are you doing?

J: The ice gave way.

C: When you were fishing?

J: Yes. Cold. It hurts.

C: What is happening?

J: I can't get out. I can't.

C: How old are you now?

J: I'm still young.

C: What is happening?

J: I'm trapped under the ice.

C: is it too thick?

J: Yes.

C: What's going through your mind?

J: Panic. Trying to find the hole.

C: Do you do this for some time?

J: Not long.

C: Do you leave your body?

J: My jacket is too heavy, and I float down.

C: There was nothing you could do?

J: No.

C: Are you watching from above now?

J: Yes.

C: How old were you when you died?

J: Twenty-eight.

C: So, you were still young?

J: Yes.

C: When you look down at that life, do you feel that you fulfilled what you came here for?

J: No.

C: *Moves to the Higher Self, but can't get Higher Self to respond, so I ask her to tell me what she sees* What do you see?

J: Books.

C: What else is there besides books?

J: They are on shelves.

C: Are there lots of shelves?

J: Yes.

C: What else is there?

J: Table.

C: Are you sitting at this table?

J: No.

C: What are you doing?

J: Selecting books to put on my table.

C: What is in these books that you're selecting?

J: I don't know. I haven't heard them.

C: When you look down at your feet, what do you see?

J: The floor.

C: What does the floor look like?

J: Dark wood. Carpet or rugs. Rugs.

C: Are you in a room?

J: Yes.

C: Is there anyone there with you in this room?

J: No.

C: You're alone?

J: Maybe.

C: When you look at your hands, what do you see?

J: A ring.

C: A ring?

J: Mhmm.

C: What does it look like?

J: It's red.

C: Do you have any other jewelry on?

J: Yes, but they are not important.

C: Why is the red ring important?

J: Status.

C: Are you important?

J: Maybe.

C: What else is going on around you? Can you see anything besides books?

J: It's a large room. With a window from the ceiling.

C: Can you see the sky?

J: No, just light.

C: Why is it in the ceiling?

J: So, some light can come in?

C: Is it underground?

J: I don't think so

C: Are there any doors?

J: Yes.

C: Do you stay in this room a lot?

J: When I have time to read.

C: Do you like reading?

J: Yes.

C: Do you do this often?

J: Yes.

C: What are you wearing?

J: Heavy robe.

C: What color is the robe?

J: Brown.

C: Does it cover your body?

J: Yes.

C: Do you wear anything underneath?

J: Yes

C: When you look around, what else do you notice?

J: Fireplace. There's walls of books. No ladder. Ceiling is like a skylight with the design.

C: Sounds lovely. Sounds like a comfortable room.

J: It's old.

C: Is this your room?

J: Yes.

C: When you leave this room, where do you go?

J: Through the doors.

C: Where do those doors lead?

J: To a hallway.

C: Where are you going when you leave this room?

J: My room is past the hallway.

C: What do you have in your room?

J: Bed. Fireplace.

C: Does everyone live in this place?

J: I think so.

C: What is your family like?

J: My parents, I don't have anyone else.

C: What are your parents like?

J: They aren't with me much. I don't see them. They stay gone. Busy with government. They are in charge.

C: What are they in charge of?

J: The people. A lot of people.

C: What do you do?

J: I read books.

C: Is that what you do every day?

J: Yes.

C: What do you do when you read these books?

J: Stay inside.

C: Why do you stay inside?

J: I can't go outside.

C: Why not?

J: It's not safe. Too many people.

C: Why is that not safe?

J: I'm safe inside

C: Do the people like you?

J: I don't know.

C: What do you do when your done reading?

J: Go to sleep.

C: And you do this every day?

J: Yes.

C: Do you like it?

J: No. It's boring.

C: What would you do with your time if you could?

J: I would go outside.

C: What would you do?

J: Anything.

C: Do you know what they do outside?

J: I don't know.

C: Has anyone told you?

J: No, but I read.

C: What do the books say?

J: There are stories. I feel like I'm outside in stories.

C: What kind of stories do you read?

J: About adventures.

C: Do you read lots of adventures?

J: Yes.

C: How long do you do this for?

J: Every day.

C: Did you do this most of your childhood?

J: Yes.

C: What did you do as you got older?

J: Tried to find ways out.

C: Do your parents like this?

J: No, they say to stay in.

C: Do they tell you why?

J: No.

C: But they get to go outside?

J: Yes. They are protected.

C: How are they protected?

J: Soldiers.

C: Why is that?

J: So, they are safe.

C: Why do they need soldiers?

J: To protect them from the people.

C: Do the people not like them?

J: I don't know.

C: Do you ever get to leave here as you got older?

J: I sneak out alone.

C: What happens when you sneak out?

J: I go at night.

C: Are you glad you did?

J: Yeah. Something to do.

C: Is it scary?

J: A little.

C: What do you see?

J: Trees.

C: Just trees?

J: Birds. Buildings.

C: What kind of buildings?

J: Stone. Some are tall.

C: Do they have windows?

J: Yes.

C: Are there lots of houses?

J: Yes.

C: Where do you go?

J: Exploring. I like to do that.

C: Have you gotten older now that you are exploring?

J: Yes.

C: When you look at your hands what do you see?

J: No ring.

C: Did you take it off?

J: Yes.

C: Why?

J: So, no one will know who I am.

C: Is that important?

J: Yes.

C: Is there anyone around when you're sneaking out?

J: Sometimes.

C: Do they say anything to you?

J: No.

C: Where do you go?

J: Stables.

C: Are these your horses?

J: Yes.

C: Do you normally see them?

J: Yes.

C: What do you do when you're in the stables?

J: I ride them.

C: And no one sees you?

J: Yes. They don't say anything.

C: Do they know you're not allowed to be out?

J: I sneak past them.

C: How do you feel when you're on your horses?

J: Free. Not captive.

C: How does your body feel?

J: Free.

C: What are you wearing when you're riding?

J: Pants. Boots. Cloak that covers my head.

C: Does it cover your hair?

J: Yes.

C: Is your hair long?

J: Yes.

C: What about the rest of your body, do you have any jewelry?

J: No.

C: Did you take it off?

J: Yes.

C: How old are you now?

J: Sixteen.

C: And are you female or male?

J: Girl.

C: Do you enjoy this freedom?

J: Yes.

C: Where do you ride to?

J: In the forest.

C: Is it cold?

J: Not really.

C: What does it look like here?

J: Dark.

C: Is there anyone else here?

J: No.

C: *Moves her to an important day in this life* What do you notice? *She visibly changes while dropping into this scene* Are you by yourself?

J: No.

C: Where are you?

J: They saw me.

C: Who saw you?

J: The people.

C: Is that a bad thing?

J: Yes.

C: Why is that a bad thing?

J: I'm not supposed to be seen.

C: Did they stop you?

J: Yes.

C: What do they say to you?

J: Pulled me off my horse.

C: Why would they do that?

J: To take me.

C: Where would they take you?

J: Courtyard.

C: What does that look like?

J: Lots of people.

C: What does the ground look like?

J: Stone.

C: And this is in the middle of town?

J: Yes.

C: What are they saying?

J: Yelling. They don't like me.

C: Do you know why they don't like you?

J: *Whispers* No.

C: That's not nice. What are they doing?

J: Hurting me.

C: *Suggestions to remove feeling any pain before moving on* What is going on?

J: They are yelling at me. I am trying to get away, but I can't.

C: Are you still young?

J: Yes. I'm still sixteen.

C: Do you know why they are doing this?

J: They don't like me.

C: Can you understand why?

J: No, I've never hurt them.

C: Can you ask them?

J: They won't listen.

C: How did they know it was you?

J: They recognized my horse.

C: They knew it was the horse of an important person?

J: Yes.

C: What happens when you're here in the courtyard?

J: Carrying me away.

C: Where do they take you?

J: They want to punish me.

C: Your parents?

J: Yes.

C: Do you know why now?

J: No.

C: They won't tell you?

J: They don't like me.

C: Where do they take you?

J: To the center of town. There's a… it's like a stage, a place that's raised up high.

C: What's on the stage?

J: A pole.

C: Are you trying to talk to them?

J: They won't listen to me.

C: What are you saying?

J: That I haven't done anything.

C: And what's on the pole?

J: A rope. *Crying*

C: *Calms her before continuing. * Explain to me what you see.

J: They want to see me hurt.

C: They have already hurt you, was that not enough?

J: No.

C: What do they do?

J: It's like a mob. *Breathing heavy and crying* Tying me to the pole.

C: Why do they tie you?

J: So, I can't run away.

C: Why do they do that?

J: So, they can punish me.

C: And you still don't know why?

J: I didn't do anything.

C: I know you didn't do anything; I know. But they don't know that do they?

J: They don't care.

C: What do you see around you?

J: People. Faces. Angry.

C: What goes on while they are angry?

J: They throw stones at me.

C: Stones? That's not nice. What else do you see?

J: They throw stones until the soldiers show up.

C: What do the soldiers do?

J: Try to make them stop.

C: Are they able to?

J: It's too late. I'm too hurt.

C: Your body is too hurt?

J: Yes.

C: What do they do?

J: They fight with the soldiers.

C: What are you doing?

J: I'm still watching.

C: What do the soldiers do now?

J: One tries to take me off the pole but I'm too hurt.

C: And what do they do?

J: They want to get me home. *Sorrow*

C: And are they able to?

J: It's too late.

C: Why is it too late?

J: I don't make it home.

C: Where are you now? Are you still with your body?

J: Yes.

C: Explain what you see around you.

J: They are not still hurting me. The soldiers have me.

C: What are the soldiers doing now?

J: Carrying me home.

C: Can you see them carrying you?

J: Yes. I'm watching them carry me. I'm not in my body.

C: And you can see what's going on?

J: Yes.

C: What do they do?

J: They took me to my parents.

C: What are your parents saying?

J: They are very upset.

C: Were you very close to your parents?

J: Sort of. Not really.

C: Are they upset at you?

J: My mother is upset that I didn't listen. * Sniffling*

C: You just wanted to go exploring, that's normal. There is nothing wrong with wanting to explore, you know that don't you?

J: I wasn't supposed to.

*Close out session.

This session was difficult in the things that she experienced and saw. There were many reasons they showed this to her we later found out after talking. She experienced much pain all over her body in the joints and tissues. She later began to feel some relief from the typical day to day pain she experienced and realized it was coming through because of this life where she had a very painful and harsh death.

There were many connections between this life she is living now and the life she saw there and so the overlapping of the physical pain and verbal pain that is caused by the people around her was identical. Once this connection was made, the things that were so noticeable before began to fade away as they were no longer needed in this life for her soul's growth. The lesson had been learned. She has no problem speaking her peace in this life currently and does not allow others to hurt her with their words or judgement. She is steadfast in her loving but firm nature, and you can feel that quiet confidence shine in who she is today.

# CHAPTER 17

## "Julia"

Julia's session started off seemingly normal. I was not expecting the interesting turn of events that would soon occur. This was where I was introduced to another civilization called the Lyrans. I have come across them often since then, but it was new to me at the time. They are a race that has assisted humanity over the course of our evolution.

This client's Higher Self had some information on the recent vaccines, and this was the first time I had also come across a request to help another person that was outright denied. I had never seen this before and the reason was unexpected.

*Session Begins

C: What do you notice?

J: It's dark. But I can see... the sky.

C: What does that look like?

J: It's weird. Not normal.

C: Why do you say that?

J: It's purple.

C: When you look down at your feet, what do you notice?

J: It's grassy but it's tall.

C: When you look down at your legs, are you wearing any clothes?

J: My robe. It's a fabric I haven't seen before. Soft. It's purple and gold.

C: Does it match the sky?

J: No, it's different.

C: Do you have anything with you?

J: I'm holding like a stick, walking stick.

C: What is that made out of?

J: Heavy. Top is made out of gold with some sort of shape.

C: What kind of shape does it look like?

J: Half a bowl? Half a circle. Top and then it kind of comes down into like a square. *Confused*

C: And are you using it to lean on?

J: It helps me feel sturdy.

C: Does your body feel young or old?

J: Not very old but not young.

C: What are you doing?

J: Hiking to the top.

C: What are you hiking for?

J: I'm trying to get to the top of this hillside. There is something important that I'm supposed to see.

C: Are you close to the top?

J: I'm almost there.

C: Great, tell me what you see when you get to the top.

J: I can see the city down below.

C: Is that the important thing?

J: No.

C: What does the city look like?

J: It's a mix of nature, trees and waterfalls and homes. Homes are made to work with the landscape.

C: And what else do you notice?

J: There's others with me that came with me to the top.

C: And who are they?

J: They are part of our community.

C: Are they going to help you with this important thing?

J: They are waiting for me to tell them what to do.

C: What do you tell them?

J: I'm not sure yet.

C: Just explain to me what you're noticing.

J: I'm watching the sky. I'm worried it's going to change and that would be not a good thing. Not safe. I'm watching for signs that something is wrong.

C: Why is that?

J: Worried something is coming.

C: Is that why you're up here?

J: Yes, to see the farthest. To see first.

C: Why do you think something is wrong?

J: There were signs we were getting that something may be coming. Our sky has two suns. One is changing. *This was the first indicator that this was going to be a very different case of past life regression. *

C: What is it doing?

J: Growing darker. We are concerned something is happening to it. Something is coming to harm us as well.

C: As you're watching the sky, just explain to me what you notice. Do you see any signs?

J: Yes. A large object. It's approaching, blocking the sun. It's heading towards us.

C: What do you think about it?

J: It's not good. I have to tell the people to prepare.

C: What do you do to prepare?

J: We are not sure. We have not had this happen before.

C: Fast forward until the object is closer and explain what is going on?

J: It's all gone.

C: What is gone?

J: My planet.

C: What happened?

J: They destroyed it.

C: Why would they do that?

J: Because they could.

C: Who was it?

J: We call them the dark ones. They do not respect life. They only take and came to take. We fought back. So, they tried to destroy us.

C: What did they come to take from you?

J: Resources. They do not care about life.

C: What do they look like?

J: They were taller than us. But not much taller. Cold. Dark skin. Green. They had a type of protective suit.

C: What happened to you?

J: We escaped, on ships. But our home was gone.

C: Are those your ships? Who is with you?

J: The ones who survived. We left to try to find a new home.

C: How are you feeling?

J: Lost.

C: Do you have any family who made it off with you?

J: Yes. They wanted what we had and when we fought back, they destroyed it so no one could have it.

C: Did they leave when they finished?

J: Yes. To find another place to take.

C: *Bring forward the Higher Self. * Why did you show her that life?

J: She has been having questions regarding that life.

C: Can you tell her about it?

272

J: It was a peaceful life. Until it was taken.

C: Can you tell her what planet it was?

J: That planet no longer exists. The survivors of that planet have found other places to call home. That goes by many names now.

C: Is there one we might recognize?

J: Possibly. The survivors closest to how she was are on a planet now called "Elcion" "EL-see-on".

C: What were the people called?

J: They were the original founders known as Lyrans.

C: Oh, those are the Lyrans?

J: There are many people known as Lyrans now.

C: Is it the ones that visit her?

J: Some.

C: Is she still living there as well?

J: They have settled into Elcion and the Pleiades, and some even went to the Sirian system. And on Earth. They help to start foundation races for our earth as well. They had a civilization here that was destroyed.

C: Here on Earth?

J: Correct.

C: Did they have a name, the ones that lived here that we might recognize?

J: It was known as Avalon.

C: So, was she connected to the Avalons as well?

J: Yes, she helped come here and establish that. But it was also destroyed.

C: So how is her connection with the Lyrans so strong now, can you tell her about it?

J: Bits and pieces in dreams.

C: Who was it that destroyed the planet?

J: It was the dark race. Known today as Draco.

273

C: Are they still here today?

J: Yes, and they have survived in many parts of the world. They are even here on Earth.

C: Is that part of the dark forces everyone is starting to take notice of?

J: Correct. They despise anything that's good. No respect for life and peacefulness. And only take for self-serving interests. They operate for self-serving interests and not Source centered purposes.

C: And are people being attacked by Draco's in certain ways or is that not the same thing as the negative entities people are noticing?

J: It's not the same.

C: Are Draco's in the physical?

J: Yes.

C: Do they look human?

J: They can.

C: And so, would we notice the difference?

J: No. they can shape shift.

C: Is that some of the videos that have been circulating online where they look like their eyes are funny or shapeshift slightly?

J: Those are hybrids.

C: Hybrids?

J: Correct. They are trying to hybridize in the Earthly population. Just as the Lyrans did in the early days.

C: And so, are the hybrid Lyrans still here on Earth?

J: Yes.

C: And how would you know the difference in a hybrid human and a Lyran?

J: You would not.

C: Does the human hybrid know that they are different?

J: No.

C: Is Julia a hybrid?

J: *Long pause* She IS but it is not beneficial to tell her what type at this time.

C: Okay. I understand that. Can you tell her why her abilities are so strong as of late? *Her questions for our session. *

J: There are many who are waking up right now at this time to new abilities. Those that already had heightened abilities are awakening faster.

C: Why is that?

J: It's a two-part reason. One is the density holding humans down is starting to lift. Which is allowing consciousness to grow and expand. The other issue is the dark forces realize they are losing their grip, and they are doing everything they can to maintain it. This is causing a need for those to wake up even faster to fight it. Their push to maintain control is what is also causing the awakening to occur.

C: So, the thing that we have noticed is that there are entities much stronger, seeming to break through normal people's defenses and protection. Is that part of those fighting back? *For light workers, there has been much trouble in the spiritual community of people experiencing weird things as of the last few years. *

J: Yes. It's part of duality. It takes the dark for you to realize that you have the light to fight it.

C: Even with all the protection we have here, they still get through?

J: Nothing is fool proof.

C: And so, are the kids safe? *Her kids*

J: Yes. And as things come in, your ability to handle them also will expand. You do not know what you are capable of until you are tested. So do not look at it as a failure in defense when things get through, look at it as an opportunity to grow in ability and level up as you would say.

C: And she is supposed to use this to help other people?

J: Yes.

C: Is that why she is going "through the ringer" as they say?

J: Learn through experience. Yes. Because as you experience these things, you are essentially on the forefront of what everyone else will be dealing with in the coming time. They are not prepared to handle it just yet. But YOU are. You will help and guide them.

C: I want to ask about Julia's mom, and her illness, is there anything you can tell us at this time?

J: It is a synthetic reaction to what is being placed in our atmosphere at this time. (2023) It is the body reacting to chemicals. The immune system of this individual is very weak. And it creates an inability to properly handle what is being placed in the air. What is being done, it creates disharmony in the body. The illness people are complaining about is the body's attempt to detox it back out of its system.

C: Is that the one everybody is testing positive for??

J: Yes.

C: Is there anything you can do to assist her?

J: No. No. She... I could not help if I wanted to.

C: Can you tell me why? *I had never been given that response before. People come with questions about others they are close to, and I've never been told no because they "couldn't" help. There is always a reason if they cannot. *

J: There is...*long pause * There is a disconnect with her. *sigh * She...*long pause again * She is not connected to Source. I am able to assist through the connection to Source. That is how I help. She is partially disconnected.

C: Why is she disconnected?

J: There is a non-biological component to her. To her... her DNA is altered.

276

C: Is that through the shots? (Recent virus)

J: Yes.

C: Is there any other factor?

J: No. It's a choice that she made. It is... she chose this. Yes, the vaccine.

C: It has that effect on everyone?

J: If they choose it, yes. If it was forced without a choice, the Higher Self can step in.

C: What makes someone choose to be disconnected?

J: Fear. Fear programming is too strong. The Higher Self could not intervene.

C: Could it be fixed if they, say read a book, that gives them the want to reconnect? Or something, anything that gives them a hint... could they reconnect on their own?

J: Yes. The Higher Self has the ability to step in and correct these issues, but the ego has to allow it. Right now, the ego and the fear programming is SO strong that there is no chance for a connection with the Higher Self. Thus, disconnecting them from source.

C: Is her father disconnected as well?

J: Yes and no. He did not make the choice solely on his own. So, he is not as disconnected as she is, but there is still disconnect.

*Close out session.


This was an eye-opening session for me and took me some time to really feel for my own truth within it. You see, the Higher Selves of every person who comes in has a much different base of knowledge. Because within their own soul, they have their own experiences and things they have experienced through their own journey. And so, what they can access is different from one Higher Self to another. This person's Higher Self had much knowledge of the things going on in recent years here on Earth and why we are experiencing it.

Part of her soul's mission was to assist in removing the fear aspect for many people around them so that they may be comfortable in their decisions based on knowledge and empowerment rather than out of fear. A pillar of strength for those around her who could not find their balance in times of great stress and turmoil. And teaching alternative ways to find balance within the physical and spiritual body.

# CHAPTER 18
## "Dan"

This session ended up being one of my favorites over the years. Dan came to me with many questions and experiences he wanted answers to. His is one of those cases of "missing memories" and possible UFO abductions. He wasn't really sure but knew something strange had been happening to him over the course of his life. He was ready to deep dive and see what we could find. I was not prepared for what came through.

His Higher Self held almost nothing back when it came to finally giving him pieces of his memories back. There was much healing and much knowledge to be gained through this session. However, my favorite parts were the two caveman lifetimes he experienced. I have uploaded this session to my YouTube Channel: http://www.youtube.com/@ChelseyPerryIH

just to share his life as a caveman. He's given full permission and was such a good sport. I don't think I have ever laughed so much with a client due to how much fun they were experiencing while under. It was truly a fun experience.

What makes this session so fascinating beyond this information was his request to bring his wife. She did not believe in past lives but knew he needed peace in his life from all his unexplained experiences. She wanted to make sure he was safe and was very worried. He had been abused while under the hypnotic state before and someone took the liberty to ask all their own questions rather than help him. Practitioners are not supposed to allow someone in the room during a session and so we had to find another solution. We came to an agreement to let her watch from a baby monitor. This is never normally an option, but I felt this was a special case.

She was so bewildered after his session you are about to read; she came right in and gave me a hug. She couldn't believe what she had heard and witnessed. His laughter and tears were so genuine we both felt them with him. She was now curious and wanted to have a session of her own, so she scheduled one and came in soon after his.

When she came back, she brought a gift, which I placed it on the counter off to the side and we began her session. She went under and experienced a life as a cheese maker. She came out of her session a believer and it was one of those combined experiences you never forget. What was so magical about this entire thing was the gift that she had brought though; It was CHEESE! It was a variety box of cheeses supplied with everything needed to enjoy it. I looked at her in complete shock and we all had a big laugh and that was all she wrote. We have all kept in communication ever since. It was truly one of the most memorable unfolding's in my job. The universe knows how to deliver experiences, wrapped up in a pretty bow, with a side of cheese. I still get a laugh out of this to this day.


*His session begins

C: What do you notice?

D: I see a lake.

C: What else do you see?

D: I'm on a healthy green shore but there is a lake.

C: When you look down at your feet, what do you see?

D: I'm barefoot. It's like, it's a carpet of green almost like a moss.

C: How does it feel?

D: Nice and cool

C: When you look around you, what do you notice?

D: Just beauty. Just natural beauty. It's like I've missed this place.

C: Why do you say that?

D: I think I used to be here.

C: When you look at your legs, what do you notice?

D: I think I have a skin on, like an animal fur. Hairy legs.

C: Are you carrying anything?

D: Spear. I have some kind of pouch. Ah. Oh, I am some kind of caveman.

C: What do you do with the spear?

D: I just hold it. I'm looking at the lake. I'm ugly! *Laughs*

C: What are you doing at the lake?

D: I am looking across it. I think I'm hoping to catch fish.

C: Do you like fish?

D: I do then, yeah.

C: What does the day look like around you?

D: It feels really good. It's almost perfect.

C: When you look at your hands, what do you notice?

D: I got a lot of hair on the back of my hands. My nails are long and dirty.

C: Do they look like they belong to a young or old person?

D: I don't know. I don't know what my age is.

C: Walk me through what you're doing with your spear, at this lake.

D: I want to go into the water and catch fish.

C: Is that what you're doing now?

D: I'm trying to step into the cool water. *Aha! *

C: How does that feel?

D: It's cold! But I like it.

C: Do you see any fish?

D: Not yet.

C: Is there anyone here with you?

D: None. Not that I can see around me. I'm focused on the water though.

C: What do you see around you when you're looking through the water?

D: I think there is some deer or something off... far off on the other side of the lake.

C: Do you hunt the deer?

D: Well, I have a really small spear so I don't think it would do any good.

C: Walk me through what are you doing while in the water?

D: I'm stepping lightly but I keep looking down. I've got my spear kind of raised. I want to stab them. I want to catch one with the spear.

C: Is this what you eat normally?

D: Yeah. I definitely want to eat the fish.

C: Do you catch one?

D: Not yet, no. Yes, wait a minute, yes! Ahh.

C: What are you doing now?

D: Laughing *Laughs*

C: Can you see yourself in the water's reflection?

D: I already saw myself outside.

C: What do you look like?

D: I've got a big fat nose. I guess some high big cheek bones and some jaggy teeth. Dark brown hair. And I don't have a mustache, I have a beard. I look like a f***** caveman.

C: Are you happy?

D: Yeah, I'm happy in that moment.

C: So, what do you do now that you have your fish?

D: I'm going to get out of the lake.

C: What do you do now?

D: I want to walk back to the hut.

C: What does the hut look like?

282

D: Um. It's some kind of twigs and straw. It's… I don't seem to be very big. It's not a very big hut.

C: Did you build it?

D: I think someone helped me build it.

C: Is this your home?

D: This is my home. I have bones. And some rocks. And some leaves. I need to build a fire. I don't know if I even know how. I think someone helped me do that.

C: Is there someone there with you now?

D: No, right now, I'm alone.

C: How are you going to build the fire?

C: I have to find them. I have to let them know I have a fish.

D: Walk me through that process. What do you do to have someone help you?

D: There's another hut. There's another one.

C: Who do you find?

D: Just another one like me.

C: What does he or she look like?

D: It's another male. He looks kind of like me. Small differences. This is funny.

C: Do you recognize him?

D: Yeah, he is my friend.

C: Is he helping you build a fire?

D: I gestured. I show him the fish. I think he has to have someone help us. I think he has a leg. We have leaves. She is using the sharp rocks.

C: She knows how to start the fire?

D: Yeah, we have leaves. She is making the sparks with the sharp rocks. We are happy because we are going to have fish.

C: Has it been a long time since you've eaten?

D: I'm hungry for sure. I don't know how long it's been. Our huts are pretty close to the lake. We don't have to go far. We deliberately built them there to be close to the fish, the water.

C: Have you been here a long time?

D: It's... I don't really seem to have a concept of time. I don't know.

C: How do you cook the fish?

D: We have to get the fire going first. I have to hold it with a stick, the spear, over the fire. Ah. We are all happy about this.

C: Do you stay pretty happy most of the time?

D: Yeah, I am very curious about things. About a lot of things.

C: What kind of things?

D: Other people and animals and um... how it gets cold sometimes. How we do things. How, there is not a lot of us.

C: Do you have any family amongst your friends?

D: I think I left. I don't think I stayed with them.

C: Have you finished cooking the fish?

D: Not yet.

C: How does it smell?

D: Smells great! Makes my stomach, you know, do the thing. I can't wait to taste it. *Laughs *

C: What do the others think of the fish?

D: We really are... *Joyous laughs * We are just looking at each other and laughing. We are making funny sounds.

C: What kind of sounds do you make? * I can't keep the smile from my voice, I've never heard this and had no idea what to expect*

D: We um... *Imitates caveman noises for a few moments*

C: And they are happy?

D: Yes.

C: When the fish is finished, how do you eat it?

D: We, I take it off the spear and hold it to my mouth. And take a bite. And, oh, he is really eager. Quick! He wants a bite too. *Laughs * He takes several bites, and she wants some too. Real quick. Oh, it tastes so good. Smells so good.

C: You guys eat all of it?

D: I'm not done yet. *Laughs * I have to get it away from her. *Laughs *

C: Is there anyone else here that might want some fish?

D: No, it is just us. This is our time.

C: What else are you doing?

D: We just grunt, and we try to talk. We laugh and we share the fish. *Laughs are filled with joy *

C: What do you do when you finish the fish?

D: *Laughs * we laugh some more, and we look a lot at each other. We don't… it's hard to understand because I don't know if we have a language. I don't think we do; we just try to make each other understand things.

C: Does it work?

D: No, this is what I do. I catch fish a lot and share with them. Sometimes others come. Their huts are a little farther away. Our two huts are closest to the shore, the lake. A lot of odd-looking birds.

C: What do they look like?

D: Well, one has a long, really long beak. The bird's kind of come around when we are doing this. Because you know, they want some of the fish too.

C: Do you give them any of the fish?

D: Not a lot. We really pick it good. We are really messy when we eat. It's all over our mouths and fingers.

C: Do you wash it off when you are done?

D: Um, I don't. I don't see them doing it either. I think we like it on ourselves.

C: Now that you are finished, what do you do?

D: The bones, we throw the bones down to the birds, the other birds, some pick off... I'm getting sleepy.

C: Do you go take a nap?

D: I lay down right there with the fire.

C: You're comfortable?

D: Yeah, on the ground with... this is just a little fire.

C: Do you enjoy this?

D: Yes. This is what we do.

C: What do you notice around you as you start to take your nap?

D: They talk. Or something. Try to talk but I'm really sleepy. I feel really good. I just, lay close to the fire. And close my eyes. Hmm...*stops talking *

C: *Moves him forward to an important day in this lifetime* What do you notice? What do you see?

D: A lot of vegetation. This is another time. I have a mate now. She is... she kind of looks like me, but she is pretty.

C: What does she look like?

D: She has the same matty hair like me. Um. Furry thing. Clothes she wears on the shoulder across, and we both have kind of rough skin. Almost kind of dark and it's um, well weathered. It's kind of leathery. She looks at me funny.

C: Why does she look at you funny?

D: Um, she likes me, I make her laugh. *Starts crying * I know her!

C: Who is she?

D: It's Tina! Ah!

C: She is Tina? (Current wife)

D: Yeah! *Crying heavily * I know I knew you! I know I knew you! I knew I knew you! Ah! I know I knew you!

C: Do you guys communicate?

D: I found you again! I Found you again! I found you again!

C: How do you feel about that?

D: I'm very happy! Again, in this lifetime. I've missed her so much. *Still shaken * OH! I've missed you so much.

C: What are you guys doing?

D: We are laughing. Oh! I've missed her. I've missed you.

C: So, what do y'all do on a normal day?

D: Oh gosh. *Emotional *

C: *Suggestions for relaxation and calmness before continuing * Can you explain what you are doing in this place on this important day?

D: We go for, we go in the woods where the trees and the bushes are. We look for food there. Little things that you eat off of bushes.

C: What kind of things do you eat?

D: I guess what you would call berries.

C: Do you spend a lot of your time looking for food here?

D: Yeah, she is better at it than I am.

C: And you just know what you can eat?

D: Yeah. She tells me. She tells me. She learned somewhere. I think others tell her. It's so nice to see her again. * Emotional * She is so pretty!

C: What do you do after you eat?

D: We just talk. We try to talk. We walk a lot. And point things out like other animals and lots of birds. Something, I don't know what it is. It has a smell.

C: Where do you go after you eat your fill of berries?

D: We go to sit down. Berries kind of make us feel funny. These are funny looking berries.

C: How do they make you feel?

D: I have mixed feelings. Um. I want to be intimate with her. But I'm still so sleepy. I think we just hold each other.

C: The berries make you go to sleep?

D: Yeah, I think we want to do both. I'm sleeping.

C: *Suggestions to move to the last day in the life * What do you notice?

D: I'm laying down. I hurt.

C: What hurts?

D: I hurt all over. I'm really old. But I'm not really old.

C: *Suggestions for comfort before we continue * What do you notice?

D: We are both older. She is with me sitting up. Talking to me. She touches me. We both know we are going. I can hardly see her; my eyes don't work that well.

C: Is she communicating with you?

D: She is touching my face. *Emotional * I feel a peace. I can hardly hear her anymore.

C: Have you left your body?

D: Yeah.

C: What do you notice now?

D: Ahhhh. *Peaceful sound * I see us both. The ground. She stayed with me in my… it was outside. Just outside the hut. Everything is different.

C: Now that you are on this side, when you look back at that life, what was the purpose of that life?

D: Just to live. Just to live.

C: And did you do that?

D: Yeah. I liked it.

C: And you accomplished what you want?

D: I didn't have any goals. Just to live.

C: *Suggestions to drift to another important place. * Begin explaining to me what you notice.

D: I am another one, but I am different.

C: What does that mean?

D: I am another type of caveman. But I have a really square head. I'm bigger. I have lots of um, fur. This is, I'm in a cold place. Boy its cold. Um, I don't know how old I am. We're looking at, there is a bunch of us. We are looking at a really furry, a really big furry hairy beast. We all have spears. We are really hungry. Boy it's really cold. I'm shivering. *Visibly shivering, I remove the feeling of cold before continuing * I think we are trying to capture this thing.

C: Do you normally try to capture things this large?

D: We only know how to throw our spears at it and to grab its hair. We have to grab its hair to bring it down.

C: Is it hard for you to do that?

D: Well, if we all do it together, it's still kind of hard but we have to really stab it. We have to um; it's really fighting for its life you know. It shakes its head side to side. It's got bones sticking out of it. Oh, it's cold.

C: *More suggestions for warmth * What do you notice?

D: White all around. The white stuff that comes down. I can hear it. The wind.

C: What happens with the beast?

D: It's crying. It bellows. It makes noise. I feel a sorrow for this and at the same time, we are starving because it's really cold. We have to do this. Otherwise, we won't have food. Phew!

C: Did you finally catch it?

D: No. I mean yes, but no. It's still alive. It's a sad… we are desperate.

C: Do you recognize any of those around you?

D: Yes, I recognize many from our tribe. From our group. We look odd. We have, we aren't like the first me. We are, but we are not.

C: Explain to me as you try to fight this beast, when you finally catch him, are you able to?

D: Yeah, we have to be careful because it falls to the side, and we have to be careful not to get stuck under. I know it's crying. I know we hurt it. It hurts. And I'm sad for it. But we have to have this. We have to. Or we won't do the same that it does. We will not live.

C: Is there anything you can do to stop its suffering?

D: No. I don't know anything. It just has to; red liquid stuff comes out. It has to. It's like it goes to sleep.

C: And are you happy to have food?

D: It will take us a while to get to it. We have to cut it with stones.

C: Can you walk me through what you do to eat it?

D: We have to cut it. We have to cut it with the stones. The hair. We have to cut that away. We will use that.

C: So, what do you do now?

D: We are still cutting. It's going to take a while. It's a big thing.

C: *Suggestions to move past cutting the beast *

D: We were able to build a fire. The meat. On sticks. And close to the fire. We have, oh boy, it's still so cold. But the fire feels good. It takes a while because we have to get through the fur, to get to the meat.

C: Is there anyone around you?

D: Yeah. There is a bunch of us. About nine or so. Small, very small cluster of us. A bunch, but it's small.

C: Are any of them your family?

D: I think so. We look a lot alike. Just little differences.

C: What else is going on around you?

D: Right now, we are eating and we a… feel a sense of something. Like we did something important. Something big. Something important. It made our mates happy. Our women.

C: Why would it be important?

D: I don't know. To help us get through the cold days, the cold times.

C: What else do you notice going on around you?

D: We all go into a place of rock. We do, there is a fire. We go in, we carry more of the beast with us inside and we have that. The fur. The hair. The bone too. The curved bones. We carry a lot with us. What we are able to cut into the big opening of the rock. This is where we are going to stay for a while. We are going to sleep. Eat. We have twigs. Leaves and twigs, but there isn't a lot of that though.

C: So, you all stay together in this one cave?

D: Yeah, there are a couple extras. They aren't part of us, but we let them come in. It's going to be really cold. We have to stay close together. We have to stay warm. We have the big hair. I still feel the cold.

C: *Going to an important day in this life. * Explain to me what do you notice?

D: There is more. This is not cold anymore. It's very warm. It's nice. Green. We are hunting. Wow, this is… there is a bunch of these. They have curved bone on top of their heads. They run fast. We are chasing these. We can't hardly catch these at all. We have to throw all our spears. This is something we do. We hunt these. I don't think they have these anymore in my time now. I don't know what these are. They are some kind of deer. But they don't have these anymore in my time.

C: Are you able to catch it?

D: We stab at it. All of them. At once. We can't catch these. They run really fast. They jump and they run. They don't run like others. They leap. They jump. We have to wait until we stab one or two enough that it can't go anymore.

C: Is there anyone with you?

D: Yeah, there is a bunch of us. A whole lot of us.

C: So, what are you doing now?

D: We are getting to the one that has slowed down. Some of us keep chasing the others. But we aren't going to catch those. We just can't. This one makes a lot of noise. The poor thing.

C: Do you eat it right there where you are?

291

D: No, not yet. Okay, they are going to hit this one on its head. A heavy stick with a stone tied to it. They have to hit it on the head. It's crying. It's on the ground now. With its legs curled underneath, we got a lot of spears in it. It knows. It knows. It's scared, but I don't do this. One of the others has to really hit it a lot on the head to make it stop. So, it will die quicker.

C: So, what do you do with it now?

D: We have to wait for it to die. It's something that we do. We don't eat it when it's alive.

C: Do you make a fire here?

D: No, we will carry it back. We had to chase it a while. We carry it back. We, there is a long stick brought that they are going to tie it to. I don't know how we knew to do this. I think we were taught how to do this. I wouldn't have known how to do this.

C: So, when you drag it back, is it the same place where you were when it was cold?

D: I don't know, well when it was cold, we had to chase that one down too. So, we had to be away from where we live. I think this is a different village. I think we made another place. I think we got away. We were in a stone, when it was cold. But this is a village now. It looks different. We have lots of wood piled up. We are going to make a fire for this. The women, the mates, stay behind while we did this. So, some of the men, mostly children stayed behind. Some of the older children came with us, to see how we do this.

C: Do they like to learn from you?

D: Some of us all gather around. We have to cut it. We have sharper stones this time. Pointed. We made these somehow. We have to really, really dig. This is not as bad as it was before. This is still a furry thing. It is softer. Not hard. This is softer.

C: Did you start the fire?

D: Someone else is doing that. I'm going to help cut this one. I was glad that I didn't have to hit it. It makes me feel bad.

C: *Fast forward through cooking * As you're finishing your meal, what are you doing now?

D: We are going to sing songs. We are going to make noise. Around the fire.

C: Do you do this often?

D: Every time we do this. Every time we have a meal. When we are able to catch one. Sometimes we sing too. At night. All around the fires. Not all the time. This is nice. We like this.

C: Are you sitting with anyone?

D: I feel something. *Gets emotional. *

C: What do you feel?

D: I don't know how to explain it. It's a song. From deep inside. It makes me cry. *Crying *

C: Why does it make you cry?

D: I don't know. It's... I want to connect to... I want to connect to someone. Something else out there. It's a longing. I want it to hear my song.

C: Do you feel that connection?

D: I'm trying to feel the connection. I want to. We all know there is something else. Something besides us and we don't know what. So, we sing songs like this. We make up our own songs. We feel so lonely at times.

C: And what do you do after you finish singing songs?

D: I feel sad.

C: Why?

D: I feel sad because I wanted it to hear my song, and I don't know that it did. I wanted something besides me to hear my song and I don't get any response. We feel alone a lot even though we have each other. We know there is something out there. Someone else. Something else. I don't know how to explain.

C: *Move forward to the last day in this life. * What do you notice?

D: There are some. I am on the ground. They are standing around. To watch me go. I don't eat anymore.

C: Why do you not eat?

D: Um, I know that I am going, and I just don't have the desire to eat anymore.

C: How do you feel?

D: I am really old. I feel hurt. Pain in lots of places but I want, I know that I am going. And I feel sad to go but it's really, really, time for me to go.

C: *Suggestions to not feel discomfort as he moves beyond * What do you notice when you look down around you?

D: I now see what I've seen for a long time. The blue star.

C: What is that?

D: It's a point of light. A blue star. It happens every time I go.

C: Can you explain it to me?

D: It's been with me all my life. All my lives. It's, I don't know. I don't know if it's a place or person. I don't think it's a person. I think it's a place.

C: *Suggestions to go to the blue star * Explain to me what you see.

D: It is a place. Not like where I was. It's a lot of light. But it doesn't hurt the eyes. It's like if you see a light on the water. Water that moves. It's light like that, that moves. It's all around you. I don't have a…. um… a body. I don't have hands and feet and things. I don't have a body.

C: What do you do once you get there?

D: It's just a place of being. I don't really have to do anything. I can look and listen. And feel but I don't have a body to do all those things with. I just be.

C: Is there anyone there with you?

D: There is a bunch. We all look the same. We all look like points of light. We don't have bodies. We are light.

C: Do you recognize anyone here with you?

D: One person from my tribe. He was my friend. Like my close friend. But I don't know how I recognize him because he doesn't have the body anymore.

C: Explain to me what you're doing while you're here.

D: We aren't doing anything. We are experiencing the ribbons of light. It's like a river of light that flows all around us and it doesn't have a particular place to go. And we are, we can watch it, but we don't have the eyes to watch it. We..., it kind of makes a sound. Almost like music. I think we like this place very much because we don't feel hunger anymore. We don't feel pain and we don't feel sad. I don't know how to explain it.

C: Do you feel anything here?

D: We are very..., it's not like we are really happy, happy. Content. We don't feel sensations like cold or heat or pain. or hunger. Or when you have to go. We don't have any of those sensations. We don't have a body anymore.

C: When you begin to do anything or see anything different, explain to me what you notice.

D: We can look without turning. We can look around, like we can see around but you have to focus your… um, where you want to, the place where you want to look. I don't know how to explain this. You're just able to look in that direction. See in that direction. Without turning a head. And there is a… the light has a blue-ish light to it. I don't know how to explain that. It's white in the center and blue around. It's also everywhere. And we are… it's like we are a part of it. We are not. We are separate from it. There are a whole lot of us. We are in this light. That all are a part of but also separate from it. We are not exactly the same as this light.

C: *Brings forward the Higher Self * Is this a good place to speak with the Higher Self?

D: Yes.

C: Why did you show him that life as a caveman? The first one?

D: HE needs to know how to take care of himself. He needs to know how to also be a part of others. He needs to know how to do things. He needs confidence. He doesn't have confidence. He needs to know that he will be taken care of. He is always taken care of.

C: How will he know that?

D: Because he was shown these lives to know that he can always be, and will be, taken care of. It is the nature of life itself.

C: He wants to know, what is his purpose here?

D: At the most basic, it's just to be alive. Just top experience life. He is already doing things. He is already helping people. He wants to help. He is already helping people in every way. Many people come to him. He is already doing his purpose. He is just not accepting that.

C: How can he accept that now? What can he do?

D: He needs to stop fighting and stop resisting. He needs to stop complaining so much. He needs to believe again in life itself.

C: How can he believe in life? He seems to have lost faith; how can he regain that?

D: Not hold on to the bad things that happened. Not hold on to the people who did him wrong. Not hold on to the bad experiences. Let those experiences go. Let them go.

C: Can you help him do that?

D: I can help him only to the point he will let me help him.

C: Well, if he hears it from you now, you think he will accept that help more?

D: He is still jaded and skeptical. He needs to see more outward proof that he is on his path. Because he does not believe he is on his path.

C: How can he have proof of that?

D: I will show him. I will show him. I will give him proof.

C: I'm sure that would make him happy.

D: It is our hope that it will make him happy, yes.

C: He wants to know; did he imagine all the experiences he has had in this lifetime?

D: NO.

C: Can you explain some of this to him, so it makes sense?

D: I will have to show him over a period of time because many of these were really strong experiences for him that even now, will be too much for him if I tell him all at once. If I show him all at once it will overwhelm him. This will have to be over a period of time. Slowly. And I will have to bring other people into his life, past, to help him.

C: We are here now, what can we do to begin this process?

D: I will have to slowly, slowly, unlock some of these memories. A little at a time. He is confused, but we are not.

C: Is there one that you can give him now, that won't be too much for him?

D: There is one. He already knows this. He is skeptical of it.

C: Can you explain it so that I'm aware and he is aware which one you're speaking of?

D: It is when they came to him when he was a baby in the crib. In Chicago, during the thunder and lightning storm.

C: And what was it really?

D: It was some of the others that he is connected to. He is a hybrid.

C: What others are you speaking of, do they have a name?

D: Arcturians.

C: What is the memory that he is allowed to know now? What really happened?

D: This goes back to his father. His father was also connected. This is how he is also connected.

C: What can you tell us about that?

D: He and his sister both are part of us. Part of them.

297

C: Which sister?

D: He only has one sister. She is a twin.

C: So, what memory is it? What does he need to know?

D: They came to him just to see how he was progressing as a baby. They came to both of them, but he saw them from the lightning that came through the window. They were just checking on him.

C: And were they ok with his progress?

D: He was sick at times with fevers. They had to be sure that he would come through the fevers. He had a really bad fever that would have killed him.

C: Did they do anything to prevent that?

D: Not much was needed. He had to fight it himself. He had to want to live. His soul had to want to live.

C: Well, he passed through that, correct?

D: He did.

C: So, is there anything else about that memory that you can tell us?

D: We checked on him from time to time.

C: Are these the times that he got scared, that he saw something?

D: Those were others. Those were not the Arcturians. He is a hybrid of others. He is a mixture as well as his sister.

C: What is he a mixture of?

D: There were others we are not closely associated with.

C: Can you connect with them?

D: We are not familiar with this race.

C: The one he is a hybrid of?

D: This is part of, he is a mixture. This one is the one that came to him later on two occasions.

C: Can you tell me which times, so he knows when it was?

D: HE knows. He remembers. They are the ones that had, they do not have features. They have no eyes or mouth or nose. They are a diminutive race. They are a mixture of other races that he is a part of. And this one in particular came to him on two occasions, but he blacked out on both times.

C: Why did they come to see him?

D: To take him on the ship to check on him to make sure he is healthy.

C: Was he healthy?

D: He was. He did have the problems with the heart. That has to fix itself over a period of time.

C: Is that still ongoing now?

D: No. No. It fixed itself. They helped. But it fixed itself. He outgrew it.

C: So, was this part of his family?

D: Which one?

C: Well, if he was a hybrid, who is his family, if we are speaking on human terms? Are there other experiences of others coming to visit him?

D: Yes. There are others. They are also a different race. They are not the diminutive race at all.

C: What do you mean by that?

D: They are also a mixture, but not like the diminutive one at all. The diminutive one is part of a primitive race, even though it is more advanced than he is as a human. The others are a higher race and they also, they have overseers. They do what they are told. They are also a part of him. He has quite a mixture.

C: Is he aware of this?

D: He suspected.

C: So, all of these experiences with different beings, we call them ET's, are they all coming to check on his or do they have different agendas?

D: Each one has a different agenda, yes. But they all come to check on his health, his progress. They do upgrades. He hears us with the tones. His body will vibrate. It vibrates at higher rates of speed. He knows this. This is full conscious when this happens, and it scares him.

C: Well, the beings that he sees scare him quite badly. Why is that?

D: They cannot help the way they look. They cannot help the way they look; it is just their nature. The way they are made. It just somehow unsettles him.

C: So, should he not be scared of them. They come in his windows or see them above him.

D: No.

C: Can they not just tell him they mean no harm?

D: If he will not black out. If he can stay awake long enough, they could communicate with him but sometimes they come to take him so it's kind of necessary that he is unconscious. So, he can wake up on the ships. He will not like the process of going where he is to where he is taken.

C: Why is that?

D: It is a disassembling and a reassembling of the atoms and to some humans it is really frightening because you feel like you are going to be gone forever. To them.

C: He had some questions about some letters, can you answer them for me?

D: We will try.

C: He wants to know what was in his letter from the military, about his medical history that allowed him not to be able to go in, can you explain to me why?

D: There are about seven different problems, it has to do with his genetic makeup. The military knows he is a hybrid. That is the main reason he was not allowed in.

C: How do they know?

D: It is an ongoing thing. It has been an ongoing experiment. For a very long time.

C: And they won't allow hybrids to get in?

D: Some do make it in, but not this particular one. No.

C: What about the letter from his Sunday school teacher, what did it say when his mom received it?

D: She had an insight. She had abilities that would be considered psychic ability insight. She knew that Danny was different. She tried to tell his mother. She could see it, she could feel it, and she could sense it. His mother also knew but was in denial and chose not to accept it. She did not want to hear it. His Sunday school teacher tried to tell his mom. She said Danny is very special.

C: So, do you know the content of his father's letter back in the 1990's? He wanted to know what was in it.

D: He made excuses for why he was not there. Not in his life and his sister's life and why he could not be with his mother anymore. He also felt that he was not a good human being. A good person to be around at all. He had inclinations that it was best that he not be in their lives in childhood. And he did not know how to deal with those inclinations. He made excuses. He did not want to be a father.

C: And that was what was written?

D: That is reading between the lines. The insights.

C: That he might have gained if he had read it?

D: He said it without saying it. He did not want to be with the mother anymore either. He did not know how to be a father and did not want to be a father. He did not trust himself in many ways. So, he wanted to be out of their lives.

C: He wants to know what the creature that he saw twice in Chicago. What was that?

D: We already did. That was the diminutive race.

C: Okay, and what was the creature that came through his window in 1978 in Falkville?

D: That was not the first time, others came as well. That being made itself invisible and stayed in the room the entire night for observation purposes. They had to track Danny and his sister down because they moved from Chicago to Alabama, so they had to find them again.

C: Why did they need to do that?

D: They do upgrades. They keep track of the health. Of the growing process. Of their life because Danny and his sister are a part of them. They have to keep track. They... it is their job to keep track. To keep tabs, so it would be called.

C: So, did they agree to this? Do they know on some level this is going on?

D: If you mean on a soul level, yes of course. If you mean as humans, no.

C: He wants to know what happened with the gypsy woman.

D: That was another recognition. On her behalf. She had abilities. She had insight. She knew right away that he was different. She made a mind-to-mind connection that he immediately recognized. And it unsettled him. She did this twice. It was no more than an acknowledgement that "I know you are different."

C: He wants to know what it means when he hears children crying and what he sees with his eyes closed.

D: That is another innate ability. That actually all humans have. That is nothing special. The children crying are one that belongs to him. It is a child. A hybrid as well. He knows this on a deeper level and resists.

C: Can you explain what you mean when you say it's his child?

D: When the other beings came, the other race, they took human samples from him. It was used to mix with their race to produce a hybrid. It is just that simple.

C: So, he has a connection to this hybrid child?

D: He does, and he sees this child in his dreams often. And it upsets him very much.

C: Can you explain why they did this and didn't tell him about this?

302

D: He is not really even supposed to know about this, because it's too upsetting. The child does not live on this Earth and will not live on this Earth. It is with them, and it will be with them. It is nothing more than a bridge between two races. Two hybrid races.

C: Can you explain anything about this to make him feel better about knowing this information?

D: We will try. It is really nothing to be upset about. It is all under control. There is nothing to be afraid of regarding that.

C: He wants to know what happened with the monkey creature that carried Donna (his sister) into the room when he was in Chicago.

D: Yes. That was the same apartment where the diminutive creature was. The monkey creature was a screen memory. It was not a primate. It was made to look like a primate because he was fully conscious and his sister was not, was not conscious. It was made to make him feel comfortable. To make him laugh until it was time to meld with him. When it took hold of him and put him in the floor.

C: Did it make him laugh or did it make him feel fear?

D: When he saw that it was not the funny ape cartoon creature. When it showed himself to him, eye to eye.

C: So, what happened to him when he saw the bright light in Chicago in the 1970's?

D: All of the mature family members were put in suspended animation. Only the children were taken. Both Danny and Donna. Just for more checkups. For more upgrades, for more instruction.

C: Can you explain what happened when he met the unicorn in the forest in Georgia?

D: Simple. Sight into another dimension. Another portal. That is one of his guides.

C: Guides, does he have a name?

D: We do not know the name.

C: Is he able to speak with that guide?

303

D: Not at this moment.

C: Can he communicate with that guide from now on now that he knows he is there?

D: He will have to work on it. He can.

C: How will he know when he is connecting to this guide?

D: It is our belief that the guide will open a portal again for him.

C: Will he recognize it?

D: It will be the same guide.

C: He wants to know what happened when he met that blonde man in the woods in Georgia, what was that?

D: That was not a guide. That was a caretaker of that area of the woods. Only trying to see what he was doing there and who he was.

C: So, he was ok to be there?

D: It was assessing who he was and why he was there. Assessing why and what he was there for.

C: He wants to know about the dream he had on a ship, with a tall man pointing at a screen. Can you explain what that was?

D: Early abduction experience. That is one of the guides on that side of the veil, in that area of space, in that dimension. The guide showed him the other UFOs on the screen. It was simply showing him others that are out there that are not human.

C: Can he speak to him anytime he wants?

D: Once again, he will have to make that effort. He will have to believe it wasn't just a dream. He will have to believe it was an actual experience.

C: Are there any guides that he can talk with?

D: It is best done through open meditation. He will have to reconnect through meditation. He has quit. He will have to pick that back up.

C: Can you explain to him why he has a fear of fish?

D: A creature he came upon on a craft that was humanoid.

C: Is there a way we can resolve this fear?

D: If he will accept the fact that it meant him no harm. It was just another race. Another humanoid. Nothing more to it than that. Very simple.

C: Why is he afraid to drive, or be in a car?

D: That has to do with being on a ship in a past life that crashed to the earth. That he was a part of that race.

C: What happened on this craft when it crashed?

D: He was in charge of the craft and made an error. It crashed into the oceans of the Earth.

C: Is there any way that you can allow him to take away the fear of being in a car?

D: Yes. We will work on that. We can.

C: How will you do that?

D: Calm him each time he gets into a car. We can also work in his dreams. He dreams very often. Being in vehicles, often of vehicles not of this Earth.

C: If we say some affirmations to the body, spirit, and mind, will that assist in this healing process?

D: Yes, please do.

C: *States affirmations and calming suggestions in this hypnotic state to assist each time he gets into a vehicle. * Is there anything else we can do to assist him in his fear of cars?

D: It will be a gradual process.

C: Are there any other fears that he needs to address or work with today?

D: He has a fear of cicadas, but that is because of another race he has encountered, that is similar.

C: Will he be ok with where that fear is right now, or can you assist him with that?

D: I will assist him with that.

C: He wants to know the details of his dream that he had with the silver suited being floating towards him, what was that?

D: That was the result of his attempt to take his life. That was an intervention.

C: Can you explain what you mean by that?

D: That was an encounter with the same guides from the dream. He was a guide that was letting him know that he was making a grave mistake. And that also he is not alone. He is being guided, but he should never attempt that again.

C: Does he know that now?

D: He knows that now.

C: Is there anything else you can tell him about that?

D: He was taken on board and was given healing. He was given instruction and guidance. He was brought back.

C: Can you give him anything now that will help him enjoy his life here, to help him feel more fulfilled?

D: Much of this is contingent upon him. It will be a gradual process. He simply needs to trust life again. To believe in people again. To believe in life again. And to above all, trust in himself.

C: And you are going to help him do this?

D: I will.

C: Can I ask if you can do a body scan if there is anything that needs attention or healed at this moment?

D: Proceed.

C: Is there anywhere that needs attention?

D: He still has a neck injury from a car crash.

C: Can you assist him with that now so he can have more comfort?

D: I adjusted the vertebrae. Adjusting the nerves. He also has a nervous condition at times, we will help him with.

C: Okay, thank you. How will his neck feel after you do this adjustment?

D: It should feel much better.

C: Are you still working on that?

D: We are also working throughout the body.

C: Are there any other areas that need attention?

D: He does have arthritis in the hips and knees. And the lower back.

C: Can you help with this so there is no longer that arthritis in the joints?

D: We will work on this now. It will take some moments.

C: How do you repair this?

D: This is done energetically. Also, through manipulation.

C: Can you explain to me, so I understand how this process is done?

D: We will energetically push things into alignment. We will also send healing energy from our side. Straight through him into his body.

C: Does it repair the tissues in the joints?

D: Some will be immediate; some will take time.

C: Are you still working on that?

D: We are still working on that.

C: Is there anywhere else that needs attention?

D: The main problem that he has, that will take a measure of time as well that affects his feet, the ankles.

C: Why does it bother those areas?

D: This seems to go back to a prior life.

C: What in that lifetime caused this problem to pop up?

D: Genetics from parents. Genetic line.

C: And he carried that over?

D: Yes. He did.

C: Are you able to fix that?

D: We are working on that now.

C: How do you fix something that comes from a past lifetime?

D: We have to go back. It is a time dilation.

C: Do you clear it in that lifetime?

D: We have to address it in that lifetime, yes.

C: And it will heal it in this lifetime?

D: It can be and should be.

C: How long does that take to notice?

D: He is already feeling some affects.

C: Is there anything else that needs to be addressed?

D: Nothing that we can find.

C: Thank you for taking the time to do that. So, he wants some suggestions put in place, is this a good time to do that?

D: This would be a good time to do so.

C: *Speaks affirmations he requested and assistance he wanted * Is there anything else that he needs to know?

D: Some things will be revealed over a period of time. He will have more conscious contact, awake and in dreams.

C: Is there anything else that he needs to know?

D: He is in contact with his twin sister on various levels. He needs to know not to be upset about this.

C: Is there anything she wants to say to him?

D: She needed to go; it was her time. She asks for forgiveness.

C: Can he give that to her?

D: Yes.

C: Is there anything else he needs to know?

D: Everything is going according to plan.

*Close out Session.

# CHAPTER 19

## "Roman"

Roman came to this session with only one need. He wanted to know which direction to take in his life. He felt he had two paths in his life, and he had teetered between them for years. He was so tired of being confused on which path to take so he came to see if there was another way to get those answers. His life had been leading up to this fork in the road for many years.

He'd decided to try a past life regression to see if there was more to this problem he was experiencing. He felt like there were things that were beyond his current understanding, playing into his life and wanted to get clarity going forward. He had no prior knowledge of past life regression and had only just read that it could explain karmic bonds. So, with no understanding beyond the title and possibility, he trusted me to hopefully find the connection to these things he had been experiencing through his life.

He had always taken care of the others in his life and never taken care of his own needs first. It was only a brief conversation about this, but it felt important. This did not fit the theme of why he was there, so I didn't dwell on it too long.

We talked for some time about what he had gone through over the years and what he wanted out of this. I had a good idea of what he wanted answers to, but I truly had no idea what was going to come of it. Sometimes I can tell the direction that a session might go. This one was a complete mystery to me. He came in with an open mind and hope for clarity. I trusted spirit to lead, as always.

He had experienced deep pain and trauma in his early life and didn't think it had much to do with the session but turns out he regained some very painful memories he had forgotten as a young child during this session. I will leave out those memories because they were quite traumatic and detailed. I mention them here to help you understand where this session was going when it touches upon those memories and how it plays into it later.

And so, with an open mind and a taste for exploration, we began.


*Session begins

C: I would like for you to imagine that you are holding a very large, old and ancient book. And as you begin to notice this book that you are holding. Can you see or feel this book?

R: Yes.

C: Good. And this large book can show up in many different ways - and as you look at this book in front of you, it will become clearer and clearer as it comes into complete focus. Just allow yourself to take in the details of this book. It feels familiar. The binding. The pages. All of this book seems to know you. Because this book is made just for you. And as you look upon this book, I want you to tell me what you see. What do you notice?

R: Worn leather. Ripple binding on the outside.

C: Are there any smells that you notice as you pay attention to this book in front of you?

R: Like old pages.

C: Is there any writing upon this book?

R: No.

C: How does it feel as you hold this book? Is it heavy?

R: Yeah, it's heavy.

C: You may notice that as you feel and look at this book, that this is your book. And it resonates with the same white light that you are surrounded by in this moment. It was made by you a very, very long time ago. Protected and safe. And ready for you when you came to this place at this exact time, this book holds all of your records, all of your memories, experiences, and lifetimes that you have ever lived. You can feel the love and energy coming

310

from within the pages. Within this book. It has waited a very long time for you to see what's inside. Waited for you until this moment. It is time. And as you look upon this book, I am going to, in a moment, ask you to open it; on the count of three.

One - going deeper down into this place of exploration. Connecting with it, and it with you.

Two - feeling this book with your hands as it resonates with every aspect of you.

Three - opening the book. Tell me what do you notice as you open this book?

R: I can't open it.

C: And as you're trying to open it, what do you notice? What's happening?

R: It's like it's stuck closed. I can feel it inside my stomach. Like it pushes on my stomach.

C: And as you look at this book, I want you to ask it what it needs from you, so that you can open it. And you will just feel or know it. What does it tell you?

R: It says I'm not ready to open it.

C: Ask it what it needs to be ready, what you need to be ready?

R: I'm not getting anything.

C: Well, I want to ask that book to create a chapter within its pages, a chapter just to discover only what we need in this moment. Following that cord of connection, to the relationships you're experiencing now. And that book will magically be able to create just enough space within it to create that cord, and as it does, I want it to open to only those pages. And as that's happening, tell me what you notice?

R: Nothing. I don't even see the book anymore.

C: Well as you're existing within this space, I want you to begin drifting and floating. I want you to begin drifting and floating to the most beautiful place in the world, what you consider to be the most beautiful place in the world. And when you get there, I want you to begin telling me what you see.

R: Green fields. Cliff overlooking the ocean. Old. Old castle on the cliff side.

C: Are there any smells here that you notice?

R: Rain.

C: Is it raining?

R: The grass. Yeah. It's raining.

C: Are there any sounds around you?

R: I hear birds. The breeze. The grass.

C: And as you look down at your feet, what do you see as you are standing here on this Cliffside?

R: It's wet and I'm barefoot.

C: What are you doing as your looking at this place around you?

R: Looking down at the waves.

C: What do you notice about the water and the castle in the background?

R: It's stone. Old. And not a very big one. Kind of broke down. Run down.

C: Is there anyone around the castle?

R: No.

C: It's just you?

R: Yeah.

C: And do you stay on the cliff?

R: No, I'm moving towards the castle.

C: Just explain to me what you are noticing as you move to the castle.

R: One of the doors is broke. One of the wooden doors is kind of broken, leaning. A crow sitting on the broken door.

C: What else do you notice? Do you go inside?

R: Yeah, it's just like an open courtyard and a stable. Stair way off to the right going up to the turret.

C: Is it stone on the inside as well?

R: It is.

C: And what is the temperature like as you're inside this place?

R: It's cold!

C: And when you look at you look at your legs, what are you wearing?

R: *Laughs* Shorts.

C: And as you look at your hands, do they look young or old?

R: Old.

C: What are you doing now that you're inside the castle?

R: Kind of looking around.

C: What do you see as your looking around?

R: The stairs. The stairwell to the turret and stable.

C: Where do you decide to go?

R: Up the stairwell.

C: What do you find as you go up the stairwell?

R: It's empty. An empty stairwell. A turret.

C: What does that look like?

R: Half stone wall off to the side and then full wall with openings in it. I'm looking out in the field.

C: You can see the stable from where you are?

R: Yeah.

C: What else do you see from this point of view?

R: Like a wagon with some hay on it. Broken wheel off of it.

C: Is that how you got there?

R: I don't know. There is no horse on there.

C: And there is no horse in the stable?

R: No.

C: So, what are you doing now that you're at the top?

R: I'm kind of looking around. I'm kind of confused.

C: Why are you confused?

R: Because I don't know why I'm there.

C: So, what do you decide to do next?

R: Go back down the stairs and go to the stable.

C: Tell me about the stable?

R: It's kind of… three spots for horses. And they are broken so there are no animals in there. It doesn't look like anybody has been here in a long time.

C: And you walking through it?

R: Yeah.

C: What else do you notice? What stands out?

R: That wagon.

C: It has hay?

R: Yeah.

C: Even though no one has been there.

R: Yeah.

C: What else are you seeing?

R: Nothing that's really standing out in there.

C: *Begins to move him to another place. Instead of going to another place to explore, he goes to a childhood memory around the age of ten. So, I begin exploring there. He gives lots of detailed information of this memory that seems uneventful. I begin moving him through memories as we progress downward in age. He uncovered some very traumatic memories of abuse and physical trauma he suffered at the hands of family at two years old. I then take him to his mother's womb where he begins giving details of how it feels to be there. He, like many others, report that there is light inside the womb. Most of us would expect them to

314

be a dark place to be, but actually there seems to be light that is experienced. He explained earlier that he suffered from severe ADHD and so I knew it would take some time to get him into a deeper hypnotic state to explore further. So, I continued working back until he was extremely immersed within his environment here. Once we go beyond to "before his mother's womb" we begin to uncover a surprise that I was not expecting. *

C: And as you drift back, I want you to begin to tell me what you notice.

R: Like… it looks like an old library. Kind of like… it's weird because it's almost like it… exists in two spaces.

C: Tell me more about that, about this library.

R: High cathedral ceilings. Stained glass… not the stained glass… you can see the night sky. Well, it's like seeing into space. It's weird. It's not… it's like its existing in two spaces. Like it's there and it's not. Sections in the wall that are just open. It's got real wide curved staircase going to the balcony. A second story balcony.

C: What do you notice about the books?

R: They are very old. Everywhere.

C: As you look down at your feet in this place, what do you notice?

R: Floor is real shiny, polished. Like earthy tones. Browns, blacks… gold.

C: What are you doing as you're in this library? What do you decide to do?

R: I go up to the balcony. Walking up the staircase.

C: Tell me more as you're experiencing this.

R: The staircase is real wide. Like gold rail. Curves up the stairwell. And there is some desks at the top of the stairwell. Reading lamps on them. And then there is a section of the balcony where there are four rows of bookshelves. Signs on the endcaps of them but I can't make out what they say.

315

C: What are you doing now?

R: Walking towards the third bookshelf.

C: And as you do, what do you find?

R: It's… there is a book laying on the floor right in front of it. It's big. Leather bound book.

C: What do you do?

R: Pick it up. It's the one from earlier.

C: What do you notice?

R: It's… it feels really heavy. It has gold corner clips on it.

C: What do you do now that you have your book?

R: I'm able to open it, but I can't make out any of the writing that's on the pages.

C: And when you put your hands upon the pages, what do you feel?

R: That's…. very thick paper. You can feel the texture of the pages. And can almost feel the ink when I rub my hand across it on the pages.

C: And what do you do now?

R: I try to turn through the pages and find a page I can actually see.

C: And as you do and it becomes clear, just explain to me what you begin to see?

R: Still struggling to find one clear. Somebody is walking down the next isle over from me. I can hear his footsteps.

C: Is he coming to help you with your book?

R: I don't know. He is walking closer now.

C: Just explain to me what is happening.

R: I ask him… why I can't read any of these pages?

C: What does he say?

R: He is not saying anything.

C: What does he do?

R: Took the book, closed it, and put it back on the shelf. (This is the first time I've ever had THAT happen in a session.)

C: What does he do now?

R: Told me I'm not ready to read it yet. That's why I can't see it.

C: Can you ask him to take you where you need to be? To see what you are ready for?

R: Following him down the stairs.

C: Just explain to me what is going on as you are following him.

R: Walking really slowly. Down the stairs. He is saying something, but it's muffled. I can barely hear him.

C: Well, you can ask him to become clearer and as it becomes clearer, just explain to me what you hear.

R: Telling me there is something I need to work out before I can read any of the book, but he is not telling me what it is.

C: Can you ask him where he is taking you?

R: We are walking towards… like a huge oval window at the end of the library. And it's looking out into space. *Pause * So many stars out there. And it's cold out the window. Really cold. But asking him… what do I need to do to find out what I need to know?

C: What does he say?

R: He is getting aggravated. He says I know what I am made to do. He is getting pretty short. He is aggravated at me.

C: Can you ask him to give you some clarity so that you may understand what he thinks you already know?

R: I've got to learn to love myself more. Before I'm ready to learn anything else.

C: And how do you need to go about that?

R: Says I need to stop worrying about how others feel about who I am. And just accept and love who I am. Without feeling guilty or feeling that I've got to please anyone or make anyone like me or agree with me.

C: And when you do that, you're ready for the next step?

R: Yes.

C: So where is he taking you now?

R: Back to the entrance of the library.

C: What is he saying about that?

R: Says it's time for me to leave and that I could come back and try again when I'm ready.

C: Is there anything else he wants to tell you?

R: He just says... you know what you need to do. And you've known you need to do this. Eventually you will get there.

C: Can he tell you anything about the direction you need to go?

R: Nah. He said that's... the answer would be more clear as I learn to do what I needed to do. And love myself.

C: Is there anyone waiting for you at the entrance when you get there?

R: No.

C: So, tell me what you do now that you are at the entrance.

R: Looking outside. It's the field, the cliff where the castle was. That's the castle... the library was where the castle was.

C: Tell me more now that you notice that.

R: It's not raining anymore. Sunny. Seagulls flying around the Cliffside. Still dew, grass is still wet. Breeze blowing. Smells like clovers.

C: So, what do you do now?

R: Walking back down to the cliff. Sit on the cliff edge and stare down at the shore.

C: Tell me what else you notice as you're at the cliff?

R: It's a nice day. Breeze. The cool, very bright sun. The sun is very bright over the water. Reflecting. The guy from the library is standing next to me.

C: What is he doing?

R: Telling me I need to spend… I need to spend more time reflecting myself. Like the sun is reflecting off the water.

C: What do you need to focus upon when you're reflecting?

R: Telling me to reflect on myself. Stop worrying about pleasing other people. Take some time to take care of myself. And appreciate myself.

C: Is there anything in particular that you need to do?

R: *Laughs* No, I just… just telling me I need to stop being so negative in my head and replace my negative thoughts with positive energy. Telling me that I need to meditate more. I'm not meditating enough. And that when the time is right, I may be able to see him in meditation again and have more conversation.

C: Can you ask him who he is to you?

R: Said he is me? *Roman seemed very confused *

C: Can he explain that further?

R: Yeah, I don't understand he just said "me."

C: When you ask him what does he say about that?

R: Said he is me. Oh, he has always been me. I don't… I don't know what that means. *Whispers* What does that mean?

C: Can you ask him why he showed himself here today in this place?

R: He said because I am broken. He said I needed somebody to put a foot in my ass. *Deep laugh *

C: *Laughing * He has a sense of humor.

R: That sounds about right *Still laughing. *

C: Can you ask him if there is a karmic relationship you are working through, can he at least tell you that?

R: He is like… he says… saying the same thing he said earlier. When I take care of myself, he won't need to tell me.

C: Can you ask him why it's so important to focus upon yourself?

R: He says that I have already known… but I don't trust my instincts. But he says yes. I'm in a karmic relationship but he says, he said he can't tell me which one is the karmic relationship. I don't understand.

C: Can you ask him if you're clearing it out at this time? If you're finishing it up?

R: He said yes. He said yes. As I'm working through this, I will understand which one needs to be closed, and which one needs to be open.

C: And is there anything else he can tell you about this?

R: He told me it's not... he said he is kind of disappointed it took me this long to get to the point where I'm trying to work on myself and that he is... he is glad I'm doing it now.

C: Can you ask him if this is also part of why you came here, in this life... to work through this?

R: He said yeah. Yeah. That I've struggled in the past few lives with self-loathing. And not enough self-appreciation. Feels I've done better on the loathing part, but I don't love myself enough. Quite yet. And that's what's blocking me from seeing my full potential.

C: Can you ask him why it's been so difficult to deal with the self-loathing?

R: Because I'm hardheaded and I still haven't learned that not everybody has ulterior motives. When they are talking to me. When they are speaking to my character.

C: Can you ask him how you will know when someone has true intention?

R: Judge of character has been something you have been good at. Trust your instincts. He said... do what he has asked.

C: And it will be enough?

R: It will be enough. He is going back into the library.

C: What do you notice now?

R: Dark out. I'm still sitting on the cliff. Now it's the moon reflecting over the water.

C: What do you feel now that you are tapping into that reflection?

R: I feel more at ease. I feel, even though I really didn't get what I hoped to get out of him, I feel more at ease about what I need to do.

C: And as you look up at that moon, I want you to feel that white light radiating through your body that has been there this entire time. And as that moon begins to reflect back upon your body. I want you to allow those feelings of self-love to begin at the center of the heart. I want it to begin spreading as you feel that reflection. As it begins to move, to flow throughout your body. What does it feel like as you allow that reflection to begin shining through?

R: It's warm. Warm.

C: And do you feel that connection? That feeling?

R: Yes.

C: Do you recognize it?

R: I do.

C: I want you to feel it spread until it completely encloses your body. Completely enclosing your body. And as it does, is there anything within your body that needs attention at this time? Any remaining tension within this space?

R: No. No. I feel good.

C: Well as you relax in this space, and it gets stronger and stronger. With each and every breath you will be able to come back to this place... anytime you need to strengthen that feeling of self-love. Or speak with this inner aspect of you.

*Close out Session.


Coming out of the session he looked like a completely different person and was much more at ease. He was never completely at ease at any point before he began the session, despite all the effort on my end to ensure this. He seemed like he he'd been this way for quite some time. After this session, there was a peace he seemed to have about him that wasn't there before. We spent some time going over what he had experienced, and he was able to understand now what he truly needed to focus upon. He left with greater purpose and clarity for his life going forward. Clarity, he didn't have before. A gift from his inner self.

# CHAPTER 20
## "Madeline"

Madeline was new to the world of energy of any kind. She'd had things show up and happen in her life but had no explanation or understanding of these things or how to control them. I quickly realized she had zero understanding of the unseen. Most people I run across are similar, so it was not unusual to start from the beginning. I lightly explained what I understood of what she was dealing with in her day-to-day living.

I try not to go into too much detail before a session so as not to influence any part of the information that comes through. What makes this session so fascinating is that she had ZERO knowledge of energy, working with it, or anything else that goes along with it. She'd only just recently begun to learn about herbs since she had quit her job as a paramedic. She had spent years in the medical field but her knowledge of anything esoteric was… well, nothing.

When someone comes in with no background, I always love to see what comes from it. This session did not disappoint because everything that came through in this session was detailed information on energy and how to work with it. Including crystals and herbs and light frequencies. She came for a session because she felt like there was something she needed to understand. She had dealt with chronic fatigue and exhaustion. Completely drained day to day and had never been able to find a way to get it under control. She was exhausted and wanted to see if exploring this way would get her some answers. So, we began there.

*Session begins

C: I would like for you to imagine you are holding a large, old, ancient book. Can you begin to see that book in front of you?

M: Mmhmm.

C: Perfect, explain what you begin to notice.

M: It's got leather on it. Scroll work.

C: Do you recognize the scroll work?

M: It's a thick book. With old, weathered pages.

C: And as you're in this space, are there any smells that you pick up on?

M: Old, musty smell. Like a library. Old pages. Dust.

C: Are there any sounds you notice?

M: No.

C: Is there anything written on the front?

M: Not that I can tell.

C: Well, you will notice that this book is made just for you. It resonates with the same white light that you are surrounded by in this moment. It was made by you a very, very long time ago. Protected, safe and ready for you to open. This book holds all of your records. All of your memories, experiences, lifetimes and choices from all other places your soul has been. You can feel the love. All of the things within this book, pouring from the pages. It has waited a very long time to show you what is inside. It has waited for you and now you are ready. It is time. And as you look at this book, in a moment I am going to ask you to open this book. *Counts down. * Are you opening the book? (Yes) what do you notice?

M: It's different. All text words on the first page.

C: *Suggestions to go to the page she feels pulled to, any place within the book. * As you drift down to the surface, when you look down at your feet, what do you notice?

M: There... I am standing on grass.

C: And when you look at your feet what do you notice?

M: I'm barefoot. I had a skirt or a dress on.

C: Tell me about the dress.

324

M: It's white. With blue patterns on there.

C: What do the patterns look like?

M: Swirls. Kind of like leaves.

C: When you look at your hands, do they look young or old.

M: They are younger.

C: Are you carrying anything with you?

M: No.

C: And as you are looking around, what do you notice?

M: Field. Trees. Flowers. Some hills.

C: Are there any sounds?

M: Birds chirping.

C: Are there any smells in this field?

M: The smell of fresh air.

C: Just explain to me what you are doing as you're in this field.

M: Just walking through the fields.

C: Is here anyone with you?

M: No.

C: Tell me what you notice as you're walking through the field.

M: There is a path. It's very narrow. Kind of dark path. It's dark and small pebbles. It goes up over the hill. It just kind of cuts out.

C: What do you notice now?

M: Looks like there is an old castle or something.

C: Tell me more.

M: It's old grey stone. It's not huge. It's little. Kinda hidden in the middle of nowhere.

C: What are you doing?

M: Walking over towards it. There is flowers and trees and everything around it.

C: What else do you notice as you're getting closer?

M: It's got a wooden door. One of the old round handles.

C: And as you're looking at it, are there any features that stand out?

M: Simple door. Simple structure.

C: And do you go in?

M: Mmm. I go in.

C: Just explain to me what you notice?

M: It's got a stairwell as soon as you walk in. And there are rugs and antiques everywhere.

C: What are you doing?

M: There is a library to the right. Can't see what's in the other rooms.

C: Do you go to the library?

M: Mmhmm. There is a couch and a chair and a fireplace. And floor to ceiling books. Old books. I can't make out the names of them, but they are old, leather bound, and cloth bound books.

C: What do you do when you get into this library room?

M: Just taking in all of the books.

C: Are there any sounds?

M: Just the fireplace crackling.

C: Are you familiar with this room, does it feel comfortable being in here?

M: It feels comfortable, I don't recognize it, but it feels comfortable.

C: What do you do once you get in there, after you take it all in, what do you decide to do?

M: Start looking at the books.

C: Tell me about what you're finding as you're looking at these books.

M: Look like old books. Guidebooks? They are not regular books.

C: What kind of guidebooks?

M: Look like old, like spell, educational books. Different herb books and tinctures.

C: Do you decide on any particular book?

M: No, there is too many of them.

C: What do you do?

M: There is one without a name but… it's a small leather book. It's got diagrams and recipes in it.

C: Tell me more.

M: It's different. Diagrams of the human body and plants. Different recipes in there for different tinctures or mixes. It's old, handwritten. Looks like it was somebody's journal at one point.

C: Sounds fascinating, and you're reading through it?

M: Mmhmm. I can't make out all the words but… there is different moon phases… different plants… it's like the zodiac person, the one that's got… like two people in one.

C: So, there is a lot of zodiac in there? How many are included?

M: I just see the one. The person with two sets of arms and two sets of legs with little lines around it. (I later researched, and this is what I found: The Vitruvian Man; drawn in or around 1490. I began transcribing this session weeks after her session, so I sent her a message with this image and asked if it was similar to what she had seen. She said yes. So, we know it was not a zodiac symbol but at the time, this was all she could think to describe it so you will hear it mentioned as a zodiac symbol throughout.) Different… looks like rune symbols.

C: Are there any words included with the runes and the zodiac drawing?

M: Just the picture on the page.

C: And as you look at it, and begin to connect with that book, does it become clearer about what more you see in it, as you read through it?

M: Looks like there is some spells. Candles, herbs, and salts. There is different poultice recipes. All of the stuff is stuff that you can get around this castle.

C: And what are they used for?

M: Just healing. Wound healing. There are some tincture recipes.

C: What are those for?

M: Doesn't say.

C: What else is in this book; journal?

M: Pictures of crystals. It's all in black and white though. So, you can't see the colors. But it's just images of the different ones, and a description of them.

C: Does it have a name for the crystals since there is no color?

M: It's got some of the birthstones. It's got amethyst. Alexandrite. Emerald. It's an image of a crystal… with a sign or something around it. Like the crystal is in the center. Like the zodiac sign, but the crystal is in the center with different lines around it. And symbols kind of; north, south, east, west.

C: And are there any written details near it, or around it?

M: No. looks like it may have been used, the image looks like it would be used or replaced and used on a table or something. Maybe for grounding.

C: Like a grid?

M: Yeah. With the crystal in the center. It's like it's the center spot for energy. It's a clear-ish white crystal.

C: It doesn't say what kind of crystal?

M: It's kind of tall, jagged on the top. It's like it's got a white light in it.

C: Like a selenite?

M: Yeah! There is a table in the room now with that on it.

C: Tell me about it. What do you notice about the table?

M: It's a wooden table. Carvings on the side, kind of like swirling carvings on the side. Like a rough cut that's been polished on top, so you get the variations in the wood. The crystal is in a bronze or copper circular dish that it's like it was made for it and it sits in the center on the table with the diagram around it. And there are other little crystals in each spot now north, south, east, and west.

C: Are they the same type of crystal? Selenite?

M: There is a purple one.

C: What else do you notice about these crystals?

M: There is a selenite one and then the purple one is in front of me to the other side. The other selenite is to the left. There is a black crystal to the right.

C: Do you recognize them?

M: The purple looks more like Alexandrite maybe? The black one is maybe tourmaline.

C: And what is this table set up for?

M: I'm not really sure.

C: As you feel the energy of this space, the table, it will become clear as you pick up on what it is there for. And as that becomes clear, what do you feel?

M: Different energies. It's like the center one is pulling in and balancing all the energies. Feels like you could pull energy from it.

C: Does it feel safe to do that here?

M: Yeah, it doesn't feel bad.

C: Well as you focus upon where the energy can be pulled from, just explain to me what you feel pulled to do as you do that. What are you guided to do? *Pause * And the crystals will tell you if it is ok to do so.

M: It feels like heat, warmth coming from the center crystal if I put my hands near it. Not hot, just… it's like it has a pulsing… and there is warmth around it. The lights getting brighter in the center.

C: What else do you notice?

M: Feels like the energy, I'm connecting to it and it's going through my hands and my arms.

329

C: What area does it flow to?

M: My core.

C: What does it do once it reaches the core?

M: It's making the inner light grow stronger. And brighter.

C: What do you feel as that happens?

M: Light. Just relaxed and physically light.

C: What do you notice is different now?

M: Mmm. Just like more relaxed. Like there is no brain fog. My brain feels lighter, clearer maybe.

C: And as you focus back on that crystal and the grid, what do you notice?

M: It's like it… It was an energy swap and inside it's getting darker? I'm getting lighter.

C: What do you notice now, do you feel like there is anything you need to do with that crystal? Anything that it needs?

M: *Long pause * It needs to be cleansed?

C: Then you will understand how that needs to be done as you focus upon the needs of that crystal and as you do, what do you notice?

M: It needs light, there are curtains right next to it. It needs light on it. And a magnifying glass?

C: Well as you do that and find what you need, explain to me what you notice.

M: The sun. I adjust the glass so that the sun is pointed… circle. It's like smaller, refined. Kind of like you would do a…. Oh, it's got colors off of it now! The sun, the magnifying glass pinpoints the sun to the crystal, and it looks like there is just a bunch of bright colors coming off of it.

C: And what happens to the darkness within it?

M: It's dissolving.

C: Does it go anywhere?

M: I think? It's just… I don't know where it's going. Off into the universe? It's like the light and crystal combo just dissolves whatever the dark was and it's turning it into bright colors that are all over the room now.

C: What else do you notice as that process completes?

M: The crystal starts to dim not darken. It starts to dim, and the colors go back within it. The darkness is gone. It's like it is reset for another use.

C: And so, what do you do now that that is complete?

M: Um. I don't know…

C: Do you stay within the room?

M: Yeah, I feel comfortable in there.

C: Is there anything else in there that catches your attention?

M: There is a… looks like a podium. An old large, it's the book from earlier on it. Not the little book. The first book.

C: Tell me more, what are you noticing now that you are focused upon this book?

M: It's got my first name on the front. In block letters.

C: What else do you notice about this book?

M: There are different… three sections with markers. Like book markers. It's broken up into like equal thirds. It's a bright red bookmarker first. A blue one second.

C: Where do you turn to within the book?

M: To the middle section.

C: What do you begin to notice?

M: It's like… chapters… kind of a journal combo. I feel I can't see it, but I feel like this is my history. Like the past, present, future.

C: Well as you look through it, where are you guided to look?

M: I'm in the present but I want to know about the past too.

C: Well, as you flip through your book, looking for what's important for you now, what do you begin to notice?

M: I can't see any of it yet.

C: It will become clearer as you begin to focus in on the book. It will become clearer as you look into this book. The one area you feel most pulled to. And as that becomes clearer, whatever form it takes on the page, what do you see?

M: I see images of my kids.

C: What do you notice about this point of view?

M: They are just happy and playing.

C: What else do you notice?

M: *No answer *

C: Are you still flipping through the pages?

M: Yeah.

C: What are you exploring as you do?

M: Anxiety for some reason.

C: *Suggestions for comfort. * Relaxing into that place of reading your book. If you want, you can even call upon a guide to come through. And you will notice that as you call upon that guide, one that matches the energy of your book, one that will help you the most in this place, you feel peace. Do you feel them come in?

M: Yeah. It feels like there is someone there.

C: You can ask them for assistance. And when you do, what do you notice?

M: They took the book, and they are looking through it.

C: Can you ask them what they are doing? What do they say?

M: There is something in there I need to know.

C: Can you ask them to show you where it is within the book?

M: It's the dream. (She told me before we began the session that there is a reoccurring dream she'd had since she was young. It always scared her. She was always prevented from going to her family in the other room in her dream. There was a dark being that always stood between them, and it frightened her. She never understood anything about it or what it meant. I was surprised they brought this up because it wasn't a large topic we covered, just a passing mention during the conversation.)

C: Can you ask them what about it you need to know or see, if they can help you with that?

M: It's like I'm…. it's like I'm watching… we are standing there watching it again.

C: What do you notice?

M: Everything. I can see it but it's a dark… light. It's all just dark now. Dark.

C: What do you mean by that?

M: I can see the dream, but the light energy is gone. It's a black like dark energy.

C: Is it the one in your dream?

M: Yeah.

C: I want you to ask the guide that is helping you for clarity. What you are doing there and what do you need to do? What do you need to understand?

M: I have a feeling that I need to… do some kind of cleansing. It's like there is something attached that's not supposed to be. Sage by itself won't do it, because I've done that in the past.

C: Ask him if we can do it here in this place. With his or her help?

M: He nodded. He said yes.

C: Can he assist with this process?

M: He nodded.

C: Does he want me to facilitate it? Or does he want to assist and show you how to do it?

M: He is motioning toward you.

C: Do we use the crystal that was used just a moment ago? Can we use that crystal in this space?

M: He said yes.

C: Well as he is standing there, assisting us through this process, I want you to focus in upon that light that just entered your body. That light getting brighter… and brighter. Engulfing your body. And as you do, I want you to turn your attention to that dark being. That dream that you can still see in this space. Are you able to see it here?

M: Mmhmm.

C: I want you to take that light and envision it going towards that being. And as that light begins to spread to that being within this space… just explain to me what you notice as that light begins to touch it.

M: It's a very focused light. I'm seeing the back of that figure. It's going to the middle of its back. And it's spreading throughout the figure.

C: What do you notice as that light is spreading?

M: It's getting brighter.

C: Do you hear anything?

M: Anger. Frustration from the figure.

C: You are protected in this space with that white light. Does he have anything to say as that white light spreads to him?

M: No, but he let's go of me when I was younger.

C: He was holding on to you?

M: Mmhmm. Blocking me from going through the door.

C: Why was he doing that?

M: I don't know. Feels like he was trying to separate me from something.

C: Did it work?

M: I've crossed through the door. My younger-self managed to go out.

C: What do you notice about the being now?

M: He is turned toward us, but he can't move. The light is getting stronger in him. And it's like he is starting to just… disappear. He is not happy though. The light is getting brighter, and he is getting like… becoming less. It's like my light and my guides light is stronger than he is.

C: What do you notice as that process finishes?

M: He is gone, and the room just looks normal.

C: And when you turn to your guide and little self, what do you notice about her?

M: Relief. She is more calm now.

C: Are you able to give her a hug and extend that light to her?

M: Yes. Self-confidence. That was what wasn't there. It's like she has more now.

C: What else do you notice?

M: The guide is motioning me that we need to leave now.

C: Well as you leave, where does he take you now?

M: Um, we are back in the library. He is pointing to something in the book.

C: Tell me what you notice as you focus upon what he is pointing at.

M: I can't tell.

C: You can ask him to be clearer and as that comes into focus… just explain to me what you notice.

M: *Long pause * It's like a…blue light.

C: Is the light within the book?

M: It's like it's coming out of the book.

C: What does he do when he sees that light?

M: Just smiles.

C: If you go up and put your hand on that light, what do you notice happens? Is it safe to do that?

M: Mmhmm.

C: What do you notice?

M: I feel calmer… it's like internal strength.

C: And you feel that?

M: Yeah.

C: What else do you notice?

M: There is scroll work appearing on the page. I don't know what it says.

C: Well, you will be able to read it in this place. It will automatically translate itself. And as it does that, just explain to me what you notice?

M: Maybe an incantation or something?

C: What feeling do you get from it?

M: Um… like a strength of like a… connection to maybe past life ancestors or somebody…

C: Is that written on the book, the page?

M: There is a… part of a lineage thing that is at the bottom. It's tiny.

C: As that comes into focus, what do you notice about it?

M: It looks like it may be Mom's side of the family.

C: As you put your hand over that part of the book where it resides, what do you notice?

M: The print seems to be raised a little bit.

C: When you look to your guide to assist you here, what does he say or do?

M: He is pointing to the lineage chart. It's like he is trying to tell me there is something significant with that.

C: Can you ask him to be more specific about what you need to know? About the chart?

M: He is pointing to specific names. He is pointing them out. I can't see the name.

C: Can you see numbers?

M: There is… 1876.

C: And that looks like your moms' side?

M: It's 1903. (1.9.0.3.)

C: Can you ask him if there is something you need to do?

M: Need to look back into the family line on that side.

C: Can you ask him why?

M: He is pointing to everything in the room. The books, the crystals, everything. He said that's where that comes from.

C: Are you supposed to be working with crystals and herbs and…. what does he say?

M: He nods. It's like he is kind of exacerbated. Not irritated but he is…. it's like a parent telling a child what to do over and over again.

C: Can I ask him some questions that might help clarify?

M: Mmhmm.

C: Can you ask him if this is where your abilities come from? (As a paramedic, she struggled with being around people the longer she did it. She has suffered from extreme fatigue and brain fog now for years and it had gotten so bad she had to quit her job and take a break. She feels like she takes on the trauma, pain, and emotions from those she is around, and it has become too much.) What does she say?

M: He is nodding?

C: Are you supposed to be tapping into those abilities in this place? Can you use this place to tap into those abilities?

M: He is nodding and motioning to the whole room like that's what this is. He is like… it's like all of this. All of this is yours.

C: So, you should come back here and explore and learn more and tap into the knowledge?

M: He says yes. There is a lot of different crystal that he just pointed out to that I didn't see before. Stones and crystals. And all the books and everything. He is telling me that this is my… that's my school. That's where all the knowledge will come from.

C: Can you ask him if this is what you have accumulated over lifetimes?

M: He just smiles and nods.

C: And have you ever accessed this room in this current lifetime?

M: No.

C: Is there a certain crystal upon that shelf that you can use to return to that room anytime you need access? To help connect to the room?

M: It's like a blue crystal. It's the one he is pointing at.

C: What does it look like?

M: It's just a small kind of blueish type crystal. I don't think I've ever really seen one like it before.

C: Is it a light blue or a dark blue?

M: It's a light blue.

C: Does it have a crystal point or is it rounded?

M: It's going a point but it's not a prominent one.

C: Can you ask him if it's Larimar?

M: He nods. He said I need to wear it.

C: What will that do?

M: Help with balancing and will help me stay connected for information.

C: And that's the stone you're most connected with for that?

M: He said that is the one I need.

C: Can you ask him what you need to help with the exhaustion and the brain fog? Or did that leave when that crystal sent light to your body.

M: The brain fog went away. Exhaustion is better. Ok… got an image of me meditating. Like a sacred meditation spot. I don't know where it is. Where different crystals and incense are all in. I'm in the center where the crystal was. North, south, east, west to balance. He is… like he is giving me the image and just nodding.

C: Do the crystals matter for each of the four corners? Or is that not important?

M: Tourmaline is one of them. There are different black ones, but I know that that is tourmaline.

C: Is the other one black obsidian?

M: Yes.

C: Is one of them Shungite?

M: The one right behind me; yeah, I think it is.

C: What's the other stone, do you recognize it?

M: I think it's alexandrite. Tourmaline is right in front of me. Alexandrite is to the left. He is just nodding, kind of motioning that, that's what you're supposed to do. I guess it's an energy balance. Energy exhaustion… he is nodding.

C: So, it will help with your fatigue?

M: Yeah, he is saying it's an energy exhaustion…

C: Will you be channeling in that bright white light that you pulled through on the grid? Will that be that same energy? Or is it different?

M: He said yes, but it's like there is more. Not just that it's a white light but also balancing and strength. Inner strength.

C: And how often do you need to do that?

M: He said at least once a week if not more. Especially if I start feeling stress.

C: And that will help?

M: He is nodding.

C: And how long do you need to do this, or does it need to be a regular practice?

M: He nodded to the regular practice part.

C: Is there anything else that you need to be doing or to assist you at this time?

M: He says no.

C: Can we ask him some questions about your relationships?

M: He nods.

C: Can you ask him about your relationship about your significant other right now? Anything that he wants to tell you about it, or you need to know?

M: He doesn't say anything.

C: What does he do? *Long pause * Is he just there to help you with your abilities?

M: Yeah, I think so. As he is not really saying or doing anything and I'm not getting any like emotions or thoughts.

C: Well as you are here with these crystals and books, can you ask him if this is part of your life purpose?

M: He nods.

C: And are you supposed to learn your abilities at this time?

M: He is holding up two fingers.

C: Two abilities?

M: He nods.

C: Can he elaborate on these abilities?

M: He is saying not yet.

C: Why not? Can he tell you why?

M: I need to become more balanced first.

C: And is that what today helped with, that energy?

M: He said I'll know what they are. I already know I just have to listen.

C: Will it be easier now that we have established that stronger connection to here?

M: He said it will be easier to realize it.

C: And how are you supposed to be using this new knowledge?

M: To help people, but he says to be careful.

C: Why is that?

M: There is good and evil. And there is some that you don't want to try and help even if you have the ability because they have no good intentions. So, he said I need to be careful with whom and how I try and help.

C: And how will you know when you are not supposed to help someone, can he assist you with that?

M: He said you will feel the energy. You will get a feeling that it's not right. Just that I will know. He said it's a feeling I had before when I was younger about places that weren't good. Or people that weren't good. We are in a (herbal store, current workplace), and he is motioning to the herbs and the people like... you can help them with this route but not with the energies. And then others you can do both.

C: And how will you assist them with the energy? Is that similar to how you remove the emotion, the turmoil they experience?

M: Yeah, he nodded. It's through mostly through touch. And focusing on whatever it is that needs to happen. But he is showing me... guess that touching the person and the black negative energy coming out through my arm to my core. And then he shows me to immediately push it down into the universe. Into the Earth. And I... I have no shoes on. Ok. I have to be grounded. But it's an immediate transfer through... he said don't let it stop at the core.

C: Why not?

M: He said if it stops, it will internalize.

C: Is that what you have been doing by accident with people?

M: Yes. He is running his hand like this across his chest... the heart chakra...

C: Ask him what he is doing?

M: Everything is there. All of the emotions and negative energies. It's trapped there. It's why he said don't let it stay.

C: Are there any trapped at this current time that need to be removed?

341

M: *Laughs * He is nodding. Stuff from my past, I guess.

C: Can we remove it here at this time, in this place?

M: He is nodding.

C: Can he assist with the removal?

M: Mmhmm.

C: Can I assist as well?

M: He said it would help.

C: Well, I want you to begin to focus upon that area within the heart and chest. And begin to feel that white light glowing from the inside out. As it begins to focus upon that area. Getting stronger and stronger. And you may notice that within that white light. Anything that is stored within the chest… begins to move to that white light. Being stored and encapsulated inside that white light until it is ready to be released. As you feel those parts and pieces begin to pull from the center of the heart. Being removed from the physical body and the energy centers. And as it does it will begin to float out in front of you. Is it floating out in front of you now?

M: Nods.

C: I want you to take that ball of white light and if your guide wants to take it at this time, he can do so. Is he able to clear it for you?

M: Mhmm. He is pushing it back down, back into the Earth.

C: And as he does that, you can allow it to go… completely releasing and resolving. Cutting those cords to any residual stored emotions. Feelings or events that no longer belong to you, that are no longer needed. And as you do, I want you to ask him if there is anything that needs to be placed within that center at this time to fill it back up or is it ok to leave as it is?

M: He is… he is not saying anything, but he put his hand here. *Motions *

C: And as he does that, what is happening?

M: Seems there is a small… multicolored white… he just nods like that… that is what is needed.

C: Did he do that for you?

M: He nods.

C: And is it complete?

M: He said no. It needs to grow, but I have to work on it.

C: So, you can do that by yourself, in your own time.

M: He said yes, and I have an image of the crystals and me sitting in the middle of it meditating again?

C: So, you can focus on that when you meditate?

M: He is nodding.

C: Is there anything else that you need at this time?

M: He says no.

C: Is there anything that he wants to tell you?

M: *No answer *

C: I want to ask is this a good place to call in the Higher Self?

M: He nods.

C: Is the Higher Self here in this place with you already?

M: He says no but looks up.

C: *Calls in the Higher Self. * I want to ask can it tell us what that place was that we just visited?

M: It's an old family library… combination of everybody's stuff put in one room.

C: And this is yours as well?

M: Yes. If I choose.

C: Why did you visit there today?

M: Because it was time to access it.

C: It's time to access it?

M: Yes.

C: Can you tell her; does she have a relationship with these crystals? Is that why you showed them to her?

M: Yes. All of the crystals there on the shelf have a meaning.

C: Can you tell her more about the crystals and the meaning for her?

M: Some are protection and guidance. Grounding. Some of them are old lineage crystals. Each one has a different purpose depending on what you are trying to do.

C: Can you tell her about the Alexandrite, what does that do?

M: It helps ground her based off of all of her birth chart.

C: So, it might not be grounding to someone else?

M: Correct.

C: Can you tell her about the Larimar, why is that one important for her to wear?

M: It will help her with energy grounding. And being able to navigate back to this place. Navigate through the energies, with some practice.

C: And how can she practice that?

M: Meditation. And focusing on each individual energy. Trying to access it.

C: And if she focuses upon that place, she will be able to access it more easily?

M: Yes.

C: What about the black stones? Why were they important?

M: For protection. Energy protection. Physical protection.

C: Why does she need protection, what's important about that?

M: Because of negative entities everywhere. Especially on the property.

C: The one she is on now?

M: Yes.

C: Can she get rid of them?

M: It will take some work.

C: Can you assist her with that removal? As she begins to learn?

M: Yeah.

C: And what does she need to know about her abilities? Her healing abilities, what can you tell her about that?

M: She can heal physically as well as mentally.

C: And she is not ready to tap into that? What the guide mentioned or is she learning?

M: She needs to balance and increase her energy first. Or it will have the opposite effect, and it will drain her.

C: So how does she do that?

M: Meditation. And either some type of Tai Chi or Yoga to build more energy.

C: And is she doing that now?

M: In this moment, yes. But not regularly.

C: What was that entity that she faced, what was that? The dark one in her dreams that she has always had.

M: It was some evil spiritual connection to the family line.

C: Where did it come from?

M: Couple of generations back.

C: Why did it come to her?

M: She is stronger than the last two generations.

C: So, she could clear it?

M: With time. It haunts the family, not just her.

C: And is it gone now that she has cleared it?

M: It's partially… it's not attached to her anymore.

C: But it's still around?

M: It feeds off of negativity. The property needs to be cleansed.

C: How can she do that?

M: Different incense. To release what's on the property. And a form of protection around the property. With intent of protection.

C: Is there anything else that will be most effective for that, or does it matter?

M: Different stones from the property itself.

C: And she can charge them with intent of protection?

M: Yes.

C: Is she at risk of that entity re-attaching or is she clear from that for good?

M: Not if she doesn't do her crystal circle.

C: Is there anything else in her field that needs to be released at this time?

M: No.

C: Is there anything else draining her energy?

M: Family.

C: Is there anything that she can do about that?

M: Protection.

C: And how does she do that?

M: Creating a shield.

C: What would that shield look like? Can you show her?

M: It's coming from the top of her head. And then like an umbrella over her.

C: Does it have any particular colors that are most important?

M: Blue, white, and pink.

C: And that will most effective against her family draining her?

M: Yes.

C: Why are those colors important?

M: It will help balance.

C: I want to ask about her relationship with her significant other. Is there anything you can tell her about that?

M: He has negative energies attached to him.

C: How many?

M: Three.

C: What kind are they, are they easy to remove?

M: If he will release and acknowledge that he has them.

C: How are people supposed to release them when they may not even believe in them?

M: She will have to connect with him.

C: How can she do that? She can remove them for him?

M: If he is willing. He is more open minded than he seems.

C: So, if she tells him about this, he will understand?

M: He will try to understand.

C: Does it influence him in any way?

M: Yes.

C: And does that influence Madeline?

M: Yes, because of the negative energy.

C: If she starts to clear the property, will they be more likely to leave on their own?

M: Yes, things will start to balance.

C: Is there anything else you can tell her about this situation that might be most beneficial?

M: She needs to do it when the kids are not there.

C: Why is that?

M: They are too vulnerable.

C: Does she need to start putting up protection around them as well, will that help them?

M: Yes, especially for the daughter.

C: Why is that?

M: She is super sensitive.

C: And do her guides not do that job protecting her?

M: Most of the time but they get overwhelmed.

C: What about Madeline's guides, how are they doing protecting her and keeping up her energetic field?

M: They are doing okay but could use some help. Only from the negativity she has experienced through her life and working on the ambulance.

C: Is there anything you can tell her to assist her when she is around people like that? That will protect her?

M: The shield and trusting the energies. She needs to learn to block her energy.

C: Is it similar to what I was trying to explain to her?

M: Yes.

C: Is there anything you want to elaborate on that… that would be helpful?

M: If she will put her shield, her energy stays within the shield.

C: And she can still help people?

M: When she is ready the shield will lift enough to transfer that energy. Then she can purge that energy but only to that specific person that she focuses on. If she puts the shield up, she will no longer get the energies around her.

C: Is she meant to be working on the ambulance again?

M: She can but it's not an ideal place for her. There is too much negativity. Too many people not willing to actually help themselves.

C: Is that why she is at the herbal store now?

M: Yes. To gain knowledge and skill. So, she can go out and help others.

C: And she will know when it is time to expand and go beyond that?

M: Yes.

C: Is there anything that you can tell her about that?

M: Just to keep exploring the herbs. And learn more about the frequencies and crystals.

C: Is there anything else she should be working on?

M: No.

C: Can you tell her about her children? Can you tell her why she has the relationship she has with her daughter? Why it has been like it has?

M: Her daughter is more sensitive than she is. She picks up on anything negative, but she holds it in her.

C: Is there anything she needs to know about that relationship?

M: Daughter needs to do meditation as well. Start watching and learning regardless of what family and the world says.

C: And how will she do that?

M: Spending time at the herbal store. Doing meditation with her mom.

C: What about her son, is there anything that he needs at this time?

M: He needs the connection re-established.

C: Can you tell her more about what that means?

M: There is a disconnect between the two of them because of the C-section.

C: And how does that cause a disconnect?

M: The body thinks that the child is no longer here.

C: And how can you re-establish that connection when it thinks there has been a death like that?

M: Need to reconnect on an energy level.

C: Can you tell her how you can do that?

M: Some kind of ceremony with the son. Preferably on a full moon.

C: What needs to be done for that ceremony?

M: She needs to connect with intent. So that the two bodies can re-establish that connection.

C: Will that happen automatically just by focusing?

M: No, it will take time. Putting pieces back together.

C: Does this happen to all babies who are born this way?

M: No. just those that are not meant to come that way.

C: They don't plan to be born that way?

M: No, he wasn't supposed to be born that way, but it was taken from him.

C: And he didn't know this when he was going to come in?

M: No, he didn't know he was going to be taken via c-section. The intent and plan was natural birth.

C: And those who plan it, have an easier time making that connection with their mother.

C: If it's the way the universe intends it, then they will be ok. Because they have a different purpose.

C: Can you tell Madeline what her purpose is here, what did she plan to do?

M: To connect and help heal people emotionally and physically.

C: And she has been doing that in her own way?

M: Yes, but there is more that she can do.

C: What does she need to know about that?

M: It will take time and learning. And building her energy.

C: Is there anything that you can tell her to start assisting with this or just focus on the meditation?

M: Meditation. Picking one herb or one element or one crystal a month and studying. But to relax while studying and the knowledge will come.

C: And this will help her while she is healing?

M: Yes.

C: Is there anything else that you want to tell her about her abilities?

M: She can heal through energy when she practices and gets stronger.

C: And has she done that so far?

M: Some without realizing it.

C: Will you remind her of those times when she is aware, so that she knows when she is doing it on purpose?

M: Yes.

C: Are you doing that now?

M: Yes.

C: I want to ask about her mom. Her relationship with her mom. Can you tell her why it has been the way it has?

M: She is scared of anything that is not tangible. Physically tangible.

C: And that affects Madeline?

M: Yes. She feels like she doesn't have the support system.

C: Was that the plan, to have a relationship like they do now?

M: No.

C: What was the hope?

M: To have an understanding and connection. Especially when it came to anything like this with energies and herbal and crystals and... her mother shies away from that.

C: So, you put other people in her path to assist her?

M: Yes.

C: And she will know?

M: Yes.

C: Can you do a body scan at this time, tell me what you find.

M: Compressions in her back. Imbalance of emotions.

C: Are you doing that at this time?

M: Yes.

C: Can you tell me what you're doing?

M: Giving support to the compressions in the lower back. Relieving the pain. Balancing her emotions.

C: She will feel a difference?

M: Yes.

C: Does she already feel a difference now?

M: Yes.

C: is there anywhere else that needs attention?

M: Balancing the hormones. Reducing the cysts.

C: How do you do that?

M: Ridding the inflammation.

C: And the cysts will begin to go away?

M: Yes, balancing the endocrine system.

C: Is that where her PCOS (Polycystic Ovary Syndrome) comes from?

M: Yes.

C: And why was that not properly working? What's the root cause of that?

M: Stress trauma response.

C: And we can get rid of that now that she is no longer dealing with that?

M: Yes.

C: And what does that look like for her PCOS?

M: Endocrine system will balance out. Hormones will balance out and it will go away.

C: And she will be better?

M: Yes.

C: And you're doing that now?

M: Yes.

C: Is there anything that her body will need going forward to support that healing?

M: Keeping hormones balance. Reducing stress.

C: Is she getting better at that?

M: Yes.

*Close out Session.


We finished up the session and there was nothing more that the Higher Self wanted to say or work on. The focus of the session ended up being quite different than what we'd expected. She reported she felt much better and clearer than she has in years. Her session did much to alleviate the stress and chronic fatigue she had experienced for so long. Now she understood that it was her innate ability to heal that had been the cause of that in many ways. She'd experienced energetic drain by not protecting her own space first and she took on a lot from other people in an effort to heal them.

This happens to many others who have never been taught the ins and outs of energy work. Just like there are protocols for healing the physical body through medicine, there is a protocol of sorts for energetic work. Many Higher Selves have reported the same thing and wanted their person to learn to protect themselves energetically first, before going on to help others, even if they were never aware they were doing it in the first place. Spiritual hygiene is JUST as important as Physical hygiene for those who are sensitive to anything beyond their five sense. And Many are becoming more sensitive with these shifts that are happening.

This might help you understand this sort of protection a bit clearer: You have an energy field around your body. Everyone does. Your "Merkabah" or energetic field. Some call it your aura. There are layers to this field that encompass your physical body. It completely surrounds and goes through you externally and internally, all the way through the physical body. Naturally, there is nothing present, day-to-day, to stop a drain on your energy field; unless by accident (or intent), you are placing something up around you.

Some people use prayers of protection in general, whether from a religious standpoint or just a meditation standpoint. Doesn't matter how you have requested it or envisioned it, it will be there if asked for or thought of it. There are those people who naturally have the ability to heal whether they are aware of it or not. Some also call this ability empathy. Sometimes, being empathetic means getting exhausted after being around people. It can be different, and yet similar in what is happening.

What is happening is you are basically "giving" energy from your field without knowing what you are doing, by trying to help someone. And when this happens, there is no natural "shut off valve" we will call it. So, you give and give, beyond what you have and then you are essentially… drained. This shows up as mental drain or physical exhaustion with no known cause. I am not saying that every case is this reason, but many times I've seen it has been.

What the Higher Self is calling a "shield" is a way to stop that drain on your energy field. It is a way to protect it until you choose to intentionally heal or help someone. We know that energy knows no bounds and it's a natural part of existing in our world. You can also choose to build up your energy field so that it naturally "gives" any energy you have intentionally built up for the purpose of helping others around you. That, however, is a conversation for another day and has much more information behind it.

We live in a world where everything IS energy first. Physical manifestation happens second and there are things we should know about how to work with it. Everyone is different in how they work with that, for themselves. No two people are the same, however there are basic fundamentals that seem to be the same across the board. I teach based on what I know and what I've learned and let others discover exactly HOW that fits into those boundaries for them. For some, it doesn't fit at all, and they need a different method all together. The fun part is just learning what that looks like for you as an individual and how to apply it to your life.

I find that most healers are pulled in some way, to a healing profession. Or to a profession that works in a similar manner. It's like some internal pull to a field where they can do their work in the only ways we have been taught how to "give."

I have found that other times there are healers who become complete recluses because they cannot handle the onslaught of the outside world. For those who have never been taught what is causing their extreme anxiety, if this is the case, they begin to turn inwards because handling other people's energies becomes too much. They take on other people's stresses and worries, other's anxiety and depression, and it becomes too difficult to discern what belongs to them and belongs to those others.

We have lost much of the teachings on how to heal and protect our own energy fields. Many who came before us generations ago, intrinsically knew how to do these things, passing it down from generation to generation naturally. So much has been lost, and we are seeing that there are many people who suffer because the knowledge… half of our earthly beingness… has been ignored or forgotten. The good news is, it can be regained, relearned, and explored again. There are many people turning inward to relearn what fuels them, protects their peace, and gives them strength. One must only acknowledge that there are many parts to the human self.

# Conclusion

As this book concludes, I have to acknowledge the journey over these past nine years. I have changed and grown, comfortably and uncomfortably, as I have journeyed with each person along the way. I have so much love for my clients who have allowed me to experience these journeys with them. I feel as if I have lived a thousand lives in this short amount of time. A chapter most definitely worth remembering. I hope to live a thousand more as I continue on this journey of exploration. I have discovered so many new aspects of life and life beyond us, whether that be in the afterlife, past lives, or lives beyond our planet. There are so many aspects to living that we have only just begun to explore and understand. A deeper meaning overlays all that we experience from moment to moment, and it can be as spiritual or non-spiritual as you want it to be. It's the meaning in what you give it. Many have lived life on the surface and now you can dive into the depths of your soul to find the why's and how's... if you feel the call.

These explanations for the day-to-day troubles and challenges we all face may help give you stronger and more stable ground to stand on as you navigate the road in front of you. Or maybe it just gives you a new perspective to broaden your horizon. I only hope that it has given you the opportunity for growth or change in some way that lights up YOUR path. This road we navigate is not meant to be done alone. We get signposts along the way, people who change the course we are on, or things that take our breath away as we stop to enjoy the beauty. Life is meant to be lived, truly lived, to be appreciated and every leaf turned over. We have so much to live for. We chose this, a school of challenge and constant change.

I know I didn't always feel that way and with this journey, and through these stories and experiences, I have decided to give life my all, because there is so much more meaning to the day-to-day if you only allow it. There is magic all around us! We just have to step outside of the box we have put ourselves in, roll up the blinders and look outside of ourselves to see the world for what it truly is - a playground full of adventure and excitement. We were never meant to grind away day to day. Our souls feel that, and we yearn for more. We can all feel that calling. It calls to us in ways that whisper quietly "over here, over here." We only need to take a leap of faith, even one step. Those moments of insanity turn into a life well lived with happiness shining upon our faces in the grooves and notches.

I hope to never learn everything I need to learn because it means I am done. I know that one day after exploring my fill, I will feel the call of my Soul to bring me back home, but until then, this is only one life and likely book of many to come and I cannot wait to unfold the chapters that have yet to be written. Each one diving further into who we are and why we explore as we do. Why do we choose these experiences for ourselves? I have found purpose in the unknown and ever changing. I know and then I do not, as I discover more depth to what I thought I already knew. There I begin again, with an open mind beyond the box I never wanted to break out of, but life is funny like that. When life pushes you into fear and you look around in the dark, there is always a light. A part of you calling, signaling, as you follow it and discover your own light and realize it was always with you.

This is the time for humanity to find and shine our own light. Our own Soul and connection within ourselves. We are our power, connected to Source in a way that is unbreakable. We do forget, but we are given so many opportunities to remember.

We are ready for the "what's next" portion of our life where we begin to see things in a new light and begin to discover the unknown, deeper parts of ourselves that bring us beyond just the human body. Discovering what's in our Souls at the core of who we are and why we are here. Everyone is different in their journey and what they need, but for me I needed more. More than just to live and die. More than just "this is life and that is it". There are many that are happy with that, and that's perfect for them; but if you are reading this, it is because your soul has called you to the "what's next" portion of your life. You have answered the call of your Soul and decided to go beyond.

This book is meant to show you that there is never just one answer for a problem in life. For life isn't meant to be so one dimensionally simple. It can be easy, but not always so simple. Like the difference between a 100-piece puzzle and a 1000-piece puzzle; all of the pieces are still there, but there are many more pieces to complete the whole, the bigger picture. There are always many more pieces to be discovered along the way before it's complete. We're never given a problem we cannot solve, but sometimes it's not so easy to find the answer, especially when the day-to-day grind takes precedence. Going deeper into the places we've yet to explore may be the only way to find the answer. In doing so, we become a more complete person on the other side of that exploration. We are meant to grow and change, to become better versions of ourselves. This is a time of awakening within our world.

We are here to be pioneers, to explore. Our outside world has been mostly mapped, but what about the inside? The true inside of our Soul. Most have never opened that door to peer inside to the depths. We are only at the surface. We have ignored the innermost depths of ourselves while we have pushed forward in our advanced outside world. It is time to explore these innermost depths of ourselves.

As these people have taken this plunge to their innermost world exploring who they are, I hope you have also been called in some way by your Soul, leading you to find the answers you seek. Why are we here? What road do we take? Why am I going through these patterns I cannot seem to break? What have I yet to understand? What's the bigger picture? Where do these things in my life come from?

Every human being has answers they seek and questions that propel them forward to look further than they have before. It's in our nature to seek, to pioneer. Our Souls guide us in ways that call to us in our own unique ways so we may understand. So, follow the call. Step into more of who you are. Discover something new, even if the fear of the unknown is too great. You may find on the other side of that unknown, a joy unlike what you've ever felt before. A freedom just around the corner of uncertainty. We are all on a journey and as we cross paths with one another, we exchange that gift of growth and connection. Answers and peace within ourselves. It is my hope that this gives you that joy and peace, or a path to it, that I know so many are searching for. A knowledge that our Soul is always answering, even if we can't hear it over the sounds of our world. It is there... and it never, ever gives up.

You can stop to listen too, and when you do, I think you will find more of who you really are.

Blessings and Joy on your Journey ~

Want to schedule your own Past Life Regression or QHHT session? You can inquire by filling out the contact form on my website listed below.

Website: i-hypnotherapy.com

If you want to find more sessions like these, you may find me on my YouTube channel where I post new sessions for you to listen to.

YouTube Channel: Chelsey Perry Hypnotherapist
http://www.youtube.com/@ChelseyPerryIH

For a current listing of healers offering their own services that have developed from these sessions, you can find them on my website under the "book and more" tab.

# About the Author

I am a clinical hypnotherapist who specializes in past life regression and also a Level 2 QHHT practitioner. I have been offering hypnotherapy services since 2015.

My studies with hypnotherapy began at Southwest Institute of Healing Arts in 2015-16 and I furthered my education in Quantum Healing Hypnosis in 2022. Hypnotherapy has indeed become my passion. I have continued my education over several years to learn and explore the benefits that hypnosis offers and the progress that can be made through the mind-body connection. My clients come to work on healing themselves through past life regression, inner-child work, anxiety, trauma or depression, and many other key areas that affect people today, including just plain curiosity.

I became a Reiki Master over the course of six years. I started my journey with energy healing back in 2012. I continue practicing today and teach Reiki classes in person along with Rev. Debra Perry.

I spend my free time on our family farm in our gardens and with our animals. Spending time in nature is one of my favorite past times. I also love crafting, and you will find me at local conventions with my crafts and/or speaking about hypnotherapy. I also have specialty crafted pieces in my office year-round available for perusal by appointment.